BORDER HACKER

BORDER HACKER

A TALE OF TREACHERY, TRAFFICKING, AND TWO FRIENDS ON THE RUN

LEVI VONK
with AXEL KIRSCHNER

BOLD TYPE BOOKS

NEW YORK

Bold Type Books
116 East 16th Street, 8th Floor New York, NY 10003
www.boldtypebooks.org
@BoldTypeBooks

Printed in the United States of America

First Edition: April 2022

Published by Bold Type Books, an imprint of Perseus Books, LLC, a subsidiary of Hachette Book Group, Inc. Bold Type Books is a co-publishing venture of the Type Media Center and Perseus Books.

The Hachette Speakers Bureau provides a wide range of authors for speaking events. To find out more, go to www.hachettespeakersbureau.com or call (866) 376-6591.

The publisher is not responsible for websites (or their content) that are not owned by the publisher.

Print book interior design by Trish Wilkinson.

Library of Congress Cataloging-in-Publication Data

Names: Vonk, Levi, author. | Kirschner, Axel, author.
Title: Border hacker : a tale of treachery, trafficking, and two friends on the run / Levi Vonk with Axel Kirschner.
Description: First edition. | New York : Bold Type Books, 2022. | Includes bibliographical references.
Identifiers: LCCN 2021034462 | ISBN 9781645037057 (hardcover) | ISBN 9781645037040 (ebook)
Subjects: LCSH: Kirschner, Axel. | Vonk, Levi. | United States—Emigration and immigration—Social aspects. | Mexico—Emigration and immigration—Social aspects. | Human smuggling—Mexico. | Illegal aliens—United States—Biography. | Hackers—United States—Biography. | Anthropologists—United States—Biography.
Classification: LCC JV6475 .V66 2022 | DDC 304.8/73072—dc23
LC record available at https://lccn.loc.gov/2021034462

ISBNs: 9781645037057 (hardcover), 9781645037040 (ebook)

LSC-C

Printing 1, 2022

For Axel's children,
wherever they may be

and for every bitch ass president
who ever deported somebody

CONTENTS

Contents

PART III: THE ATTORNEY

PART IV: THE ANTHROPOLOGIST

AUTHOR'S NOTE

THIS STORY IS not about me. It could be said that it's about Axel; he is, after all, the titular character. But that's not exactly right either. This story, really, is about the relationship between us and how it is possible for two people who seemingly could not be more different on paper—a young, southern, white academic and an undocumented, Afro-Latino, New York hustler—to still share something. It's a relationship that, when this book is published, will have spanned more than seven years. To convey it with depth—and all the complexities, pitfalls, and power dynamics therein—it was also necessary to question the borders around what is considered acceptable nonfiction. For instance, portions of this book are written from Axel's first-person perspective. These passages are based on hundreds of hours of recorded interviews. The best were selected and transcribed by me, and then Axel and I edited them together many times over for strength and clarity. Frequently, passages of several interviews have been combined or rearranged to create the most engaging narrative. In anticipation of any criticism or skepticism that this methodology may inspire, we ask: Why should the author be allowed to rewrite as much as they please, as well as have access to an editor, but not the subject?

In this book, conversations between Axel and me are also often based on recorded interviews or text messages, though they just as frequently come from my memory or his. At every step, we have worked together to ensure that these recollected conversations are as true to the originals as possible, while still conveying a clear and compelling story. Rest assured, Axel read every page of every draft of this book, and any time he flagged something that was inaccurate or that he remembered differently, he swiftly addressed my error. All irregular spellings were recommended by Axel himself to better portray his unique pattern of speech. The intention from the start was to give him space to speak for himself, to tell his story on his own terms, even when he contradicts or criticizes my account of events. It is, no doubt, an imperfect attempt at—what word to use? Equity? Parity? Solidarity? However, it is an attempt, and one that we hope will push narrative nonfiction in a direction that is not only more compassionate toward its subjects but also more wary of its own narrator-centered point of view.

To accomplish such a daunting task, I have developed what I believe is something of a unique interview style, one that differs somewhat from the journalistic or anthropological standard. I would ask Axel to talk about a subject at length—perhaps a particular event in his life or his perspective on a certain aspect of migration—and then, throughout the years, ask him to retell that same story to me over and over again. The repetition provided us with much more material, which in turn led to much richer passages in Axel's voice. It also has its challenges: Axel and I must grapple with the inconsistencies bound up in all narratives—whether intentional or otherwise—and sometimes Axel's way of thinking about a particular subject changed over time. We have tried to embrace and move deeper into these issues, rather than obscure them.

One of the reasons I believe that this new, experimental way of writing has not been attempted before in mainstream nonfiction (at least that I know of) is because it is much more laborious. For seven years now, Axel and I have stayed in near-daily contact. Our project has taken over both of our lives. Our interviews are incredibly long and nonlinear. What might take an average journalist or social scientist five hours of work (say, one hour of interview, plus three hours of transcription, plus one hour of analysis to pull the best quotes) can easily take us ten times as long. This additional labor is shouldered not only by me, of course, but by Axel as well. For this reason, I have tried to ensure that he is well compensated. Not only have I helped support him financially since we met, but he will be paid like a coauthor for this project and will receive a substantial portion of the profits for every book sold for life. We again see this as a crucial departure from mainstream nonfiction, in which subjects are not only routinely uncompensated, but their unpaid labor is justified through the invocation of some kind of abstract journalistic integrity or objectivity, the measure of which is never defined except through the adamant denial of payment.

Other notes on methodology: Axel and I have sometimes changed or obscured minor facts throughout the book. For instance, Parts I and II are told in chronological order, but Parts III and IV contain a few select passages that have been arranged outside of strict chronology. However, at no point does this slight disjuncture in temporality impact the actual claims made in the book. Additionally, several vulnerable characters' names have been changed, as well as their identifying characteristics. In the service of protecting them, I have not marked which names or features have been altered.

However, this book does claim that Axel and other migrants were abused by certain self-identified "migrant activists" and "human rights defenders" in Mexico, whose names I have not changed. All of these claims have been thoroughly vetted and fact-checked. Axel's identity has been partially obscured in this book for his own protection, but, in reality, the migrant activists who pose him the greatest threat already know everything about him, as many were in charge of his immigration cases in Mexico. They know his real name, date of birth, and, of course, what he looks like. It would not be particularly hard for one of them to have Axel killed. We are both incredibly worried about this, but it is a risk Axel insists on taking to bring the abuses he and other migrants have suffered to light. At the behest of our publisher's attorney, we have struck several instances of even more shocking and egregious misconduct by migrant activists than those included in the final draft of this book. We hope that others, especially anthropologists, will risk something of themselves and pick up the detective work where we left off.

One might ask how Axel, a down-and-out deportee with little formal education and no resources, was able to uncover such systemic corruption when no one else could. It hasn't been easy. One reason is that many of these "activists" act much more brazenly in Mexico than one would assume, relying on migrants' and journalists' transience to cover their tracks. Another is that I kept coming back when no one else would, and I stayed much longer than anyone else who looked like me would stay, especially the prestige journalists who routinely parachute into migrant shelters for a two-day story.

There will no doubt be objections to our versions of things, as well as the inevitable accusations that neither Axel nor I is Mexican, and so we have misunderstood or misconstrued the subtleties of Mexico in general and Mexican politics in particular. My answer is this: Our goal has never been to give an accurate portrait of Mexico as a whole or of how "the real Mexico" works. Such portraits are impossible, even and especially for Mexicans themselves, just as there is no "whole" or "real" United States. Instead, we have endeavored to provide the account of a friendship that must at every point struggle against Axel's systematic abandonment by three states—Guatemala, Mexico, and the US—and if something distinct yet wholly partial is glimpsed of Mexico in that account, all the better. As Axel and I often tell people, the Mexico we are familiar with is not one many Mexicans would recognize on its face. But we hope that, if the reader stays with us, something much deeper will resonate, no matter their nationality.

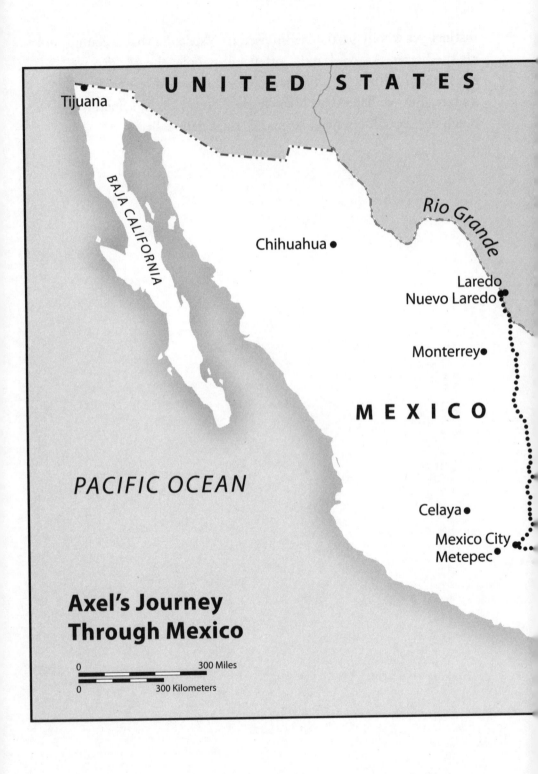

UNITED STATES

Tijuana

BAJA CALIFORNIA

Chihuahua •

Rio Grande

Laredo
Nuevo Laredo •

Monterrey•

MEXICO

PACIFIC OCEAN

Celaya •

Mexico City
Metepec •

**Axel's Journey
Through Mexico**

0   300 Miles

0   300 Kilometers

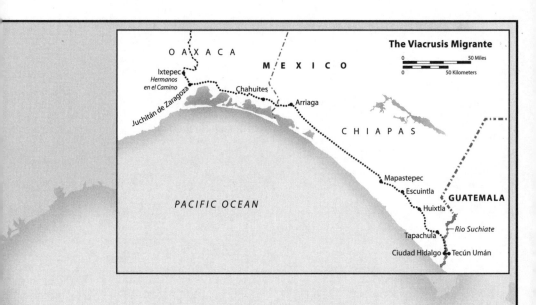

The Viacrusis Migrante

0 ___ 50 Miles
0 ___ 50 Kilometers

OAXACA

MEXICO

Ixtepec
Hermanos en el Camino

Chahuites

Juchitán de Zaragoza

Arriaga

CHIAPAS

PACIFIC OCEAN

Mapastepec

Escuintla

GUATEMALA

Huixtla

Rio Suchiate

Tapachula

Ciudad Hidalgo ● Tecún Umán

Gulf of Mexico

YUCATÁN

ISTMO DE TEHUANTEPEC

BELIZE

Ixtepec

GUATEMALA

HONDURAS

Guatemala City

I hate traveling and explorers.

—CLAUDE LÉVI-STRAUSS

PART I
THE PRIEST

CHAPTER 1

THE VIACRUCIS MIGRANTE

THE FIRST THING you should know about migrant caravans is that nobody ends up in them who has somewhere better to be. Nobody. No matter what people tell you, no matter who they say they are or what they pretend to be, if they're on a migrant caravan, they're out of options. In this way, every caravan is the same. I have yet to find an exception.

The second thing you should know about migrant caravans is that actually no two of them are the same. It all depends on who's in charge. Sometimes they're led by a priest, and the kind of priest who starts a caravan is usually charismatic and well connected and has some sway in the area. He's on amicable terms with the local police forces, for instance. Or if not amicable terms, then at least reasonable ones, and he can therefore negotiate safe passage through Mexico. This priest almost certainly runs a shelter, a place that hosts migrants passing through on their way north. And if the priest is powerful, you can bet his shelter will be top notch as well. It will have bunk beds to crash on, three decent meals a day, and even showers, all of which will actually work, though none will have hot water. Not that you'll care, considering that you've been trekking through a sweltering jungle or desert all day. But many migrant shelters aren't run by charismatic priests, nor are they luxurious, and the worst aren't really shelters at all. They're dumps with dirt floors and holes in the ground for toilets,

3

and the only food you'll find is beans, a scoop of lukewarm beans that have been sitting in a greasy pot for god knows how long. Obviously, you want to end up in one of the better shelters. But, when you're from another country, sometimes it's hard to know which shelter will be good and which will be bad. Sometimes you'll travel to where someone said a shelter would be, and its doors are locked. Nobody home. Or sometimes there won't be anything at all. No building, no nothing. Like it just vanished. Or maybe the person who told you about it was lying. Maybe they were just screwing with you, or maybe they wanted you to die.

This brings me to the third thing you should know about migrant caravans—and really this is directly related to the first thing and indirectly to the second: you can't trust anybody you meet on a migrant caravan. The kinds of people you encounter on caravans are sad and desperate characters who probably gave you a fake name. They are not your confidants. Never offer up any personal information, especially in regard to where you're traveling. And definitely do not show them where you've stashed your money, even though everyone already knows it's in your underwear. It's always in your underwear. But no one can be completely sure unless they catch you with your hand rummaging around in your crotch, so don't do that. And don't take anyone else's general untrustworthiness personally because, if you're being honest, you probably can't be trusted either. You're probably also using a nom de guerre. You're probably also hiding where you're from, and where you're going, and have your birth certificate tucked down the front of your pants right next to your cash.

But here's the tricky thing, which is also the fourth thing you should know about migrant caravans: you have to trust the people you meet on migrant caravans. Not everyone, obviously, because you actually can't trust anyone. Caravans are full of thieves, or at least degenerates. Drug users, drug smugglers, drug dealers. Sex predators and sex pests and pedophiles. Murderers, or people who openly boast about murdering, which is not the same thing, as well as attempted murderers, who are less likely to exaggerate their botched attempts and are, therefore, somewhat more credible. But you have to choose someone, and you must choose carefully, because migrant caravans are full of vultures, predators, and prey, the worst and waste of humanity.

Or at least that's what anyone on a migrant caravan will tell you. But, as I just said, you can't trust what people tell you on a migrant caravan. And yet you have to. Because you are running for your life. Because you have never been to Mexico and have no idea how big this country is or how to get from one end of it to the other. Maybe you can't read. Or you can read, somewhat at least, but you can't read maps. Or you can read maps and books just fine, but none of that seems to matter anymore, because you need to travel from where you are, in southern Mexico, to the US border, and ahead of you lie two thousand miles of some of the most hostile terrain on the planet. Thick jungle, sweltering swamps, barren deserts, poisoned rivers. Immigration is everywhere, or if they are not everywhere then the threat of them is. Their shadows haunt the buses and trains and hidden pathways that circle backwater towns. Ideally, you'd have someone to guide you through it all—a coyote, a pollero, a human smuggler. But they're expensive, and, let's face it, you're probably broke. Besides, you can't trust a coyote. They're in the caravans too, scoping out business opportunities, leaching off of suffering, sowing disunity. Though if you do have some money, coyotes can be a bit more trustworthy, for the right price of course, and, remember, you need to trust somebody.

But if you don't have money, then a migrant caravan is a good place to find a travel companion, seeing as how everyone around you is trying to get to the same place. You can't distrust everyone, after all, because that would be paranoid, and you need somebody to watch your back. It's safer to travel in groups. Gang members, kidnappers, and thieves—and if you're one of those things, you're likely some version of all three—join the caravans as well, pretending to be migrants to gain your trust. And then, just when you let your guard down, just when you get comfortable and fall asleep or unzip your fly to take a leak—that's when a gang member will strike. He'll rob you or kidnap you or worse. So you find someone to trust, who is also someone you don't trust, and who feels the same way about you. That's why you confide in them in the end. Because they're kind enough to trust you. Because they're smart enough not to.

I'm telling you all this now because I wish someone had told me then, back before I joined a migrant caravan. And I especially wish I'd known it before I met Axel. It wouldn't have changed how I feel about him or the fact that I'd risk my life a thousand times over if it meant bringing him back home. But maybe I would have also been more prepared. Maybe I'd have understood that my whole life was about to be upended, and that his would be as well. Maybe I could have warned him. But no one tells you any of this stuff. You don't know until you're in it, and then it's too late.

I JOINED A migrant caravan because I didn't know what else I was supposed to do. I'd come to Mexico to be an anthropologist, of that much I was certain, but the problem was that I wasn't exactly sure what an anthropologist was. Fortunately, I met Armando Amante. He was the one who invited me to join the Viacrucis Migrante.

"What's the Viacrucis Migrante?" I asked.

"It's a migrant caravan," he said.

"Oh," I said, trying to feign like I knew what that was.

Armando Amante looked at me like I was crazy. "You don't know what a migrant caravan is?"

I looked down apologetically and said no, maybe not. This was back in 2015, back before most people had ever heard of migrant caravans, if you can imagine such a thing.

"Well, in Mexico, a caravan is like a big group of protestors," he said. "Everybody joins up together. And a migrant caravan is a big group of migrants, people from all over Central America fleeing their countries. Because there's safety in numbers, right? If you run through a checkpoint by yourself, immigration will catch you for sure. But if you run through it with a hundred other guys, they can't do anything to stop you. You see? And a Viacrucis Migrante, well, sometimes those are the biggest caravans of all. But they only happen once a year, during Easter. Last year's Viacrucis was huge, over a thousand people. Father Solalinde helped lead it."

My ears perked up at the mention of the name. Father Alejandro Solalinde was more than a priest—he was one of the most powerful people in all of Mexico. He was also technically our boss, though I'd never seen him in person.

Solalinde became famous after founding a migrant shelter in southern Mexico called Hermanos en el Camino, which meant "Brothers on the Road," or "Brothers on the Path," as in the Christian path, or the righteous path, or the path that led to heaven. But the priest didn't have much interest in heaven, which made him all the more interesting to me. Instead, he seemed to be fixated on hell. Not the hell of the next world but the one in Mexico, the one that Central American migrants endured trying to reach the United States. He led marches to illuminate their suffering—how they were attacked by gangs and drug cartels on their perilous journeys north—and held press conferences about the brutality of immigration officials and police. Journalists from the *New York Times* and the *Los Angeles Times* and all the other *Times* routinely quoted Solalinde's scathing indictments of corruption and violence in the country, and he frequently drew comparisons to Mahatma Gandhi, Nelson Mandela, and Martin Luther King Jr. There was even talk of a Nobel Peace Prize nomination.

Then, just months before I arrived in Mexico, state forces kidnapped and disappeared forty-three students in the southern state of Guerrero, in what later became known as the Iguala Massacre. In response, millions of people rallied across the country to demand a national investigation. One of the most outspoken was Father Solalinde. He openly condemned the presidential party, the PRI, and made it known that he believed the students were murdered on government orders. From the news coverage, Solalinde seemed like a hero. He was someone who pursued justice at all costs, even if it meant risking his life. I had to meet him. Not that I knew all that much about Central American migration, or that Solalinde knew anything about anthropology. But, as I already said, I didn't know much about anthropology either. Back in the US, I'd taken some classes and read some books, but I'd never conducted any real fieldwork before. So I applied for a research grant to move to Mexico, and, to my surprise, I was selected. I was going to be forged in fire.

To start my research, I decided that I'd travel to Hermanos en el Camino and volunteer my services, however inept they might be. I had no idea how a would-be anthropologist could be of service to an internationally renowned priest. All I knew was that I was preoccupied with a deep yearning to be part of a cause, as young people so often are, and to find someone who might recognize my rough potential and mold me into something useful. So I packed a single bag, left my apartment in Mexico City, and boarded a fourteen-hour bus bound for Hermanos, hoping that Father Solalinde might be that person.

But after working at the shelter for the better part of a month, I hadn't so much as glimpsed the priest. He was always away on some speaking tour or attending an important meeting in the capital. Word in the shelter was that Solalinde was fighting a new secret policy called Programa Frontera Sur—the Southern Border Program. Little was known about the Program, except that Mexico was catching and deporting as many Central American migrants as possible, as quietly as possible, at the behest of the United States. Nearly overnight, a quasi-army of immigration agents, federal police, and soldiers descended upon southern Mexico. They came in fleets of souped-up four-wheel-drive vehicles with machine guns mounted on the roof. Scores of new mobile immigration checkpoints appeared out of thin air, just long enough to detain hundreds of people, then disappeared again, only to materialize elsewhere. In Hermanos, it felt like an overwhelming and mysterious force lurked just outside our walls. It wasn't uncommon to see someone who, in an effort to avoid the new checkpoints, had walked the bottoms of their feet clean off in the jungle, and migrants stumbled into the shelter in various states of shell shock after being beaten and left for dead. A war zone had opened up in southern Mexico, funded by the American government, and no one in the US seemed to know.

Stuck within the relative safety of the shelter walls, however, I mostly spent my days doing chores—chopping firewood for the cafeteria's woodburning stoves or scrubbing toilets in the men's dormitories—and I began to feel restless and disheartened. It was ridiculous, I realized, to have expected that I would waltz in and catch the priest's attention. So when Armando Amante proposed marching with the Viacrucis, I jumped at the chance. At the time, Armando was also working as a volunteer at the shelter. He was originally a migrant from Honduras, but had settled down in Mexico after the staff at Hermanos helped him obtain a visa. Now that he was no longer under threat of deportation, he was itching to expose what was happening to his compatriots under the Southern Border Program.

"Is Solalinde leading the caravan again?" I asked.

Armando spat on the ground and said absolutely not. After Solalinde's participation in last year's Viacrucis, the Mexican government forbade him to ever partake in another caravan. Under the Program, all the activists and priests were being silenced by the PRI. The problem, said Armando, was that priests were too traditional and obedient. Everything was sacred and pious to them, which meant—at least according to Armando—that everything was tedious and dull. They didn't fight back. "But this year is going to be different," he said. "Me and my friend Irineo, we're changing things. No more priests. And no more Solalinde."

I shifted uneasily.

Armando insisted that Solalinde wasn't living up to his reputation. Leading another caravan could have been a way for the priest to stick it to immigration, he said, to show that he wasn't afraid of them, but instead he chickened out. So Armando was going to do it himself. The goal was to march from the Guatemala-Mexico border all the way to Ixtepec, Oaxaca, where Hermanos en el Camino was located. The three-hundred-mile stretch was one of the most patrolled areas in all of Mexico, with potentially dozens of mobile immigration checkpoints funded by the Southern Border Program. The new Viacrucis Migrante, said Armando, would intentionally target these checkpoints. It would overwhelm them with as many people as possible and then keep charging north. "That way we'll draw attention to the Program," he said, "and we'll expose what's really going on."

I asked whether something like that was safe.

But Armando just shrugged his shoulders. "Viacrucis Migrantes have been happening for years now," he said, "and the government has never stopped one before. Never. This is our chance to stand up to them. To call their bluff."

"But if Solalinde can't do it," I said, "surely we can't."

"Man, what is it with you and Solalinde?" asked Armando. "Look around you. The guy's never here. You can stay if you like. Scrub some more toilets or whatever. But if you want to know what being a migrant is really about, and not just the boring everyday bullshit that goes on inside this shelter, you should come."

The next day, I bought a one-way ticket to the Guatemala-Mexico border for March 23, 2015, two weeks before Easter Sunday.

WHEN I ARRIVED in Ciudad Hidalgo, a little pueblo nestled into the leafy-green crook of the southern border, Armando stopped returning my calls. Not a good sign, I thought. But the town was small, so I wandered around until I found him at the local cybercafé, a business that's still popular in southern Mexico, since most people can't afford a computer themselves.

"Is everything okay?" I asked. "I couldn't reach you."

"Oh, don't worry," he said. "It's just that you were asking too many questions, so I turned my phone off. You need to relax, man. We're not so big on planning."

Another bad sign.

"Fuck this fucking priest," seethed a man hunched over a computer at the back of the café.

"Levi," said Armando, "I want to introduce you to the co-founder of the 2015 Viacrucis Migrante: Irineo Mujica."

The man didn't turn around from the computer. Armando explained that he'd met Irineo in Chahuites, a small town just south of Hermanos en el Camino. He ran another migrant shelter there affiliated with Father Solalinde's humanitarian network.

"Irineo's trying to reach the priest," said Armando.

"Who, Solalinde?"

"No, not Solalinde. The local priest here in Hidalgo."

"I thought the Viacrucis wasn't going to have a priest."

"We're not," snapped Irineo, wheeling around. He was older than Armando, though it was hard to tell exactly how much older, since he was incredibly disheveled. Beneath his matted hair glared a pair of dark, hooded eyes, and he was wearing an unwashed t-shirt that was obviously turned inside out. "It just looks better in front of the cameras to have a priest send us off. But the fucking guy has disappeared on me." He turned back to the computer.

Armando explained that Irineo had booked the priest to lead a prayer at the start of the Viacrucis. It was meant to be a kind of olive branch to Solalinde and the other clergy in the area, a way to show that the Viacrucis still respected them, so that they wouldn't denounce the march even if they disagreed with it on principle. But the priest had ditched us. Clearly a bad omen, everyone could agree, even though we weren't supposed to care about priests. It didn't help that nobody could remember his name.

Another guy walked into the cybercafé. Armando introduced him as the Viacrucis Migrante's third cofounder. "His name is also Armando," said Armando.

The other Armando had big ears and a shy smile. "Armando Mejia," he said as he shook my hand. "Nice to meet you." He said that, like Armando Amante, he was from Honduras, but he'd also been living in Mexico for some time.

"We're tocayos," said Armando Amante.

"What's that?" I asked.

"It's just a fun word here in Mexico," the Armandos explained. It meant "name twin." Any two people, even if they were strangers, became tocayos once they met and realized they had the same name.

"The son of a bitch is avoiding me," snarled Irineo. He pointed at the Armandos. "You two, go to the church and see if you can track him down. And you, gringo, come with me." I glanced uneasily at Armando Amante as he ducked out the door. Whatever airs Armando had put on about starting the Viacrucis himself, it was clear that Irineo was actually the one running the show. I was worried he wanted to get me alone in order to grill me, to demand to know what a lost American kid was doing on his march anyway, but the reason he requested my company became apparent as soon as the Armandos were out of earshot. "So I hear you have a scholarship," he said, turning his empty pockets inside out.

We walked to the local hardware store. I paid for a length of beige cloth, two cans of spray paint, and a soda for Irineo. One can of spray paint was black, to connote seriousness, and the other was red, to evoke spilled blood. When we met back up with the Armandos, they said an attendant at the church told them that, though he wasn't supposed to say so, the priest had skipped town. The other priests would have strangled him if he'd endorsed the Viacrucis publicly.

"Bastard," spat Irineo.

We unrolled the cloth and cut it into two banners. Then we stood over them in silence for a long time. I didn't understand why we weren't talking, so I kept my mouth shut.

Finally, Armando Mejia turned to me. "Levi, you studied Spanish in school, right?" I said that I had, and he handed me the spray paint. "None of us did. So sometimes the spelling gets a little confusing."

"Oh," I said, sensing their embarrassment. "Of course. Um, what should I write?"

After some debate about the tone and tenor of the banners and which words should be emphasized in the blood of red paint, the first banner read:

VIACRUCIS MIGRANTE
NO MORE BLOOD

And the second:

SOUTHERN BORDER PROGRAM
EXTERMINATION OF MIGRANTS
UNDECLARED WAR

Only one thing remained: to recruit some actual migrants. Irineo directed us to a shelter on the other side of the Rio Suchiate, in the small town of Tecún Umán, Guatemala. There were no border guards or checkpoints, and it didn't cross my mind until later that we had, technically, entered Guatemala illegally. The houses on the other side of the border were strange. Some were almost falling apart but had unusually large and expensive-looking metal doors that were padlocked shut. Armando Amante nodded toward one. "That's where the goods are stored before they get sent north."

"Goods?" I repeated.

"The cartels' goods. Drugs and people."

When we arrived at the migrant shelter, Irineo strode into its center, cleared his throat, and called for everyone's attention. About a dozen curious onlookers gathered around. Then Irineo gave his pitch. He spoke emphatically about the plight of migrants in Mexico. About how dangerous it was with the gangs, cartels, and corrupt police. He talked about the long-suffering migrant and the sacrifices every single person in front of him had made already.

The message didn't sound that different from Solalinde's, I thought.

But, Irineo continued, things had only gotten worse. If any of them tried to cross Mexico alone, they'd almost certainly be caught. It was all because of the Southern Border Program, a secret plan designed by the Americans to turn Mexico into a bloodbath. But they had a chance to fight back. They could join us, the Viacrucis Migrante, a caravan that was beginning right now, right here, in Tecún Umán.

"So, who's with us?" called out Irineo, concluding with a raised fist. A bit much, I thought.

There was a nervous silence, and then people began to stroll away. Only one migrant remained, a young man about my age. Undeterred, Irineo asked his name, but the young man said, very shyly, that he didn't want to say given the circumstances.

"Never mind," said Irineo. "Look at him, he's small, but he's strong. We'll call him el Chaparrito." Shorty, in Mexican slang.

Irineo had arranged for a photo op back on the Mexican side of the border, which was short and chaotic. First, many of the reporters—unable to reach Armando Amante now that his phone was turned off—weren't sure where they were supposed to meet us, and we wandered around town aimlessly until we finally ran into them. Then Irineo made us all pose behind him for the cameras while he gave interviews.

"That piece of shit," hissed Armando Amante as Irineo instructed us to hold the heavy canvas banners a bit higher. "He always does this. I'm just as much the leader of the Viacrucis as he is, but he takes all the attention."

Then, from out of nowhere, a lone trumpeter in clown makeup appeared and began blasting an oddly forlorn melody. He was neither particularly skilled nor welcome, and someone yelled for him to kindly shut the fuck up, he was ruining the television interview. But instead of leaving, our would-be serenader simply stood there in silence, mopey and dejected, until someone remembered that they'd booked him ages ago to provide a bit more pomp and circumstance for our departure. It dawned on me that I was possibly making the worst mistake of my life. My safety now lay in the hands of insane people. I considered making a break for it and abandoning the whole affair entirely, but then the photoshoot was over and Irineo was pushing me down the road, waving goodbye to the cameras.

Ciudad Hidalgo quickly faded into an alternating patchwork of small farms, deserted houses, and jungle. We were all alone. For some reason I couldn't quite discern, we were still holding the banner, which pressed itself against our waists when the wind blew across the open farmland. We walked that way, silent and steady, for many hours. After the sun set, the quick silhouettes of birds or bats darted against a dark purple sky. We heard the sound of a vehicle slowing behind us, and then two short honks. It was a neon orange truck—immigration. I could see the muscles in Armando Amante's shoulders tense. A tall man stepped out of the vehicle and gave a cheerful wave. He said that the National Institute of Migration had heard about our march and sent him to ensure our safety.

"It can be dangerous out here," he said, gesturing to the empty fields. "Not everybody is friendly, you know." For the rest of the caravan, immigration would "escort" us to our destination.

There was nothing to do except thank him and keep trudging down the road. Above us the sky turned into a black vacuum, and from the darkness came the soft song of insects calling out from empty space. Only the headlights of the immigration truck illuminated our path. No priests, one migrant, and us, in the great unseen expanse of southern Mexico.

When we reached the outskirts of the nearby town of Tapachula, Irineo said he knew of a hotel that took cash and didn't ask questions. A place where our immigration tail wouldn't find us, just in case. He led us down a dark alleyway that snaked between a pirated video store on the right and some kind of combination dance hall–barbershop on the left. The hotel lobby was unlit save for the glow of the attendant's small television at the front desk. The place smelled like raw sewage and bleach. Irineo asked for two rooms, then held out an empty palm until I filled it with a stack of pesos. He would bunk with el Chaparrito tonight, he said, and instructed the rest of us to share the other room. I thought it was odd that Irineo wanted to sleep with a stranger, rather than with Armando Amante, but kept quiet. The attendant waved us down the hallway without a word. The deadbolt of our door had been punched out, and the old man showed us how to wind a coat hanger through the hole as a "lock." Any passerby would be able to peep in or enter as they pleased. The room was "hot as hell itself," as Armando Amante muttered, and had no windows. A single but surprisingly bright lightbulb hung from the ceiling over two bare mattresses. The toilet had no lid and was encrusted in dried urine. The shower was curtainless.

"So," I said, trying to mask my growing sense of dread. "What was all that with immigration? They're just going to follow us now? Is that normal?"

"They know that they can't stop us," said Armando Amante. "It would look bad to detain a bunch of peaceful protestors. So they sent a babysitter to spy on us instead."

From down the hall came the drone of late-night television game shows, the wails of a baby, and periodic shouting—a couple having an argument, or sex.

"Well," said Armando Mejia, "I suppose we should get some sleep."

I offered to share a bed, but the Armandos said not to be silly and switched off the lightbulb. In the dark, I heard one Armando mutter something to the other. Something glanced softly against our door then continued on down the hall. Someone farted. I was twenty-four years old, thousands of miles from home, and an accidental founding member of the 2015 Viacrucis Migrante, the migrant caravan that—though I would have sworn differently that night—was about to change the course of Mexican history.

CHAPTER 2

WAKE UP, WHITE BOY

THE NEXT MORNING, Irineo woke us with a bang on the door. I quickly rinsed off in the shower—who knew when my next one would be—and walked back through the hotel alley and into the sunlight. Irineo stood on the street corner, one leg cocked atop the curb, shaving his neck with a dry disposable razor. El Chaparrito stood obediently beside him.

"Time to get new recruits," was all he said and hailed a cab, which I paid for. I still basically knew nothing about Irineo. Whenever I tried to make small talk, he acted as if he couldn't understand my American accent. He acknowledged me only when requesting more money, which he justified by stating that I, as a US citizen, had an obligation to redistribute my wealth to poor Latin Americans like him. That I, in fact, had no wealth to speak of mattered little. Several days later, when the first stories about the Viacrucis were published by the reporters from Ciudad Hidalgo, I would learn that Irineo was forty-four years old, Mexican, and, in addition to his migrant shelter in Chahuites, ran a small nonprofit called Pueblo Sin Fronteras. Other than that, he was a mystery, an unknown small-time activist looking to make his mark with the Viacrucis.

The Shelter of Jesus the Good Shepherd for the Poor and the Migrant lay at the edge of town. The name sounded better in Spanish. After Irineo gave his spiel—which he seemed to have memorized—he asked el Chaparrito to testify to the crowd that everything he said was true. El Chaparrito stepped forward, his head down, and repeated that, yes, everything Mr. Irineo Mujica said was the truth. On the Viacrucis he had been treated fairly and was fed three meals a day. Strange, I thought, since el Chaparrito had only been with us long enough to have eaten dinner and breakfast. Apparently, Irineo had coached him in the hotel room.

The response in the Good Shepherd, however, was decidedly more enthusiastic than in Tecún Umán. Many of these migrants had been stuck in Tapachula for weeks, or even months, now that the Southern Border Program had blocked all routes out of town. The crowd spilled out onto the street, and more figures emerged from the edge of the jungle—whole families who said that they were sleeping in the bush because there wasn't enough room in the shelter. Irineo shouted that we were leaving in five minutes. Anyone who wanted to come with us should ready themselves. Amazingly, people started to fall in line. Then we were off, marching down the road. Just like that, our ranks had grown from five to fifty.

In the main square of Tapachula we gained another twenty people, migrants who had gone to the city center to beg or to sell what little wares they could hustle up. They saw us marching by, singing and chanting like some kind of lumpen carnival, and joined in like they'd been expecting us all along. But the thrill of our embarkment into the wilds of Mexico dissipated as soon as we hit the highway. It was easily over a hundred degrees, and the black pitch road was twenty degrees hotter still. My back was drenched in sweat. My phone overheated and shut off. As we exited Tapachula, the orange immigration truck pulled up behind us.

Like any good anthropologist would do—or at least what I imagined any good anthropologist would do—I'd packed a notebook and an audio recorder, and I busied myself trying to learn everyone's names and countries and where they hoped to go. The first person I met was Ever Hernández, who said he was seventeen and had fled Honduras with his family after his mother's ex-boyfriend sent a team of hitmen to kill them. Ever pointed out each of his eight family members, who walked quietly behind us, including his mother, who was in her sixties; his older brother, Iván, who had a constellation of stars tattooed across his right eyebrow; and his sister, Celia, and her infant son, a little boy everyone simply called "the Russian" because of his shock of blond hair. As Ever spoke, his head jerked reflexively to peer back over his shoulder, as if an assassin might be right behind him. I asked if he thought his family was still being followed, and Ever said that, yes, it was possible. He didn't feel comfortable being exposed on the road, even with so many other people around. Then, as if to put the matter out of his mind, he asked what an anthropologist was anyway and remarked that he thought it had something to do with digging up bones.

No, not usually, I said. He was probably thinking of archeology, or maybe paleontology, which was a common misunderstanding. Most anthropologists worked with people, living people, and I was interested in Central American migrants, about what their lives were like now, in the present, and about what they dreamed they might be someday in the future.

There was always someone new to talk to. Jeferson, Andarson, Jenry, Wiliam—strange spellings of familiar names. Remnants, I believed, from centuries of colonization and military intervention at the hands of the US and Great Britain. Another man refused to give me his name but said he was from Nicaragua and a former Sandinista guerrilla. He professed to have lost his mind in the war and claimed to trust no one, not even himself. Most of the women I tried to interview immediately declined. A strange man in a strange land was to be avoided. But a mother named Mildred, who was traveling alone with her three children, said that I didn't look like much of a threat to her, with my scraggly hair and skinny arms. But then, after a moment's pause, she added that, before she left Guatemala City, she had taken her preteen daughter to see a doctor, where they both received birth control shots.

"That way," she said, "even if you did have bad intentions, we couldn't get pregnant."

Then another woman tapped me on the shoulder and demanded to know why I hadn't written her name down yet in my little book. Was I avoiding her because she was trans?

I said of course not and asked her name.

"Shakira," she said.

"Shakira what?"

"Shakira Shakira," she sang, sashaying. She was wearing a bubble-gum pink crop top with matching pink cargo pants. I noticed that she wasn't carrying any kind of bag at all, which meant this outfit was the only thing she owned in the world. She said that she was from Honduras but was heading back to Miami, where her boyfriend was waiting for her.

By midafternoon, I gave up the interviews due to exhaustion. We'd walked thirteen miles, half a marathon, and still had another half to go. The land was varied and wild. At first, it was deep, verdant jungle, with leaves and vines that stretched out toward the road as if to suffocate us. But then the pavement would turn abruptly, and we'd find ourselves in a burnt ochre desert. Then the road would plunge back into lush vegetation. At first, I pondered how such a landscape of contrasts could exist, but soon what once felt exciting became mundane, and what was mundane became monotonous, and what was monotonous became excruciating in the sun of southern Mexico. I could feel large blisters blooming across the bottoms of my feet. Still, I was grateful to be wearing tennis shoes—most people only had cheap plastic flip-flops, which mercilessly sliced into their skin with each step. At dusk, we stopped at a gas station just long enough to buy duct tape, which some of the men unflinchingly wrapped around their feet and between their bleeding toes, a gritty bandage of last resort.

When we spotted the first immigration checkpoint, it was night. In the distance, the light of the checkpoint shone a dazzling white. Fortunately, it didn't appear to be particularly large or well equipped. I could just make out four dark figures pacing against the glow. Armando Amante conducted a quick head count. That way, if anyone was snatched, we'd know.

"Seventy-two," he called out to Irineo.

"Good," Irineo replied. "We should have enough." He sketched out a basic marching formation in the dirt: women and children in front, with men in the back. In order to look less threatening, he said. I was about to ask whether that didn't also put the women and children in the most danger, but then Irineo grabbed me by the arm and dragged me to the front as well. "Get your ass up here," he said. "And wave that recorder of yours around. There's no way they'll fuck with us if they see a gringo recording them." I did as I was told.

From the back of the march, the Armandos began to chant over and over again, until everyone joined in and our voices carried out across the road. It was a strange chant, I thought, a song about how migrants were not criminals but international workers, even though this was a crowd of people who might not have ever had access to a steady job in their lives. Behind our rear guard, the orange truck rolled along silently. I suddenly feared that this was all a trap, that we were now being squeezed between the checkpoint and the truck with nowhere to run. Being an American, my implicit understanding of the police was that they would sooner shoot us than to have their authority so brazenly flouted. We were less than one hundred yards away. The border patrol officers were holding something. Guns? Handcuffs? No, it was just their cell phones, recording us. One man even had a handheld camcorder, which he pointed directly in my face, and I made sure my bandana was securely over my nose and mouth.

Then we crossed into the pearly white light of the checkpoint, so bright that we all had to squint our eyes, and I held my breath, anticipating the officers' inevitable lunge toward us. But they stayed where they were. And then we were through, out of the light and back into the shadows, and a triumphant and incredulous cry erupted from the crowd. Armando Amante counted us all again. Seventy-two. We had done it. We took on an immigration checkpoint, and we won. I wasn't able to articulate it at the time, but, looking back now, that was the moment something changed inside me. It came like a slow thunderclap. I entered that checkpoint in southern Mexico from the old world—in the midst of paupers, led by a company of fools—and I stepped out into a new one. A world in which we could take matters into our own hands. From that moment on, I began to feel like I was being followed by something. Something that sat unseen just over the horizon. Something that I didn't have a name for yet, but something that was coming to find me one way or another.

BY THE TIME we finally stopped in the tiny town of Huixtla, it was well past midnight. Irineo announced that the local priest had agreed to let us sleep on the church grounds, and we filed into an old annex. The orange immigration truck honked good-bye and coasted down the dark road, its beady-eyed brake lights disappearing around a corner. It would be back in the morning. The interior of the annex was unfurnished, and half of the ceiling was caved in, the remnants of which were still scattered across the floor. People simply stepped around the debris and stretched out underneath the open hole. Two nuns stood by the front door, silently distributing stacks of tortillas. Someone handed me a styrofoam plate of beans and a cup of hibiscus water, and I wearily flopped down in the corner of the room. I must have nodded off, because suddenly the Sandinista was standing over me, his eyes gleaming maniacally, screaming, "Wake up, white boy."

The whole room froze. I rose to my feet gingerly, as if confronted by a wild animal.

"You better not go to sleep," he crowed. "Or else."

"Or else what?" I said, trying to force a chuckle, as if I wasn't terrified.

"Or else this." The Sandinista mimed raking a knife across his throat. He held my imaginary decapitated head between his hands and brought it down to his crotch, thrusting wildly. "I'll skull fuck you while you sleep, white boy."

The room roared with laughter. Someone wolf-whistled. A young mother glared at me disapprovingly before pulling her drowsy toddler away from the commotion, as if somehow the ruckus was my fault. The Sandinista, reveling in the attention, continued to undulate his pelvis. Fully emasculated, all I could do was gaze dumbstruck at my own erotic demise. All my excitement from the recent victory at the checkpoint disappeared instantly, as did any illusion I had about fitting in.

Armando Amante tugged my arm. "What are you doing down here? We're waiting for you in the priest's house."

I let him pull me away, grateful for an excuse to leave, to belong somewhere else. The priest's house was conjoined to the church, and the dining room table was filled with food in anticipation of our arrival—cheese, chicken, beans, rice, and an assortment of fruits and salsas. Irineo and Armando Mejia were already there, seated around the priest and a few other people who I assumed worked for the church. A nun offered me a glass of water. I sat at the only open seat left, near the end of the table. Irineo and the priest were in the middle of a heated discussion regarding the clergy who didn't support the Viacrucis. The priest said something about how cowardly all the other priests in the area were, and how someone needed to step up to immigration and show them who was actually in charge. But then again, he sighed, we couldn't possibly understand the pressure he himself was under. He was already catching hell just for receiving us. Armando Mejia asked if he knew what Solalinde thought of our caravan, and the priest grunted as he chewed, mulling the name over. He said that he wasn't sure what Solalinde was playing at, but that he seemed to know something we didn't. That was the thing with Solalinde, said the priest. He always knew more than anyone else, and even if you didn't like him—which was understandable, because after all he was a son of bitch—you should still take note of whatever the son of a bitch was doing. Because sooner or later you'd be adjusting your whole life around him.

"Fuck Solalinde," said Irineo. "We don't need him anymore. We're doing it without him."

"Maybe," said the priest.

I tried to feign nonchalance, but I could feel the blood pounding in my ears. Irineo or Armando Amante speaking so irreverently about Solalinde was one thing, but another priest? And it wasn't even the irreverence, really, but the caution in his voice, the implicit understanding that it was all a game, but a game whose rules would become clear only after the fact. If even this priest didn't understand what was going on, it seemed impossible that I ever would. I thought again about the Sandinista's threat. I wasn't an organizer, and I definitely wasn't a migrant. I didn't know what I was, other than lonely.

SOME MORE THINGS that no one tells you about migrant caravans: There are no toilets, and no one has toilet paper. A significant portion of your food is scavenged from the jungle and nearby farms, but it probably isn't ripe yet, so you'll gnaw on green mango and rock-hard avocado, both of which will cause bowel movements so horrific they're almost awe inducing. Everyone knows that the fastest and cheapest way to score some protein is a can of tuna, and every gas station in southern Mexico keeps them in stock for this reason. Teenagers will fall in love while sharing the oily cans of fish. Adults will also fall in love, or at least have sex.

NGOs will donate condoms but not toilet paper. Some small pueblos will hear that you're coming and cook meals to welcome you. These meals are usually just beans and tortillas, but they are a gift, and the people who cooked them will speak of when they were once migrants as well. Other towns will want nothing to do with you. You won't have enough underwear. There definitely won't be enough tampons—NGOs will donate pads but not tampons. You will have to drink whatever water is available, no matter how obviously impure, and suffer the consequences later. If you are an American, most migrant shelters will insist you use the staff bathrooms because the migrant ones aren't "suitable" for you. You'll seriously never have enough underwear. Almost no one brushes their teeth, because there are no toothbrushes and even less toothpaste. Makeup will be scarce, razor blades scarcer. Men will grow scruff and women will grow leg hair. Teenage girls will insist on wearing pants despite the heat to cover their unshaven skin. Eventually a secret market of razor blades and makeup will form, with people lending what they have in exchange for favors, but the favors will vary depending on who you ask and what you ask for and whether you are a generally pleasant person. There will be a less secret market of drugs and alcohol, though demand will remain centralized within a significantly smaller group, mostly men, who think they're being slick, but in reality everyone knows what they're doing.

You will cry in the dark. You will begin to suspect that someone or something is always watching. You will feel eternally alone. You will thank God the children don't understand what's happening, just as much for yourself as for them. They will laugh and play despite everything. They will think that charging through an immigration checkpoint is a game. You will buy them candy to keep them quiet and happy. A robust and legitimate market of sugar products will emerge before any of the secret markets, with several entrepreneurial individuals investing in bags of bulk candy and then selling them piece by piece for a markup. In the end they will probably make more money than the drug dealers and can fund their entire journey through Mexico this way, selling sweets one peso at a time. If these same people apply for an official work permit, the Mexican government will deny them. The Mexican government will deny everyone work permits. The Mexican government will probably deny everyone asylum wholesale, despite what they promise in the media. Despite what they promise you. No matter what they say, they do not want you here. I knew almost none of this yet.

THE NEXT TOWN we marched to was Mapastepec, a tiny place where everyone slept outside in the main square. Whenever we happened upon a gas station, I purchased several armfuls of snacks and passed them out—waters, cookies, and candy, as well as the occasional pack of cigarettes to share among the men, especially the Sandinista. If I could not win their love, I thought, perhaps I could buy it. And I did see a return on my investment. After a few days, people began to call me by my name. At the beginning of the march, I introduced myself with the anglicized pronunciation of Levi. "Like the jeans," I'd say. My tocayo was Levi Strauss. But that kind of Levi sounded strange in Spanish. It was hard for native speakers to pronounce. So I switched to the other pronunciation, as in Claude Lévi-Strauss, the great anthropologist. A new tocayo, I supposed, and to pass the time I tried to think of all my others. There was Primo Levi, the Italian chemist, author, and partisan. And there was "levy" like a tax or the archaic terminology for a military draft. There was also "levee," as in a protective dyke, a floodplain, a landing place. When I asked Armando Amante if inanimate objects counted as tocayos, he rolled his eyes.

"Do all anthropologists ask such weird questions," he said, "or is it just you?"

While we marched, I tried to find out more about the Southern Border Program. I learned that it was conceived in 2014, the same year that nearly seventy thousand unaccompanied minors from Central America were apprehended by border patrol after crossing into the US. Their arrival was sensationalized by the media and eventually dubbed the "Border Crisis," which caused headaches for politicians on both sides of the aisle. Republicans were in a bind because if they remained tough on immigration, they appeared heartless and betrayed their supposed commitment to family values and Christian charity. Democrats had the inverse problem—if they accepted the children, they'd be accused of political sentimentality and of allowing immigrants to drain national resources. So the Obama administration cut a back-alley deal: the US would quietly send Mexico millions of dollars every year, and Mexico would keep Central Americans from reaching the border at all costs. The program especially targeted women and children, since they were much more sympathetic to American audiences and could potentially whip up another media frenzy, a recurrence that the Obama administration was obviously hoping to avoid. The Program's power lay in its secrecy. It had no clearly defined policy, law, or centralized supervision, which allowed it to silently adapt itself to hunt down migrants using increasingly efficient and brutal methods, without having to answer to anyone.

The most obvious evidence of the Program, however, was that migrants were no longer allowed to ride the Beast. The Beast was a train passage that had been a symbol of Central American migration for decades. Tens of thousands of migrants used to ride it to the US each year, braving the elements and gangs atop its rickety cars. The Beast was dangerous, but it was fast. If you rode it hard and pushed your luck, you could make it across Mexico in two weeks. Even better, you could do it for free, without hiring a smuggler. But after the Program, immigration forces swarmed the tracks. Every week there was a new report of agents pulling hundreds of migrants off the speeding train, or even shooting at them as the cars whipped by. Migrants had no choice but to navigate the jungles and deserts of southern Mexico on foot—vast swaths of isolated country where gangs and drug cartels roamed. No one knew exactly how many migrants went missing in those obscure and veiled corners of Mexico. But people kept walking into the unknown because it was still safer than facing the foot soldiers of the Program.

WITH EACH IMMIGRATION checkpoint we passed, our ranks continued to swell. Soon we were easily over 150 people. Every time I turned around, it seemed like more migrants had materialized behind us. I watched a man I'd never seen before peek from behind a tree and observe the Viacrucis carefully. Then, after a moment's consideration, he dashed from the jungle and fell in lockstep with the rest of the marchers, as if he'd always been expecting us. I squinted into the thick underbrush and wondered how many others were in there, watching from the shadows.

We were in Arriaga, at the Home of Mercy migrant shelter, when the rumors started. Whispers that immigration was preparing to bust us. No one knew when they would strike, but everyone agreed it was only a matter of time. It didn't help that, after marching for nearly a week nonstop, Irineo abruptly announced that we were to remain in Arriaga until further notice. He refused to say anything more and then began to disappear for hours each day, which made me suspect that he really had caught wind of a raid and was now sneaking away to make frantic phone calls and beg god only knew who for help.

The rumors didn't stop our numbers from growing, however. If anything, they helped us. Our first day in Home of Mercy, every migrant in the shelter decided to join the Viacrucis. More people showed up the next day, and the next. We were now over 250 strong. The more migrants we enlisted, the more insistent the rumors became, and the more agitated we all felt. Small fights broke out in the cramped quarters. Outside, the orange immigration truck looped dilatory circles around the shelter. For the first time in my life, I had the sensation of being prey.

To escape the pressure cooker, I wandered through Arriaga, which was like a ghost town. Just a year ago, it had a thriving downtown that catered to the hundreds of Central Americans who arrived each day on the Beast. But after the Program, Arriaga's economy dried up. The restaurants, hotels, bars, and brothels were all shuttered. Empty train cars sat motionless on the tracks, and one was tipped over on its side, like the calcified carcass of an ancient animal.

One night, as I lay down to sleep on the concrete floor of the common area, I heard shouting from the computer room, which Irineo and the Armandos had converted into their private sleeping quarters. Then Armando Amante flung open the door and stormed out, muttering something about how he couldn't take it anymore, how Irineo was fucking him, fucking all of us. I lay awake thinking about Father Solalinde. Where was he? Did he know that we were in danger? Surely if anyone could fix this mess that Irineo had gotten us into, it was the priest.

I wasn't the only one who had this thought. Armando Mejia told me he'd floated the idea of contacting Solalinde, but Irineo was having none of it. The latent threat of his authority being subverted, however, apparently lit a fire under him. The next day, Irineo announced that we would be leaving in an hour. We were to make a beeline for his shelter in Chahuites, a two-day march, and there was suddenly no time to spare. While everyone packed their bags, I sat outside on the curb next to Ever. He said he had something to tell me. He looked around to make sure the coast was clear, and then whispered that he wasn't seventeen. He was actually twenty-six, but he told everyone he was a minor because he was gay, and to be gay and a migrant was a bad combination, especially when you were as small and skinny as he was. So it was better to just say that he was seventeen, still a child, and therefore somewhat beyond suspicion. I would later learn that this wasn't an uncommon tactic for queer people on the migrant trail. In fact, most people obscured at least some identifying information about themselves—they lied about their ages, their hometowns, and their names. Even Armando later told me that his last name wasn't really Amante.

But before I could respond to Ever, there was a shout from down the street. Then a stallion, unbridled and randy, came charging toward us, and we had to scramble to our feet and dive behind a tree for cover. The horse was alabaster white from nose to tail, except for its two-foot-long erection, which was a dark gray in some places and pink in others, and swung wildly beneath its belly. Every few paces he would bray, rear up on his hind legs, and kick the air. Several men from the caravan, the Sandinista among them, began to whoop and holler at the horse's bobbing phallus from behind a small patch of bushes.

Two boys appeared, barefoot and out of breath. The older one swung a lasso at the stallion's head but missed, and a man's voice cheered him on to try again. Another shouted that he knew how the horse felt, to let him have his fun. The stallion bolted and tried to leap over a shoddy barbed-wire fence. One of his hind legs clipped the top wire and dragged it down before he darted through an empty field and retreated behind a house. The boys scampered over the fence in hot pursuit. It felt like a sign, but an empty sign, a symbol of something that none of us could quite comprehend.

Then we all lined up and marched into the desolate town center, where Irineo had arranged a cluster of journalists for another photo op. We dutifully chanted and posed for their cameras, and Irineo gave another interview in which he said that the Mexican government was being paid by the Americans to slaughter migrants. The whole time I kept peeking around the corners of houses, hoping to catch another glimpse of the horse, but I never saw it again.

WE ARRIVED IN Chahuites unscathed but on edge, and the state of Irineo's shelter did not help. It was, in a word, disgusting. By far the worst migrant shelter I had ever seen. The structure itself was cinderblock and split into two main spaces. On one side was an empty room, with no ventilation or electricity. It slept approximately twenty people lying down snugly on the floor, which was so dirty I thought it was packed earth until I scraped away the muck with my shoe and saw there was concrete underneath. On the other side was Irineo's bedroom, where Armando said that I should stash my backpack, so I wouldn't have to keep an eye on it for the rest of the evening.

There was an outdoor bathroom, if you could call it that, which consisted of a toilet sitting atop a small platform, with a threadbare sheet hanging in front to provide some semblance of privacy. The toilet could only be flushed by pouring a bucket of water into the bowl, as was customary in rural Mexico, but this one frequently clogged, causing a torrent of water and feces to flood down the platform's steps and into the common area. Next to the toilet was the shower. It had a hole chiseled into the wall at crotch height, like a glory hole, which allowed someone waiting outside—when the toilet was occupied—to piss directly into the shower drain. The whole shelter gave me a terribly ominous feeling, as if some unseen evil was slithering across the floor in the dung and grime. It was surely better, I thought, to sleep in the jungle or risk crashing in the town square than to stay in this hellhole.

An enterprising neighbor had already fired up her comal and was hocking quesadillas to a cluster of hungry migrants when an SUV bumped down the street. For a moment, I thought it was a government vehicle, but then it parked next to the entrance of the shelter, and a small man, much shorter than I had imagined, opened the back door. I recognized him instantly. It was Father Solalinde. I felt an overwhelming sense of relief. We were saved. Irineo shuffled toward the priest and shook his hand. Neither appeared particularly pleased to see the other. Then Solalinde turned and greeted the neighbor cooking the quesadillas by name, and she laughed and said welcome back, Father, would you like something to eat?

No, he said, but could we please use the privacy of her yard for a little meeting? It would only take a minute.

We followed the priest into the patch of scrubby grass, where several chickens clucked around our feet. I was ecstatic. Finally, I thought, this was it. I had waited so long. Solalinde was going to take care of everything.

"What's all this nonsense about a caravan?" The priest spoke softly, and he mostly looked at the ground or out into the distance, as if he was contemplating something from long ago, or yet to come. Irineo tried to reply, but Solalinde cut him off. "I told you, Irineo. I told you so many times not to do this. That my contacts in Mexico City said caravans would not be permitted this year."

"Father," started Irineo again, but the priest silenced him with a wave of his hand.

"This is not a caravan. Do you understand me? From now on, this is a Viacrucis and a Viacrucis only. A pilgrimage. A religious procession of Christians during the Holy Week of Easter."

"Yes, Father," said Irineo. "The caravan has always been religious—"

"No, not caravan. Do not say that word again."

"The Viacrucis has always been religious—"

"Now you're getting it, Irineo." The priest raised his voice only slightly, but it was a palpable change. "Caravans are political. Pilgrimages are not. See the difference? And no more of this silly anti-government nonsense. Don't you understand what you have done? They are almost here. They are ready to take all of you away. If you call yourselves a caravan again in public, that's it. They will come. And if that happens, I cannot and will not support you. Not even I have that much power."

Then the priest said that he had to make an important call. He'd meet us in the town square that evening, where he would announce his official support for the Viacrucis Migrante, a holy, nonpartisan pilgrimage that was definitely not a caravan. After Solalinde disappeared back behind the tinted windows of his SUV, Irineo grumbled something about the priest swooping in and stealing all the fucking credit, but he ultimately seemed to accept what was now clearly out of his hands.

I showered quickly in the shelter to freshen up for the priest's speech and was pissed on twice through the glory hole. There was no soap. I dried myself with a dirty t-shirt and then walked to the town square. When Solalinde stepped up to the mic, there was a murmur in the crowd. His speech was short and to the point. He spoke about Christ and sacrifice. He spoke about Easter and the resurrection of the body. He spoke of pilgrims and pilgrimage. Throughout the speech, he almost entirely avoided the words "migrant" or "migration." Then he announced that he would welcome the Viacrucis to his shelter in two days for Easter Mass. Everyone cheered. Banda music suddenly erupted from the town square's loudspeakers. People began to dance in celebration. Solalinde quietly slipped into his SUV once again, which was parked on the same side of the street as the orange immigration truck.

When I returned to the shelter that night, the light was still on in Irineo's bedroom. I knocked and opened the door. Irineo was sitting on his bed in his boxer shorts. On his knee was a young boy in a pair of dirty white briefs. Judging by his face, he was approximately twelve years old. The boy was leaning against Irineo's bare chest, who had his hand on the boy's lower stomach. Several men I recognized from the Viacrucis, but whose names I didn't know, were lounging on a bunk bed nearby.

"Sorry, just grabbing my backpack," I said, slinging it over my shoulder. Without a word, Irineo swiftly closed the door behind me, and I heard someone start to laugh inside. I had only been in the room for a matter of seconds.

I lay down on the floor of the common area and closed my eyes. From up above I heard the sound of clanking and someone cursing to himself. Then a torrent of foul-smelling water washed over my legs. I realized why no one else was sleeping in this spot. It was right below the toilet. In the dark I could just barely make out a man, his pants around his ankles, desperately trying to herd his own turds back into the toilet. There was nothing to be done but stagger to my feet and find another place to lie down. Except I couldn't sleep at all, of course, and, as I stared up into the starless sky, I swore that I would never set foot in the hellhole of Chahuites again.

THE NEXT MORNING, Solalinde hired four buses to drive us to Juchitán, the last town north before Hermanos en el Camino. I was in a horrible mood. I should have been elated. Solalinde was finally here. We were safe. There was even a new rumor going around that, with our ever-growing numbers and the powerful priest's protection, the Viacrucis might continue on from Ixtepec and all the way up to Mexico City. And yet I still couldn't shake the strange feeling I'd had since the start of the Viacrucis. It was partly the sensation of being pursued, of being stalked from the shadows by unknown figures or forces. But now it was also a suspicion that I'd seen something I shouldn't have. That there was something right in front of me that I needed to make sense of but for some reason I couldn't quite put together. It was then, as I was walking down the dusty main street of Chahuites—miserable, alone, and still stinking of another man's excrement—that I heard his voice from behind me.

"What the fuck you doing here, cracker?"

I turned and looked him in the eyes, and right then, I don't know how, but I understood that whatever had been following me all this time—call it fate, call it bad luck, call it the stars aligning or the black spaces between them—had finally found me.

CHAPTER 3

THE MIDDLE OF THE NOWHERE

THE MAN IN front of me looked like hell, or rather someone condemned to hell who was nevertheless trying to make the best of it. His polo shirt—originally a dark shade of yellow, but now sun bleached and streaked with mud and days of dried sweat—was tucked neatly into a pair of oversized jeans. On his right hip was a leather cell phone holster, which he touched lightly every so often, like a cowboy instinctively reaching for a pistol. The top of his head was bald and sun beaten, but an unruly forest of black hair shot from its sides, speckled with bits of leaves and pollen and other unidentifiable detritus. I had the distinct impression that I was face to face with a mad man.

"Did you just call me a cracker?" I said.

"Look buddy, I'm just tryna help you out."

"Help me out?"

"Yeah man, help you out. Can't you see?"

"See what?"

"That you're about to die." When he spoke, his arms flailed wildly around his head, as if he was flinging the words out of his body, and his hands constantly rummaged around in his pockets for loose cigarettes. "Look around you, buddy. You're surrounded by gangsters. You gonna get yourself killed."

I surveyed the relatively demure scene: People standing in line for the buses. Two teenagers holding hands under the shade of a tree. Ever fetching his mother some water.

"Dude, I don't know who you are," I said, "but I've been traveling with these people for weeks." I remembered what Solalinde told us to say. "This is a pilgrimage. It's peaceful."

"Peaceful, huh?" His fingers trembled as he brought a smoke up to his lips. I wondered if he was on drugs and thought about making up an excuse to leave. But I couldn't remember the last time I'd spoken to someone in English, and it felt invigorating if irksome, like I could finally think clearly.

"Who even says 'cracker' anymore?" I asked.

The man smiled as if he knew me. "Well, if I can't call you cracker, what do I call you instead?"

I gave him my name.

"Yo, like the jeans? Damn son, that's a weird name. You sure you don't like cracker better? Ah man, I'm just screwing with you. So, Levi-like-the-jeans, how does someone like you end up in a shithole like this?"

"I'm an anthropologist," I said.

"Well, that's certainly a fancy word."

"It means I'm a researcher."

"Like a writer?"

"I'd like to be a writer someday, I guess."

"But is somebody paying you to be here or what?"

"I have a research grant, a Fulbright."

"A full what?"

"A Fulbright. It's like a scholarship from the US government."

"You telling me the feds are paying you to be here?"

"No, of course not. Well, I mean, technically yes, but it's not what you think."

He squinted and then spat on the ground. "You ever published anything before, Levi? Something I can read? Something that proves that you're a—what'd you call it?"

"Anthropologist."

"Yeah, that."

"Um, I haven't really published anything academic yet. But I did just publish a poem in this British magazine. I don't think you could find it online, though, it's a pretty small publication."

"A poem?"

"Yeah."

"Poetry?"

"Yeah."

"Are you fucking with me?"

"What? No."

"Listen man, are you a cop? Like DEA or CIA or some shit? That's how this works right? If I ask if you're a cop, then you gotta tell me the truth."

"Dude, I'm not a cop."

He brought his face close to mine and stared me in the eyes. I couldn't tell if he was joking around. "You wanna know why I believe you ain't a cop?"

"I'll bite," I said, trying not to flinch.

"Cause you really believe you ain't in danger, dummy. But you're wrong." He pointed to a Guatemalan named Louie, who was palling around on the corner. "That guy's high outta his mind. I've seen him deal drugs to three different people already, including that guy"—he pointed at the Sandinista—"who I can just tell is somebody you don't wanna fuck with. And this dude over here"—he pointed at a Honduran who everyone called el Lobo—"is a coyote. He's been recruiting people all morning, promising to take them north as soon as your little march ends. Now look me in the eye and tell me you already knew all that."

I said that I didn't.

"Yeah, that's what I thought, Levi-like-the-jeans."

"What'd you say your name was?" I asked.

"I didn't," he said coolly.

I felt a tug on my arm. A boy I didn't recognize, with a wide face and squinty eyes, began to speak very quietly. So quietly I almost couldn't hear him. He said that he had arrived in Chahuites all alone, but, by the grace of God, Irineo had taken him in and was helping him apply for a visa, so that he could make a new life for himself. The boy said he was so grateful to Irineo, that he loved Mexico in general and Chahuites in particular, that he was being fed three meals a day, and that he believed in the Virgin of Guadalupe. At first I thought that the boy was going to ask for money, like so many other children did when they were traveling alone, but he just continued to talk and talk, barely above a whisper. He never asked for anything.

From the doorway of one of the buses, Armando Mejia announced that we were heading out. Then the boy waved goodbye and trotted back toward the shelter. It was odd, no doubt, but I was distracted by this new man, who stood a few paces away staring at me.

"So," I said. "You coming?"

"I'll think about it," he said.

I shrugged and boarded the bus. It was only later, as we were driving down the road, that I realized I had just spoken with the boy who was sitting on Irineo's lap the night before.

WHEN WE PULLED into Juchitán, the mysterious man was already smoking a cigarette next to one of the other buses. He lifted a hand and waved me over.

"Axel," he said.

"Huh?"

"My name's Axel. Like the thing that holds the wheels together. Cause like an axle, I keep on rolling, baby boy."

I wondered if Axel and axle were tocayos, even if they were spelled differently. "So you decided to join the Viacrucis after all."

"I decided that me and you got some shit to talk about."

He said his full name was Axel Alfredo Kirschner, that he was thirty-seven years old, and that he was looking for someone he could trust. Because ever since they'd deported him to Guatemala, it was like he'd been stuck in a dream, and nothing made sense anymore.

"Where'd you grow up?" he asked.

"Georgia," I said. "In a tiny little town. You wouldn't have heard of it."

"Sounds like something an undercover cop would say."

I laughed. "It's called Camden. Camden County. But I haven't lived there for a while now."

He asked me other things. Specific questions, one after another. When was I born? Did I have siblings? Pets? What high school did I go to? What were the names of my parents? "You got a wife?" he asked.

"A girlfriend," I said. "Her name's Atlee. But she's in grad school right now, so she's not in Mexico."

My answers seemed to reassure Axel a bit, and he began to tell me all kinds of things about himself, strange and intimate things, things that you don't normally tell someone when you first meet them. He said that he guessed he should start from the beginning, which always meant birth. He was born in a coastal pueblo of Guatemala during the country's civil war, when the right-wing dictatorship was burning all the villages suspected of housing leftist rebels. In the chaos, Axel said, his mother was raped by a man, a military man on vacation, believe it or not, who claimed to be in the German navy. She was fourteen years old. That's how he came by the last name Kirschner. After he was born, his mother found a boyfriend, and one day the boyfriend heard a rumor that the military was coming to raze their village that very night. They packed a bag and fled to the US, where Axel's mother crossed the border with him swaddled in her arms. They made the jump in Tijuana but decided New York sounded more promising than Los Angeles, mostly because the name was in English.

"Long Island to be specific," said Axel, "Port Washington to be more specific."

That night I would look up Port Washington and learn that, at the time, it was one of the richest zip codes in America, a suburb so opulent that it had inspired the fictional town of East Egg in *The Great Gatsby*. Axel's mother found work as a maid cleaning mansions, and the boyfriend—who called Axel his stepson when he was in a good mood, but only when he was in a good mood—landed a maintenance gig at a local golf club.

Axel slid his phone out of its holster and showed me a picture of his mother. She still looked young and had very fair skin, which was puzzling. If I'd passed Axel on the street in New York, I would have probably assumed he was black or Afro-Latino. In fact, when glimpsed from the right angle, with his large ears and toothy grin, Axel bore something of a resemblance to Barack Obama. I considered asking about his biological father again, because maybe I'd misunderstood something, but then I thought better of it. Besides, once Axel got talking, there was no stopping him. He had already launched into his school days. He said he grew up a normal, all-American kid. He made As and Bs in high school and was kind of a geek, but a popular geek who got along with everybody. He even went on a school trip to London as a freshman, he said. That was before 9/11, and things were different back then. More chill. He traveled with his Guatemalan passport and never had a problem getting back into the US. He didn't learn he was undocumented until he was seventeen. That was the first time, he said, that he felt "stuck in the middle of the nowhere."

"What do you mean the nowhere?" I asked.

"You know, the nowhere. It's like a place but it ain't a place. It just comes, man. It comes all at once and you feel like you're lost."

"Maybe you're the poet," I said.

His speech was peppered with other bizarre phrases. Sometimes he said "feets" instead of "feet." He pronounced "geek" with a soft g, so it sounded like "jeek." There was no standardization to his speech, other than that his accent was definitely from New York. But I couldn't place it, and the words came out strange, like he was a native speaker, but a speaker from a long-forgotten sixth borough where the dialect had been separated from the rest of the city for generations.

His voice was so unique that I pulled out my recorder and asked to conduct an interview.

"No thanks, baby boy," he said. "Axel don't do interviews."

He frequently spoke about himself in the third person, as if his life had happened to someone else, or as if there was another being inside him who occasionally took over. "The main thing you need to know about Axel is that Axel works a lot," he repeated again and again. He said that after high school, he received an associate's degree in computer science from a community college. But afterward he couldn't find a real job because of his undocumented status and started working under the table at a local yacht club. Some rich guys paid him in cash to maintain the boats. He scrubbed the barnacles and reconfigured the navigation systems. But the gig never covered all the bills, so he mowed lawns in the summer and shoveled driveways in the winter. Sometimes he washed dishes at a Mexican place down the street from his house. When things were really tough, he scavenged aluminum cans and cashed them in for five cents apiece. But the thing he said he was best at was fixing computers. "Man, gimme any device—computer, smart phone, tablet, TV, anything, no matter how busted—and I'll get it purring again like a little kitty cat."

Honestly, it was hard to believe that this man knew anything at all about computers. I chalked it up as a bit of exaggeration, which was common on the migrant trail. Necessary, even. A lot of migrants, especially men, tended to hyperbolize their past lives. The amount of money they made, the number of fights they won, the size of their dicks—everything ended up being a little bit bigger than it was the last time they told the story. Regardless, there was something about Axel I was starting to like. We were obviously quite different in many ways, and his situation was clearly more dire than mine had ever been, but I also saw something of myself in him. Back in Georgia, I'd grown up in a blue-collar family and was comfortable with hard labor. I'd worked alongside men like Axel on construction sites and in restaurant kitchens, men I often felt I had more in common with than most of my fellow Fulbright scholars. I took pride in possessing the kind of scrappiness forged only by occasional economic desperation. I wouldn't have been able to survive on the Viacrucis for very long without it, and I said as much to Axel.

"So that's why you're here," he mused. "You're still just a baby anthropologist, so you gotta do all the sucky work no one else wants to do."

"Something like that," I said. "But I don't think it's that sucky, actually."

"Well, that's cause you ain't a migrant, buddy. Believe me, this is sucky."

Maybe it was because of my own alienation, and the overwhelming sense of isolation from and ennui about the Viacrucis, but when I talked to Axel, he gave me a sense of camaraderie and purpose that I'd been searching for since first working in Hermanos. We didn't just share a language; we shared a certain cultural sensibility that was different from everyone else around us. Axel described the migrant trail, obviously, as someone from the US would. And in some ways, he was much more stereotypically American than I was. He knew nothing about Mexico, he said, and everything in the country seemed to be working against him. He hated spicy food. The local slang was impenetrable. Southern Mexico was smack dab in the middle of the nowhere. This led to revelations that were just as hilarious or brilliant as they were bizarre. He remarked, for instance, that each day, in order to steel his nerves before running through the jungle, he'd listen to 50 Cent's "In Da Club," which he considered to be the pinnacle of American civilization. I agreed wholeheartedly.

"Most of these people here don't even know who 50 Cent is," spat Axel. "Ain't that freaking sad?"

He described how to chop down a stalk of bamboo, fill it with rocks and sand, and use it as a makeshift water filtration system in the jungle. He found a discarded soda can and showed me how to turn it into a fishing trap by cutting the bottom and bending it inward, his fingers deftly shaping the sharp metal, so a fish could swim inside but would skewer itself trying to swim back out again. It was a method he claimed to have used successfully several times since crossing into Mexico. Then he said that the secret to migration was never masturbating. Because when you masturbate, you lose your energy, and when you lose your energy, you get caught. He hadn't masturbated since he was deported because he needed all the strength he could get.

Without thinking, I said that was an absolutely insane thing to believe. Then I realized it was the first time I'd felt comfortable enough to contradict someone on the Viacrucis.

Axel just ignored me and kept talking. Of all the things he missed about the US, he said, there were three he longed for in particular. The first two were air conditioning and sirloin steaks. Not just the cool of the AC, though obviously that was part of it, but the literal sensation itself, of what it felt like to step inside and feel truly inside, with the chill of the house on his skin as he sank his teeth into a piping hot steak he'd bought with his own money.

But the thing he missed the most, the thing he brought up over and over again, was being a dad. He had a son, who was six, and a daughter, who was two. They were still in New York, he said, with their mom. That's where he was headed. Back to New York to be with them. Just mentioning their names, he started to tear up. He told me about when his son was born, and what it was like to hold his tiny hand. He talked about combing his daughter's hair, and the perfect ringlets around her ears. He said that the only thing he could think about anymore, the thing that consumed and defined him, the thing that pulled him through the jungle like gravity itself, was being a father. He asked if I knew what that felt like. I said that I didn't.

That evening Father Solalinde led a procession through the town of Juchitán. People hung their heads out of windows and watched us from doorways, murmuring in Zapotec, the local indigenous language. We paused to pray at one church, then another, then another. Streamers twirled between buildings. Children waved from windows. A priest from one of the churches spoke and described the Viacrucis not as a pilgrimage or a caravan but as a great wandering, akin to those who followed Moses out of Egypt and into the desert. He spoke of the parting of the sea, of drowned armies, and what it meant to be delivered and lost at the same time.

After the procession, I asked Axel to tell me about his deportation. It was getting dark. People were busy finding a place to sleep that wasn't too dirty or searching for an electrical outlet where they could charge their phones and call their families.

"You still got that recorder, Mr. Anthropologist?" he asked. "Pull it out. It was an accident. All of this happened cause of an accident."

IN ORDER TO tell you how I got deported, I gotta tell you another story first. Cause the accident happened just a little ways from Schreiber High School, which I graduated from. Believe it or not, I had a lotta friends back then. That's the thing about growing up in Port Washington, everybody knows everybody, and I was always over at somebody's house hanging out, going to parties, hitting up shorties, you know what I'm saying? And one time my friend who lived down the street, Gina, she invited me to this pool party at her house. It was, like, one of those classic high school scenarios where her parents was gone for the weekend and she threw a party while they were away. And we was having fun, swimming, a couple beers, not doing nothing too crazy, right, cause we was actually pretty good kids. And then all of a sudden Gina runs up to me and is like, "Axel, you gotta go."

"What you mean I gotta go?"

"My parents just came back early and my dad can't see you here."

And at first I thought she meant, like, the party was getting busted and we all had to bounce, so I jumped outta the pool and hopped the back fence. I dropped to the ground and was hiding there in the grass, just listening. But I didn't hear nothing. And then I realized no one else was moving. All my other friends was still chilling, splashing in the pool, acting like nothing had happened at all. And through the cracks in the fence I saw her dad come out. And I thought that was it, he was gonna freak out, cause he was this big tough New York cop, right? But he just waved hello to everyone, and everyone waved back, and then he walked into the house again all casual. And for a moment I thought everything was cool, and that the party was gonna keep going.

So I stuck my head back over the fence and shouted, "Yo, Gina, what's the situation, baby girl?"

And then Gina ran over to me like she had a secret and was like, "Axel, I'm sorry, but you know my dad hates Spanish guys"—that's what they used to call us back then, Spanish guys, even though I ain't Spanish, I'm Guatemalan—"and he can't see you here. Get your head down."

I remember I just sat there for a little while behind the fence, not knowing what in the world to do, and eventually I just kinda jogged through a couple people's backyards, hopping over one fence and then another, and went home. That's how it was back then on Long Island. There was a lotta people who didn't like Spanish guys, and if you was Spanish you just had to deal with it, you know what I'm saying?

But anyway, that was back in high school, a long time ago, and I ain't the kinda guy who holds grudges. I hadn't even thought about Gina for years until the accident. It happened just after Christmas. I was driving my son to kindergarten, and unfortunately I fell into this car accident. It was January, the road was slippery with ice, and I was sitting at a stop sign when this lady skidded out and rear-ended me.

Believe it or not, it wasn't something that was that aggressive—just my taillight, her bumper, something that coulda been fixed on the spot.

But then the lady got outta the car and started asking me for all these freaking documents—my license, my insurance card, my registration. And I said I didn't have them on me at the moment, ma'am, that I musta forgot them at home. But she said she needed some kinda information about me for the insurance company. So I apologized quick and reached into my pocket and pulled out my fake that I bought down in Queens.

And, oh boy, that's when things changed. Like, I felt her mood shift in that moment, from her feeling kinda sorry to being suspicious. That's also when I realized there was a man sitting in the passenger's seat, who I guess was her husband, and when I looked at him he got out the car. And I hate to say it, but they was white, know what I'm saying? And the white guy approaches the white lady, and she hands him my ID. They start whispering to each other and then eventually the white guy turns to me all pissed off and says, "We're calling the cops."

And I was like, "Whoa, whoa, let's calm things down. How about this? I just got paid last night. Why don't I give you the five hundred bucks in my pocket for the bump in your fender and we'll forget all about it?"

And then the guy went off, like, "I knew it. I knew you was a fucking illegal. We ain't taking any money, you immigrant piece of shit. We're calling the cops." And then he threw the ID down at my feet.

I just remember thinking I had to act cool, cause there was nowhere to run. When I was younger, I woulda just bounced, took off on foot right there—forget the car, forget the insurance, forget everything. But I'm a dad now, and my son was buckled up in the back seat. I couldn't just leave him. So instead I had to stand my ground and play it cool, which honestly scared me to death, but what else was I gonna do? And remember when I said that if you're from Port Washington everybody knows you? Well, when the po-po showed up, the guy who got out the car was Gina's dad. Swear to god. And I knew right then I was gonna get deported.

He took one look at my face and said, "Well, well. If it isn't Mr. Axel."
For years he had it out for my family, cause we was Spanish and lived
down the street and my stepdad fixed cars in the driveway, which
Gina's dad always hated for some reason. But until then, he'd never
had something on me personally, cause I had always kept my nose clean.
He went through my pockets and found the fake, which he said was a
felony in the state of New York, and then he grabbed me and put me in
his cruiser. As we drove away, I saw my son in the back seat of my car
crying, and the red and blue lights was flashing through the window
and across his little face.

They took me to the precinct and ran a background check to see if I
had any old arrest warrants, which of course I didn't. I always behave, I
don't consume drugs, I don't mess around with any sort of narcotics. All
I do all day is work, work, work. So when my record came back clean,
the guy at the desk originally said I was free to go, that this was all just
a minor dispute, and since I wasn't even responsible for the accident the
police didn't need to get involved.

But then Gina's dad was like, "No way. This guy's dirty. He had
a fake driver's license in his pocket. We gotta at least check him out in
Nassau."

And so they transferred me to Nassau, which is where immigration
is. ICE. When I got there, there was already some big tough Latino
agent waiting for me—we didn't say Spanish by that point any more,
we said Latino—and the Latino-looking agent took my biometrics and
came back and told me that he couldn't find me in the system, so that
meant I musta been in the country illegally.

How could I lie? They knew the truth. So I said yeah buddy, that's
right, I was from Guatemala, but that I had immigrated to New York
when I was a baby, so there musta been a way to work things out. But
the agent just shook his head and said I had two options. The first option
was that I could fight my case in the States.

"That one. That's the option I want," I said. "Lemme fight it." Cause
obviously I didn't wanna leave my kids, right? But then he said they'd

keep me locked up during the entire case, and when I asked how long that woulda been, the agent dude said it woulda took two or three years probably. And that's when I said, "Shit, what's the second option?" and he told me I could sign this thing called Voluntary Departure, which was like a deportation but that it wouldn't stay on my record, and if I signed it they'd let me go in a couple days.

So obviously I said yeah, of course, send my ass back to Guatemala. I got kids, I can't be locked up for years, not seeing them, not supporting them. I grew up without a dad. I ain't gonna let that happen to my kids. So I figured they could deport me to Guatemala, and then I'd find a way to cross back into the States within a couple months, right?

I spent the night in a jail cell with some tattooed gangster mother-fuckers from El Salvador, and then the next morning they handcuffed our hands and our feets and shoved us on a bus with a buncha other immigrants and drove us all the way down to Texas. I don't even know where in Texas. I ain't never been there before, so it was all just Texas to me. We drove for a whole day without stopping, and then finally we pulled up to this detention center, a huge building made outta bricks and barbed wire. Then they pulled me into this courtroom, and a random dude in a suit walked up and said that he was my attorney. Then the judge asked if I wanted to stay in the States, and the guy who said he was my attorney said, "Say no." So I said no.

And then the judge said, "Okay Mr. Axel, in that case you'll have to sign final departure documents," and then banged her little wooden hammer like they do in the TV shows. And then—and I'll never forget this—she looked me dead in the eyes and said, "Good luck."

I wanted to say, "Good luck? Bitch, you coulda been my good luck. You coulda let my ass stay." But instead I just said thank you.

Then they chained me and all the other immigrants up again and drove us to the airport. And everyone in the airport was looking at us like we was criminals, like I was dirty and had stole something or beat somebody up. And I wanted to shout at them that it wasn't even my fault, man, that the white lady was the one who rear-ended me. But then I was on the plane and it was lifting off the ground and I was looking out the window, just watching the land drop away, like the whole world was falling from beneath my feets.

I slept on the streets in Guatemala. It's embarrassing to say it, but when they deported me, I didn't have nobody or nothing. When I finally got to a pay phone, I called my mom and told her I had got deported and asked if she still knew anybody in Guatemala who coulda helped me. But she said no, she didn't know nobody there no more. Then I called my wife, Monica, and asked her to count the little bit of cash I had saved up in the house, to see how much she could send me, and not to worry, I was gonna use it to get a coyote and get back home immediately, like nothing never happened at all.

And you know what Monica said? She asked if I knew what it felt like to pick your baby up from the cops cause your husband had got arrested for bothering some white people. And I said no, baby girl, it ain't like that. And I tried to explain the situation, but then she just said that rent was due in two weeks, and that her babies didn't have no food in the fridge, so I needed to be a man and figure out how to get home by myself.

And I thought, damn, at some point she was right about it. My kids needed the money more than me, and besides, if I hustled my whole life in New York City, then I could certainly hustle in this little place called Guatemala. And since Guatemala was technically my country, I shoulda finally been able to work legal, right? Especially with me speaking English and being good with computers, I thought I could easily find a job at a call center for a bit, save up, and then make the jump north. So I went to a call center, showed them what I could do, and they offered me a job on the spot.

"Perfect," I said. "When do I start?"

And they said as soon as I filled out all the paperwork and gave them my DPI.

And I was like, "No problem, what's a DPI?"

And they said it was like a Guatemalan social security number, the thing that proves you're allowed to work legit. So I went to the *government office and was like, "Yo, I got a job, hook me up with that DPI."*

And the lady working behind the desk walked away and was gone for a while, and then she came back and said, "Mr. Axel, I'm sorry, but we don't have a DPI on file for you."

"No problem at all, just make me a new one. I got a job offer at this sweet ass call center and I need it before I can start."

And she said that I didn't understand, it wasn't that simple, that actually the government had no record of me existing.

"What you mean, shorty? Look at me. I'm right here in front of you. Axel, in the flesh. There can only be one."

Well, she said there used to be a record that I existed—my paper birth certificate—but that it was destroyed in 1998 after a hurricane. Hurricane Mitch. She said that she had a record that my record was destroyed, but that the record of the destroyed record was the only record, and that what I needed was the original record, not the record of the record. So I asked how to get a record that wasn't destroyed. And she said with an attorney, that's how, cause the process to get the destroyed record undestroyed was complicated, and that with an attorney the whole procedure would take a year at least.

And I was like, "How much is that supposed to cost? Look, I just got deported. I got my kids waiting for me up in the States." And she said she didn't know, probably like forty thousand quetzales. I did the math. And that's when I started to panic, cause forty thousand quetzales is like five grand in US dollars. And then I said straight out to her, "Listen, sweetheart, how the fuck am I supposed to come up with five thousand dollars if you won't give me permission to work in this country?"

And then she said not to call her sweetheart and called security to kick me outta the building. I went back every day for a week, tryna find somebody who would help me, but nobody did. So I found a job under the table selling fish out of a cooler in the market.

Well, one day this dude comes up to me all chill and says, "Hey man, that looks like some nice fish. How much for the whole cooler?"

Bro, I thought I hit the jackpot. I gave him a fair price. Then he lifted up his shirt to show me a gun in his waistband and said I had a week to pay "us" a cut of all the money I made. And then he left. Now, I'm tough. Axel can get ghetto, you feel me? And I didn't even know who those "us" motherfuckers was, so I just shrugged it off. What else was I supposed to do? But the same guy kept coming back asking for his money. And so eventually I told him straight up, "Look dude, I don't know who you are, but I just got deported. I'm selling fish out a damn cooler, does it look like I'm making any money to you?"

And immediately he got up in my face and I could feel him press the gun into my side. And he said that he was from MS-13 and that the next time he came, if I didn't have his money, they was gonna kill me. And he also said that I better not try to run, cause he knew I was sleeping out by the cathedral at night and they'd find me. And that's when I said fuck it, this ain't my country. The government don't recognize me, the gangs are tryna kill me, and every day that passes is another day my babies ain't got their daddy. So if I gotta cross Mexico on foot, that's what I'm gonna do. And I bounced, simple as that. So that's why I'm here, Levi. Stuck in the middle of the nowhere. I'm going back to my kids. Ain't nothing gonna stop me. I'd rather be in a casket in the States than alive in Guatemala.

CHAPTER 4

ONLY DESPERATE PEOPLE

THE NEXT MORNING, on Easter Sunday, we gathered on a side street off the main square. Eventually, Father Solalinde appeared with Irineo at his side, said a quick prayer, and then we marched out of town, the orange immigration truck faithfully in the rear. On the highway, Solalinde took his leave to prepare the shelter for Easter Mass. Now that he had publicly endorsed the Viacrucis, camera crews from the biggest networks in Latin America were awaiting our arrival. Before he climbed into his SUV, Solalinde added that he'd unfortunately received word that immigration was still gathering forces nearby. We needed to book it to Ixtepec as quickly as possible. But once we were inside Hermanos en el Camino, we should be safe.

Not even news of immigration could dampen our spirits. Now that we were on Solalinde's turf, no one believed that la migra would dare to cross him. At some point, the highway met a creek, and at the bridge many of the men stripped off their shirts and jumped into the water, whooping and hollering. I spotted Axel standing to the side and asked if he wanted to join, but he said no. There was no way he was going to let his guard down.

"Dude, you don't understand. Solalinde's a big deal. You're safe now. You can relax."

"Nope, no way, buddy. Relax is a word Axel don't know no more."

Instead, we leaned against the bridge and watched the revelers leap into the water. Axel pulled a wad of paper out of his pocket. "Lemme show you something," he said, spreading the dirty pages across the railing. The pages were black-and-white printouts of maps, but it was hard to tell what they portrayed. "This is how we did it," he said.

"Did what?"

"Found you, baby boy. The Viacrucis."

I picked up one of the pages and held it up to the sun. "Where is this?"

"That's just south of Chahuites. Where we was running right before I met you. We used the maps to go deep in the jungle. To avoid the immigration checkpoints."

"Where'd you get them? This doesn't look like Google Maps."

"Nah, man. It's way more legit." He pointed to three men walking nearby. "You see those guys? That's Jimmy, Meme, and Charlie. They're from Honduras. We met back in Tapachula and been traveling together ever since." When they heard their names called, the three men turned and waved in our direction. Axel said that Jimmy was the oldest and the de facto leader of the three. He was lanky and leathery, and kept multiple cigarettes tucked behind both of his cauliflower ears. Charlie had the kind of stocky shoulders only earned through hard labor since childhood. Meme was light skinned and slender, a jumpy kid who always seemed on edge. Axel said he called them the Catrachos, a nickname for Hondurans.

When he'd met the Catrachos just over a week previous, they didn't realize that riding the Beast was no longer an option under the Southern Border Program. They were stranded in Tapachula with no money, and none of them could really read. Jimmy had graduated from elementary school and could partially decipher a map, but the names of the pueblos in Mexico were confusing and kept getting jumbled in his mind. Was Huehuetán north or south of Comaltitlán? Or was that Mapastepec? Or Pijijiapan?

They were almost ready to throw in the towel and turn back when they met Axel.

"Honestly, I didn't know nothing about being a migrant," he said, "but I knew how to read. And how to work a computer. So we decided to help each other out."

In a cybercafé, Axel coaxed a dusty desktop back to life. He spent the afternoon debugging it, until it was just fast enough to run a bootleg copy of Google Earth. "Not Google Maps, you hear me? Google Earth. It gives you hi-res of the jungle to see exactly where the streams and hilltops are. That might not sound like much, but it ain't an easy thing to do on a computer so old and busted. But I worked my magic."

The plan was simple. To avoid the immigration checkpoints, many migrants walked through the jungle, but normally only at its edges, so that they could follow the roads and train tracks north to the next town. Immigration agents expected that, and raids were regular and brutal. Under the Program, it was rumored that immigration earned commission for each migrant they apprehended, so it made sense for agents not to spend too much time hoofing it in the deep bush with the snakes and spiders. The real pesos were made kicking back under the shade of a checkpoint and catching migrants by the busload.

That's why Axel mapped out routes in the heart of the jungle. "If we coulda gone deeper, we woulda," he said. But it came at a cost. While they might elude immigration, they now risked encountering the cartels who sometimes ran drugs through the unsurveilled territory, and the narcos would put a bullet between any prying eyes. To avoid them, Axel and the Catrachos decided to travel by night whenever possible. They kept two rules. First: no lights. A flashlight in the jungle was a bullseye and would attract all kinds of attention, both human and animal. Second: no walking. It was run or get left behind. The first night was the scariest. When they pushed through the lip of the jungle and stood in the pitch of its mouth, Meme got spooked. No way man, he said, jumping back out of the undergrowth. Axel pulled him into the vegetation and held him there for five minutes until their eyes and nerves acclimated. Eventually, they could see small rivulets of moonlight trickling through the thick leaves above their heads. Then they started to run.

Axel's story was interrupted by the Russian, who was wriggling in his mother's arms next to us. "Here mama," said Axel, scooping up the toddler, "I can carry him for a while." He swung the Russian up onto his shoulders, where the boy, delighted by his new vantage point, pointed and babbled at the swimmers below. Irineo whistled and shouted that the fun was over, that Solalinde would be missing us soon if we didn't hustle up. Shakira watched from the bridge, playfully catcalling to the shirtless men as they bashfully dried themselves beneath her gaze.

Axel resumed his story. He and the Hondurans ran until signs of all other humans disappeared. They ran across bogs, over mountains, and through sugarcane fields, seeking out the hardest and toughest terrain to ensure that no one was following them. They ran until they felt like they had discovered virgin territory, places so remote that it seemed like no one had ever been there before. But inevitably they would stumble upon yellowing water bottles, lone sandals, discarded KFC buckets full of bones. Who had left these tokens? Once, in an open field lit by the moon, they found a pair of jeans hanging on a tree limb, the fabric stiff and mineralized, like someone had hung them to dry long ago and then was startled, fled suddenly, and never returned.

Axel plotted the digital routes, but the jungle itself was Jimmy's territory. When he was a child, his family lived off the land, hunting armadillo, iguanas, and snakes. He could spot the trails that no one else saw, the subtle markings that signaled they weren't alone. Keep moving, he'd say, or we'll have company. "Only desperate people," said Axel, "fucked in the head people, would do what we was doing."

In the dark, it was impossible to know if they were following the map exactly. If they felt lost, the crew had to hike laterally until they hit a road and could check the street signs to make sure they were still headed in the right direction. By the time they arrived in Huixtla, they were half dead. "You're so tired," Axel said, "that you don't think about the fact that someone might be watching you."

In town, they picked up two more Hondurans, both named Roberto. Tocayos. Roberto Stanley was an older, pudgy man with gray in his beard, and Roberto Victor was a quiet, obedient teenager who followed at his heels. The Catrachos dubbed him Junior, even though there was no relation. It was the Robertos who said that they'd heard about something called the Viacrucis Migrante, some kind of march that had passed through about three days prior. "From then on, we had one goal," Axel said. "Fly to the Viacrucis. It was torture for real. We didn't carry no food or water, cause it was too heavy, and most the time there was nothing to eat, so Jimmy gave me cigarettes. I got addicted. Can you believe that shit? Thirty-seven years of no smoking. Then I get deported and boom, baby, I'm running through the jungle with nicotine pumping in my veins."

When they weren't near a town, they slept in the trees, securing themselves by cinching their belts to the branches. The ground was too wet, and there could have been snakes or scorpions. But up in the trees, Axel said, the mosquitos were so bad they had to smear mud across their skin for protection, which made them look like animals or primordial travelers from another realm.

I had never heard these kinds of details about the migrant trail before. There was something so ingenious about Axel's approach, just as measured as it was hellbent. When I spoke to other migrants about their time in Mexico, they usually didn't have much to say. They talked about their lives back in their home countries or what they hoped awaited them in the US, but Mexico was simply a place that one passed through as quickly as possible. Or maybe they were just wary of telling a stranger their plans. With Axel it was different. He had no country back in Central America. For him, everything was just as confusing and alien as it was for me. And yet he'd designed a way to evade the Program unlike any other I'd ever heard. I was hooked. I had to figure out who this man was.

At the front of the march, I watched Irineo answer a phone call, listen in silence for several seconds, and then scream, "Shit."

The Armandos and I jogged over to him. Irineo said the call was from Hermanos. After the swim in the river, the Sandinista and a few other guys snuck away and hopped on a local bus. Immigration promptly pulled it over and arrested them. Terrified, I looked around for Shakira. I'd last seen her talking to the Sandinista by the river. If she were detained, she'd be in more danger than anyone else. Trans women were much more likely to be assaulted and killed than other migrants, and no small part of that was because of bigoted police. Thankfully, I caught sight of her bubblegum pink outfit bobbing along at the back of the pack.

"They've got us surrounded," said Irineo, glancing at the orange immigration truck behind us. "And that motherfucker is relaying information to them. If anyone else breaks away from the group, they're going to pick them off one by one."

The rest of the march was decidedly more tense. We walked in silence, glancing over our shoulders at even the slightest noise. But we made it to the outskirts of Ixtepec without further incident. In the distance were a fleet of media vans and camera crews. Axel tapped my shoulder and asked if all the commotion was really for us.

"Dude, I told you," I said. "Solalinde's legit. He's famous."

"So this guy really is powerful?"

"Yeah, man. One of the most powerful people in the country, probably."

"You think they'll put my pretty ass on TV?"

"I mean, look at you. How could they not?"

"You know what, Levi-like-the-jeans? You're smarter than you look."

When the cameras were ready, Solalinde led a procession through Ixtepec. We stopped every so often so that he could read scripture aloud. Christ was beaten. Christ was crucified. Christ rose again. The doors to the shelter had been decorated with calla lilies. The local Zapotec women arrived to greet us in their embroidered huipiles and gold jewelry. Solalinde offered mass on the shelter's covered patio in front of a life-size crucifix. In the evening, the priest started a bonfire by the train tracks, and its light flickered over the sleeping body of the Beast. He announced that he was negotiating the release of the Sandinista and other men from immigration detention, but this should serve as a warning to anyone else thinking about abandoning the Viacrucis.

Shakira asked if that meant we would continue on to Mexico City.

Solalinde pursed his lips and said that such matters were for another day. Tonight we should rest a bit and celebrate.

THERE WAS A reason that Hermanos was considered the gold standard in migrant shelters. It was a literal compound, with a cafeteria and kitchen, as well as dorms for men, women, and queer migrants—the third being a recent addition—though most people opted to sleep outside on foam mats, which was preferable in Ixtepec, where the only relief from the heat was the salty, humid breeze that comes rolling in off the Pacific. The shelter also had a legal aid office, pop-up medical clinic, rudimentary soccer field, computer room, and a small library with a surprisingly sophisticated selection, including Borges's *A Universal History of Infamy* in the original Spanish, an English translation of Dostoevsky's *The Brothers Karamazov*, and a copy of *Dubliners* by James Joyce, bequeathed by yours truly. Such luxuries were made possible by the international donations, both cash and material, that poured into the shelter as Father Solalinde's fame grew. Each day the floors were swept, the dishes were scrubbed, and the food was served. All in all, it wasn't a bad place to crash for a night or two if you were heading north.

After dinner, Armando Amante dragged an old speaker onto the patio. Its dull electric hum floated across the shelter, and everyone who hadn't been interested in the mass began to huddle around. A cellphone was passed toward the front and hooked up to the speaker, and reggaeton rang like a shot across the courtyard. A collective cheer rose up as Armando grabbed the mic and began coaxing bashful individuals into the circle forming in front of the crucifix. Celia pushed the Russian onto the dance floor. He was naked except for his diaper, and for a moment he wobbled on his little legs, looking around uneasily at all the faces watching him. But then he raised his arms above his head, his tiny fingers reaching outward, and let out a shriek of joy. It was all the permission we needed. Meme shimmied over to the Russian, spasmodically miming his dance moves. Ever swayed with his mother to the beat. Someone changed the song to a salsa number, then cumbia, and the younger kids drifted away and were replaced by their grandparents. For once the atmosphere felt tranquil.

Then Armando Amante cut the music off. There were angry shouts and whistles. "Calm down, calm down," he boomed into the microphone. "Ladies and gentlemen, we have a very special guest scheduled for tonight." A soft prelude began to play, orchestral strings, dramatic and moody. The door of the women's dormitory flew open. As the music began to build, a silhouette slinked across the square in what looked like, in the shadows, a ballgown. A train of fine fabric swooshed across the dirt. Then Shakira stepped onto the patio. She was wrapped, throat to ankles, in a floral bedsheet. Everyone was transfixed. Shakira catwalked across the length of concrete, lip-synching into a hairbrush. She stopped in front of a man and trailed her fingers against his cheek.

The rest of the men howled, and I winced in anticipation. Surely, I thought, these callous and angry men would never permit a drag show. But then the man's body softened, his eyes glassy and out of focus, and he nuzzled his face instinctively into Shakira's palm. Just as quickly, she snatched her hand back and spun away. The man let out a small cry that sounded almost like a child, and he lunged at Shakira, trying to catch her hand, but she danced just out of reach.

Then another man called out to Shakira, his arms outstretched. Then another, and another, begging to be gazed upon, to be touched, to be chosen. The life-size crucifix loomed behind her, Christ's face bloodied and anguished, his body arched toward the heavens.

"Shakira," blurted the first man, "do you love me?"

"No," she said, not even bothering to look at him, and the crowd roared.

"Shakira," another man called out, "do you love me?"

"No."

A chorus of desperate, bewitched men called out *Shakira, over here* and *I love you, Shakira* and *Please Shakira, just one kiss.* Men who were constantly hungry. Men who had been shaped and hardened by heavy labor and rough fathers. Men who had seen other men—men who they once loved—die in violence. All these men asked Shakira to love them, and each time she refused. And with each refusal they became, for but an instant, transformed into softer and more desperate beings. Axel whooped and punched my arm. "Goddamn, baby boy, why didn't you tell me this was what the motherfucking Viacrucis was really about?"

And for a moment together, with Axel's arm swung excitedly around my shoulder—and with Shakira sashaying in front of the crucified Jesus, and Irineo nowhere in sight, and Solalinde making calls behind the scenes—it felt like everything was finally going to be alright.

CHAPTER 5

THE KIDNAPPER

WHEN I WOKE it was dark and steaming in the barracks. Someone was crouched over me, frantically shaking my shoulders.

"Bro, wake up."

The screen door was cracked open. Soft light spilled across the stained concrete floor, illuminating splotches of toothpaste, leaking water bottles, and bare mattresses holding splayed and hunched figures. Above the bald head, a lone ceiling fan spun stale air lazily across the room.

"Levi." Calloused palms moved across my face. "Get the fuck up, man."

"Axel?" He was so close that I could smell the tang of old cigarettes on his breath. It was such an intimate position, I thought, though we had only met days ago.

"Bro, you gotta help me." He grabbed my arm and pulled me from the mattress to the door. Outside, the Hondurans stood huddled behind the dormitory, their bodies tense and flighty. I was still in my boxers.

"What's going on?"

"Look, by the clotheslines." Axel pointed around the corner. "Don't let him see you."

I spotted a dark shape looming above the hundreds of still-sleeping bodies in the early morning. A big man, hulking.

"That guy tried to kidnap us."

"What? When?"

"A few days back, in Escuintla. Before we joined the Viacrucis." The others murmured in agreement.

"You've had a kidnapper following you? Why didn't you tell me about this earlier?"

Axel tensed at the question. "Bro, I was tryna tell you yesterday, but then immigration snatched those guys by the river and you walked off to talk with the other big shots."

"Dude, but I didn't know—"

"There's a lotta shit that you don't know, Levi."

I looked away, sensing the distance I had accidentally placed between us. I started to apologize, but Axel cut me off.

"Levi, you was the one who said the Viacrucis was gonna protect us. I trusted your word on that. But the kidnapper looked right at me just now. He coulda recognized my face. What do we do?"

"We tell Beto," I said.

Alberto Donis, Beto for short, was Father Solalinde's right-hand man in Hermanos. While Solalinde was meeting with government officials in Mexico City or on speaking tours around the world, Beto handled the day-to-day, tackling the grittier aspects of running a shelter otherwise unbecoming of an internationally renowned priest. He was tall, around thirty, and handsome. When he stood in the heat of the day, the sun shone off his bronzed face like a polished statue. Rumor was that years ago, Beto had been a special investigator in the Guatemalan police force. And that he was good, too good. After several successful sting operations against MS-13, a price was placed on Beto's head. He fled for his life, and, while passing through Hermanos en el Camino, Solalinde recognized that he was no ordinary migrant. The priest said that he needed someone with Beto's particular skill set and asked him to help run Hermanos. The stories were almost certainly exaggerated, I thought, if not entirely fictional, part of the mystique that followed Beto around the shelter, like the smell of his strong cologne and the gazes of curious women. What was true, however, was that after he met Solalinde, Beto became a one-man anti-gang unit.

Beto's primary targets were the MS-13 and Calle 18. Neither gang was originally from Central America. They were both founded in Los Angeles by Salvadoran immigrants during the Reagan years. By the early 1990s, the United States had begun deporting gang members wholesale rather than housing them in the federal prison system, essentially exporting the problem to El Salvador. The country was just emerging from a twelve-year-long civil war that had severely weakened its government and depleted its national resources. Both the Carter and Reagan administrations had backed the right-wing dictatorship during the war because its leaders permitted American corporations to run amok and untaxed so long as they got a cut. In such an unstable climate, El Salvador was simply unprepared to respond to sophisticated, transnational criminal syndicates like MS-13 and Calle 18. The gangs quickly evolved into something closer to amorphous paramilitaries, cutting deals with corrupt officials and spreading into other war-torn countries like Guatemala and Honduras.

But it was the Southern Border Program that gave them the opportunity to penetrate lucrative new markets in Mexico. Before the Program, the gangs mainly stuck to the Beast, charging migrants small fees to travel through certain areas, or robbing everyone atop the speeding train cars. Though there was already some evidence of MS-13 participating in human smuggling pre-2014, in reality they were more like pirates, plundering and pillaging all the poor souls who happened to cross their paths. After the Program, however, there were rumors that MS-13 began partnering with various Mexican cartels to smuggle Central Americans through the country, especially with Los Zetas cartel, who could easily repurpose their drug trafficking infrastructure for human smuggling as well. Los Zetas had trucks and halfway houses to stash migrants all over the country. They knew which police officers and immigration agents and local politicians to bribe. They even had scouts on the US-Mexico border and moles inside the US border patrol, so that they could traffic people into the country with ease.

The one thing that Los Zetas didn't have, however, was a rapport with migrants. The cartel was from the north of Mexico, and their accents and mannerisms were completely different from those in Central America. That's where the gangs came in. I'd learned quickly while working for Hermanos en el Camino that migrant shelters, even superlative ones, were prime targets for gangs and cartels. They were cloistered microeconomies of the world's most desperate people, all in need of coyotes or drugs or sex. So members of MS-13 or Calle 18 would disguise themselves—throw on some rags, mess their hair—and walk through the front door like any other migrant. Then they'd funnel people into the hands of Los Zetas. It was never clear how structured the partnership between the gangs and cartels was in practice—they clashed just as often as they collaborated—but there was an obvious incentive to work together. Within a few years, the fee to be smuggled from Guatemala to the US went from around $3,000 to as much as $20,000. And if some poor souls happened to be robbed or kidnapped along the way, who cared? It was just part of doing business, and under the Program, business was booming. The great irony was that—though it has never been proven—it was likely that the US was at least partially funding the Southern Border Program through the Mérida Initiative, an enterprise largely orchestrated by the Obama administration to ostensibly combat cartel violence in Mexico. But instead the Program created a prolific new black market beyond the cartels' and gangs' wildest dreams.

Beto's job was to stop them, and he teamed up with the local police force to run counterattacks. It was a unique and tense collaboration, and the only one of its kind, at least as far as I knew, with Solalinde's peaceful liberation theology tangled up in a Mexican SWAT team—the same police force that, when not cracking MS-13 skulls, was likely harassing and robbing migrants in southern Mexico. It was decided that Axel and I would talk to Beto alone. Seven guys rushing into shelter headquarters together would be sure to draw attention. The rest of the crew would stay out of sight and call us if they saw anything sketchy.

Beto was in his office thumbing through a stack of paperwork. He took one look at us and stiffened. "Close the door," he said. "What is it?"

"There's a kidnapper in the shelter," I said.

Beto looked at Axel. "What's your name?" he asked.

Axel mumbled something unintelligible. I could tell that, given his undocumented status, he was reluctant to speak, seeing as Beto was aligned with the cops. But that was the problem with the police. In situations like this, there was simply no one else to call, which unfortunately left little room for moralizing. "Dude, I know this is a lot for you right now," I whispered in English, "but I really need you to grow a pair."

He rolled his eyes. "Axel," he said. "My name's Axel."

"And?" I said, elbowing him.

"And this dude tried to kidnap us." Axel paused. I realized he wasn't just wary of Beto. He was wrestling with a deep, inarticulated fear, the animal terror of being hunted. "You gotta believe me, man," he finally blurted. "This guy is a killer for real. And he's looking for us right now. He saw me. He saw my face. He's gonna kill us. I bet that son of a bitch has killed like a hundred people."

"Whoa, slow down," said Beto, signaling to the chair in front of his desk. "I need details."

Axel rubbed his eyes and wrestled a crumpled cigarette package from his pocket. The encounter with the kidnapper happened approximately five days ago, he said as he sat down, back in a town called Escuintla. Axel and the Hondurans arrived in town after a twenty-four-hour trek through the jungle. There was no shelter in the pueblo, as he remembered it, but they slept in a small church that kept its doors open through the night. At dawn, Axel slipped out of the chapel to scout for the best way to leave town. As the group's informal leader, it was something he always did, he said. After he found what looked like a good entry point into the jungle, he walked back to the church. That was when Axel saw him: a large man in an old truck pulled right up to the chapel's front steps so it blocked the entrance. The Hondurans were gathered around him. Axel sensed immediately that something was off.

"I don't know how to explain it," he said, "other than that this was a bad-looking dude. His eyes was lost, like he had no soul. When I walked up, Jimmy looked at me as if to say: Get outta here, don't get close. But I was the boss of the crew, know what I'm saying? I had to see what was popping. So I walked over anyway. The guy was saying he was a coyote and could take us for cheap to Guerrero. That's where he said he was from, which was kinda far, like a few hundred miles north. That's a few hundred miles of not walking. All we had to do was give him the names and numbers of our family. And once we got to Guerrero safe, he'd call them up and have them wire the fee. We wouldn't have to pay nothing up front, right?"

"Guerrero is where lots of migrants go missing," said Beto. Much of the state was in open rebellion against the government, and the chaos of the warring factions made it a perfect place for cartels to smuggle migrants away from prying eyes. Mass graves, many of them containing the bodies of migrants, were discovered in Guerrero each year.

"Makes sense to me," said Axel. "Cause this dude was acting so freaking sketchy. For example, he offered to feed us right there in a restaurant, just to prove he could. We was six people at that time. How you gonna feed six grown men, seven counting him, every meal without getting paid beforehand? And then transport everyone to Guerrero too? That shit ain't cheap, and nobody offers you nothing for free on this journey. Nobody. He knew we was starving and was tryna take advantage of our hungriness. So I said no thanks, real polite like that. No thanks, buddy. But he wouldn't leave. And then he said something real creepy. It got us shivering, man. He said that he already had everybody spotted out, including me—like, what towns we had been at, what shelters we had stayed in, everything. How in heavens he woulda knew that if he was just showing up in Escuintla by chance? He wasn't working alone. So I was like hell no, this guy can only be one thing: a kidnapper. Anda pescando, that's how they say it in Spanish, right? He was fishing, fishing for migrants."

Axel hustled everyone back inside the church, hoping that the man would eventually lose interest and leave. But the guy kept his truck parked right in front of the entrance, surveilling them. The only option, said Axel, was to sneak away. They split into three groups. The Robertos left out the front door, to give the illusion that they were breaking off solo. Jimmy and Meme snuck out a side exit and then circled westward around town. Axel and Charlie hopped out of a window and went east, crawling through some bushes around the side of the square.

"But the craziest thing was," said Axel, "when we was sneaking around the plaza, I looked back, and I saw the dude smiling at me. Like he knew what we was doing and didn't even care, like, 'Go ahead and run. I'll just find you again.' That was spooky. But then we all joined back up in the jungle and I was like, okay, we're good. And then we found the Viacrucis and we thought we was safe. Levi even said that no one woulda messed with Father Solalinde, right? But here this dude is, showing his ass in the priest's own house."

Beto typed something into the computer. "Look," he said, turning the screen toward us. "This is our database. We take a headshot of every person who enters the shelter." Beto clicked through each photograph one at a time. "Tell me if you see him."

"Stop," said Axel, about a dozen clicks in. "That's him."

The man looked like a caricature of a gang member. Glassy-eyed, shaved head, grimace, with the tail of a tattoo snaking up his beefy neck.

"He told you he was from Guerrero?" asked Beto.

"Yeah, that's right. Guerrero."

"When he registered with us this morning, he said he was from El Salvador." Beto clicked on the screen a couple more times. "A person with this same name checked into the shelter two months ago. And again two months before that." The man had been showing up at the shelter over and over again. A poor strategy if you're a migrant headed north, but a pretty good one if you're a gang member fishing for a catch. Beto stood, anxiously ran his hands through his perfectly coiffed hair, and then poked his head out of the office door. Another staff member appeared. He was slight, maybe twenty, and probably used to be a migrant too, I thought. Hermanos en el Camino was full of people like Beto, who had fled their homes and stayed in the first place they decided was safe.

"Esteban," said Beto, motioning him to the computer screen. "I want you look for this guy. Six feet tall, tattoos on both arms. When you see him, report back. Don't approach." Esteban nodded and slipped out the door.

Beto pulled a cell phone out of his pocket and hit a number on speed dial. "It's Beto," he said. "We've got a situation here. . . . Yeah. . . . One guy as far as we know, possibly gang or narco. . . . No, I need you here now. . . . Fine." He hung up.

Beto turned back to us. "Where are the other people you were traveling with?"

"Behind the men's dormitory," said Axel.

"And they can corroborate what you told me?"

"Absolutely, my dude."

Esteban opened the door. "Bad news," he said. "The man is outside the shelter, hanging out at the taco stand. He's got two other guys with him."

"Gang members?" asked Beto.

"No, migrants, I think. Looks like he's buying them food."

"See I told you." Axel slapped his hand against the desktop. "That's what he tried to do with us. He's fattening up the little piggies before he eats them."

Beto peered out the window. "We need someone to bring him back to the shelter so he can't run away." The room was silent. Beto turned to me. "It needs to be you."

"Me?" Up to this point, I had barely spoken a single word. I was fairly certain that Beto didn't even know my name. He was aloof, and I was unimportant. Until now, apparently.

He nodded. "You're not Mexican and you're new here. He'll never see you coming."

I thought about protesting, about saying I was just an anthropologist and shouldn't get involved. But what had I expected? To join the Viacrucis without getting my hands dirty? I watched Axel take a nervous drag on his cigarette and felt a genuine tenderness for him. I'd spent months in Mexico searching for a purpose. Now I had one. I could help him.

"Alright," I said, steeling my resolve. "What am I supposed to do?"

"You need to lure them back inside," said Beto. "Say that the headshots we took this morning were accidentally deleted, and they need to retake them. And say they forgot to sign some documents. I'll print some forms that they can fill out." I had to hand it to Beto, the guy was a pro. He was going to beat the kidnapper with good old-fashioned Mexican bureaucracy. "Now hurry up," he said. "We're wasting time. And whatever you do, don't make him suspicious. For your own sake."

I put my hand on Axel's shoulder to steady myself.

"Dude, I know this is a lot for you right now," mimicked Axel, "but I really need you to grow a pair."

I tried not to smile and failed.

As I stepped out of the shelter, I had the sudden impression that I'd been ushered onto a stage and forced to act in a production that had been performed a thousand times before. Except I didn't know my lines or even the role I was supposed to play. I'd learned quickly to use my skin in Mexico. Being a white American, I normally had two options in a dangerous situation. The first was to puff up my chest, flip my long blond hair in the sunlight, and act impossibly more important than I was. Speak loudly and carry an American passport. The US government has sent me to conduct this important blah blah blah, and if I don't report back soon then they are going to go absolutely blah blah blah, and trust me, bucko, you do not want to be around when the yada yada hits the fan. Cops and immigration agents respond to this strategy in Mexico for the same reasons they respond to it in the US—they revere power. Once, in Mexico City, I got out of a sticky situation by tucking a few hundred pesos into my passport, putting on my white American voice, and demanding that the low-level schmuck stop wasting my time. The key was to be simultaneously benevolent and dismissive: "Look buddy, you can take this money and buy some drinks for the fellas at the station, maybe get your girl a new dress, or I can call my boss back in Washington and you can finally learn what it's like to tango with the big boys." The cop ate it up. He actually thanked me and apologized for wasting my time. And it wasn't technically a lie. In the event I actually went missing in a Mexican jail, I supposed the State Department would have to come looking for its Fulbright scholar eventually. But the obvious problem with that strategy, besides the general sleaziness of slipping into the skin of empire, is that crazy people, desperate people—say frontline grunts kidnapping migrants for MS-13, for instance—do not give a damn about your stinking government. They will shank you just to call your bluff.

That left me with the second option, which was on the opposite end of the spectrum: become the idiot gringo. There was a small cast of morons I could choose from. The enthusiastically lost tourist was one. Glossy and fantastically inept foreign correspondent was another. Hippie backpacker might work, I thought, given my incredibly disheveled state, though this also implied broken family ties and therefore fewer people willing to come looking for a corpse. In the end, I decided to lean into the role I knew best—I'd play a bumbling, wannabe anthropologist confused by almost everything around him.

The taco stand was maybe fifty paces from the shelter gates and tucked into a grove of scrubby trees. It was little more than a ramshackle lean-to with some wobbly plastic tables arranged outside in the earth. Behind the plywood bar was just enough space for a greasy stovetop to fry whatever meat was cheapest at market that day, usually some bit of chicken or end of pig. The occasional iguana. Extension cords curled out of the stand and into the bone-dry undergrowth, siphoning electricity from some unseen generator or fuse box. One spark and the whole place could go up in flames.

The man leaned his back against the bar, with his large arms splayed across its stained and pockmarked topography. I was acutely aware of how skinny I had become during the Viacrucis. The guy had me beat by a hundred pounds, and a good amount of that was muscle. He could throttle me with one hand and finish his tacos with the other. His potential victims looked almost like children beside him, hunched hungrily over their plates. They were younger than I expected and had the wispy mustaches of teenagers trying to pass. In front of them, a daytime talk show droned on a small television jammed into the crotch of a tree. I chanced a glance at the shelter and saw Axel's bald head gawking from the doorway. I waved him back. The kidnapper had a clear view of the road. If he got spooked, or if the police showed up too early, he might make a run for it. Or, if he had a gun, he could hunker down behind the bar, maybe take the woman at the grill hostage. Or me.

In the distance came the low rumble of a train pulling into Ixtepec's station—the Beast, now mostly empty of human cargo. I had the thought right then that the Beast had been a little too perfect. It was an image—the huddled masses hurtling north on a monster made of iron—that belonged to a simpler world, one in which real machines carried real people seeking jobs in American factories that really existed. It stirred something deep in the psyche Americana, where the drama of the hardened poor could play out for the benefit of journalists and activists and politicians. But that world was gone now. When the Southern Border Program dismantled the Beast, it was about more than simply enforcing borders or deporting migrants en masse. It was about making the two teenage boys in front of me invisible. It was about pushing them into the grimiest bars and hidden halfway houses and places exactly like this, an obscure taco stand on the outskirts of town where they could vanish a thousand times over and no one would care.

A blast from the train horn shook me out of my philosophizing. I took a deep breath, fixed an insane smile on my sunburned face, and marched up to the taco stand. I rapped the top of the plywood bar with my hand.

"Buenias días," I said, mispronouncing the words and really laying into the gringo accent. "Como estáns?"

The teenagers looked up from their tacos. "Buenos días," they said in unison. The kidnapper sniffed, said nothing, and turned back to the television.

"Llegarons este mañana?" I asked, which translated roughly to "Yous arrived on this morning?" in broken Spanish.

"What?" said the kidnapper.

"I am new volunteer at shelter," I chirped. "Yous arrived on this morning?"

"Sí," said the teenagers.

"Oh hoorays. Nice to meets."

The teenagers chewed.

"Tacos?" I said. "Is morning. Very early for taco time, but taco smell is tasty." I waved overenthusiastically at the woman cooking at the comal, trying to replicate the bizarre energy characteristic of white tourists in Mexico excited by everyday life. She raised her spatula in return, bemused.

"We haven't eaten in forever, man," said one of the teenagers. "We've been walking for days."

"Oh wow, so tired. Yous travels together?"

"Who is this guy?" spat the kidnapper. It seemed to be a rhetorical question. He reached into his waistband, and for one horrifying moment I thought he was going to pull out a gun. But it was just a cell phone. He shot off a text, and I wondered who else might be listening nearby.

"We met this morning," said the other teenager, nodding to the large man.

"Oh I sees," I said. "Listen, I is new volunteer at shelter. I make big accident. I delete pictures you take when arrive. So sorry. You come do pictures in shelter again please?"

"We have to take our photos again?" asked the first teenager. The way they talked, I could tell they were from rural Honduras, just two small town kids.

"Look, buddy," said the man. "They don't need to take the photos. We're about to leave. Get lost."

It was then that I saw the backpacks tucked underneath one of the plastic tables. They were already packed and had no reason to return to the shelter. I had to think of something else. I drummed my fingers apprehensively against my leg and felt the recorder in my pocket. I pulled it out. Sweat prickled on the back of my neck.

"You know, I is anthropologist. You does interviews with me? Chats about travels?"

"What's an anthropologist?" asked the boys.

I cursed myself for choosing such an obscure discipline. But before I could answer, the large man lunged and slapped the recorder into the dirt. "You son of a bitch," he snarled. "No god damn interviews. I said get the fuck out of here."

I stooped to recover the recorder and glanced up at the teenagers from the ground. Their eyes were wide with shock.

"Okay, there is no problemos," I said, standing upright again,
brushing the dirt off my knees. "No problemos, muchachos. No
interviews necessaries. But maybe we make pictures in shelter before yous leaves? So families knows yous was here in case somethings happen?" I swallowed. "Somethings bad?"

The kidnapper glared at me but stayed silent. I grinned hyster-
ically and made unwavering eye contact. Sweat poured down my
back.

"Maybe that's a good idea," said the first teenager, looking at
the other.

"Yeah," said the second. "We can take the pictures again."

"Hoorays." I clapped my hands. "We be so quicks. Oh, we also
has some teensy-weensy documents for to sign." I threw my arms
over the teenagers' shoulders and steered them toward the shelter.
"Come, come, Señor Fuerte," I called back to the kidnapper.

Señor Fuerte—Mister Strong Man—lumbered behind us,
likely wondering if he should bolt but so close to his prey that he
couldn't give up the hunt. As we walked through the gates into the
compound, I spotted Esteban sitting in the shade, watching us.
"Camera is here," I said. Another volunteer was already manning
the tripod outside of Beto's office, snapping pictures of a string of
waiting migrants. We filed in line, and Esteban quietly closed the
gates behind us. I chanced a glance around the shelter but did not
see Axel. The teenagers shuffled toward a plastic folding table and
began filling out a stack of forms. The tattooed man stood in front
of the camera, clearly annoyed.

From the other side of the gates came the sound of engines
roaring and tires skidding across gravel. Doors were thrown open.
Boots hit the ground. Then a small army charged into the shelter. They wore ski masks and waved automatic weapons. Someone
yelled, "Get on the ground," and the kidnapper looked up from

the camera, baffled, just as an assault rifle was shoved in his face and he was thrown into the dirt. Beto suddenly appeared from his office and yanked the teenagers backward through the doorway to safety. More uniforms were still charging through the gates and skirting the perimeter. Behind them the Beast loomed on the tracks, brooding and empty. The SWAT team cuffed the kidnapper and dragged his limp body out into the street. They threw him into the back of an idling truck and jumped in after. Then they were off again, peeling out, spraying gravel over the crowd of shell-shocked migrants spilling out of the shelter, with Axel skipping after them, triumphant, shouting, "Bye bitch!" middle fingers in the air.

The whole operation took less than two minutes. Afterward, a jagged adrenaline coursed through the shelter. People milled around the fresh tire tracks, still unsure of what had happened, swapping rumors. A police officer arrived to speak with Axel and the teenagers. He wore slacks despite the heat and spoke in facts.

"We ran a background check," the officer said, flipping open a notepad, "and identified the man as a known MS-13 gang member. He's already been deported several times before to El Salvador. We believe he is involved with other disappearances in the area, but we have no proof."

"Well yeah," said Axel.

"But," said the officer, tapping the notepad with his pen for emphasis, "we cannot hold this man for long. We have no evidence. He has committed no obvious crime. A few days, maybe a week. Then he'll be deported."

"He'll just cross right back the next day," said Axel.

The teenagers did not stick around. I don't know where they went, but by late afternoon they were gone. We never saw them again.

Axel and I, however, became inseparable. From then on, we spent most of every day together conducting interviews, sharing meals, and swapping stories. Axel was a somewhat eccentric character, no doubt, but correctly identifying the kidnapper proved that he was also incredibly attuned to what was happening on the ground, in ways that I and even the other Viacrucis organizers were not. I realized that Axel was something of an organic anthropologist—someone who was a migrant and yet wholly different from the norm, someone who saw things that others didn't see. We quickly established a symbiotic partnership. I would inform Axel of the latest news from the Viacrucis higher-ups, and he would share what he was hearing from other migrants. For instance, after I told him that I'd heard from Armando Amante that Solalinde really was considering escorting the Viacrucis up to Mexico City, Axel informed me that another train was scheduled to pull into Ixtepec the next day. Several migrants—tired of all the uncertainty and delays—were going to board it, he said, despite the fact that immigration was practically crawling all over the tracks. Sure enough, the next evening a train pulled up, and a couple dozen people disappeared.

One night, while lying in bed, I received a friend request from an account named Ruffrider Quest. It was Axel. A few of the account's photos were of him alone, standing in a single beam of light on a dark street or throwing up the peace sign next to a well-muscled pit bull. He had other pictures with a little boy and girl. The boy looked exactly like him, with the same big ears and goofy smile. The girl was still a toddler and wore a flowery dress. The pictures were hard to place. They were closely cropped and didn't have much of a background. Just a patch of grass or a cinderblock wall. But it was strange. The scenery didn't look like any part of New York that I'd seen before.

I should have known that night, when the spider bit me as I slept, that it was a bad omen, a sign of other creatures moving in the dark. But instead I swatted blindly at my leg, then rolled over, fell back asleep, and by morning had almost forgotten that it happened at all.

CHAPTER 6

BROWN RECLUSE

THE THING ABOUT a brown recluse spider bite is that, at first, you don't know it's a brown recluse spider bite. The fang marks leave two barely visible bumps. Just an ant bite, you think, and go about your business, scratching at it absentmindedly. But underneath, the flesh rots.

I secretly hoped that the sting operation would finally land me on Solalinde's radar. That he'd see how competent I was, and how I was willing to take risks for the cause. But if the priest ever learned of my involvement, he never mentioned it. There were bigger things for him to worry about. After nearly a week of silence, Solalinde stepped outside of his quarters and announced that he would lead the Viacrucis to Mexico City after all. He had spoken to his contacts, he said, and decided that the government would not likely retaliate. That night there was more dancing. The sky sparkled with stars. A warm breeze fluttered across the palm trees and felt like a sign that the whole world was beckoning us to run into it.

The next morning, immigration descended upon Ixtepec. They set up checkpoints on every road out of town, and no one was allowed in or out without having their documents inspected. They also brought backup—a cadre of federal police with enough vehicles to detain nearly every person in the Viacrucis. Solalinde declared that under no circumstances was anyone allowed to leave the shelter. So long as we stayed inside, he said, we should be safe. I didn't understand why—if immigration really was out to get us—they didn't just batter down the doors and detain everyone posthaste. Some of the shelter volunteers conjectured that the agents wouldn't dare because they'd be crossing a thinly veiled line that had divided the power of church and state since before Mexico was even a country. Others, like Irineo, said that the Mexican constitution protected pilgrims, and that state officials were banned from entering migrant shelters unless explicitly invited inside. I pored over the constitution on my phone but found no such law. Regardless, the strategy held true: immigration remained within sight of the shelter gates, but they kept a respectful distance. Through the trees and underbrush, we could just make out the glint of orange and white trucks several hundred yards away, and, almost comically, men in dark sunglasses peering at the shelter through sets of binoculars. Each day, the siege strangled a little more air out of the shelter. The food supply started to dwindle. Anytime shelter volunteers went into town to buy supplies, the police would question them, and they often came back empty handed. Then the shoddily installed plumbing system busted from overuse. Water had to be rationed, the toilets backed up, and the farthest corners of the shelter walls began to stink. We realized people were defecating in them at night.

"We're marking our territory," joked Axel. "Like the dogs they think we are."

Then my phone stopped working. I couldn't call or text anyone. Axel was offline too. I looked around and a murmur rippled across the shelter. No one could get a call out.

"They're jamming the signal," said Axel. We walked the perimeter, looking for clues. On the far side of the soccer field, Axel stopped and pointed. "Look at that truck. Does it got a weird antenna on it?" The vehicle had some kind of contraption on its roof, like a small satellite dish. Axel got a funny look in his eye. "I'll be back," he said, then dashed away, zigzagging through the soccer game.

"Wait," I called. "Where are you going?"

"To find the most badass computer they got in this bitch."

Ten minutes passed, and my phone still didn't work. Then half an hour. The reality of the signal jam began to set in. There would be no way to call for help if immigration raided us now. I wouldn't even be able to warn my family. I desperately tried to punch my girlfriend's number into my phone. Nothing. After an hour, I saw Axel jogging back across the soccer field.

"Try it now," he shouted.

Lo and behold, I had one bar. Just one, but it was enough to shoot off a message. "Dude, you're a miracle worker."

"I'll be honest, bro, I don't know how long the signal is gonna last for. This is just a temporary defense."

"Does Solalinde know?"

"Yeah, I was just with him and Beto. They was making calls to Mexico City to let them know these bastards is jamming us up."

"How'd you do it?"

"Oh, you know," he said, smirking. "I already told you I'm a computer geek."

The signal was spotty from then on, but every time it went down, Axel was eventually able to get it running again. I imagined the police on the other side of the fence losing their minds, trying to figure out how Solalinde kept thwarting their jammer. Most people in the Viacrucis didn't even know that Axel was the one keeping us safe. I knew. Beto knew. Solalinde knew. But other than that, it was very hush-hush. Axel had a whole other side to him that no one else could see, but every time I asked exactly what he was doing when he disappeared, he'd quickly change the subject.

Every few days, Solalinde held a meeting to strategize with the Viacrucis organizers, but it was always the same: The timing was not right, things were too tense, immigration might strike at any moment. Irineo was not happy. Solalinde stole his march, and now it had ground to a halt entirely. "Levi," he said, pulling me aside one evening. "Aren't you tired of this old priest trying to make up his mind? I'm starting to think the only way to Mexico City is on the Beast. Let's get as many people in the shelter together as we can and just go, yeah? You in?"

No, I said, I was not in.

"C'mon, Levi," he said, suddenly chummy for the first time. "What are we waiting around for? If people want to follow me, they should be able to follow me. You really want to stick around and do nothing?"

"I don't know," I demurred. "Won't we be immediately detained on the Beast?"

"Nothing's going to happen. I still ride the Beast all the time."

I highly doubted that, but even if it was true, Irineo was Mexican. He couldn't be detained by Mexican immigration, and I told him as much.

But Irineo just waved my concerns away. "Think it over. And while you're thinking, do you have any money? I'm trying to buy supplies for the trip."

After dinner, I told another shelter volunteer named Julio about Irineo's proposition. "Ride the Beast with Irineo?" he scoffed. "With all these kids and old people? That's absolutely ludicrous."

"But then why would he want to do it?"

"Because Irineo's an idiot," he laughed. "Haven't you noticed? No one here respects him. He's just angry that Solalinde's stealing his spotlight. Look, be patient, okay? Whatever we end up doing, it's better to be here than with Irineo. The guy's a moron."

Sensing a sympathetic ear, I said that Irineo had been driving me nuts, actually. All the secrecy he'd cultivated around the caravan. Always putting himself in front of the cameras. And constantly asking me to pay for everything, just because he said that he was Mexican and didn't have any money.

"Mexican?" said Julio. "You know Irineo's American too, right?"
"What?"

"Irineo's American. He has dual citizenship. He lived in Arizona, I think. He's up there all the time holding fundraisers."

I was furious. "Are you kidding me? He's always hounding me for cash. Wait—are you telling me this dude knows English but has been forcing me to speak Spanish with him the whole time?"

"Yeah, he just thinks it's funny to hear your accent."

ONE AFTERNOON, A migrant I'd never spoken to before asked if I knew where Levi was.

"I am Levi," I said.

"No, the other Levi then," he said.

"I don't think I know another Levi," I replied, confused.

"You know, that guy you're always with."

"Axel?"

"Oh, I thought your name was Axel," he said. "Anyway, can you tell him that I heard another train is coming tonight?"

"Sure thing," I said. How migrants came by this information, I never knew. It seemed accurate, however, because Beto ordered the guard at the front door to keep an extra close eye out for anyone trying to leave that night. But after sunset, I noticed that Shakira and several other people were missing.

"Do you think they're out by the train?" I asked Axel. "We've got to convince them to come back."

"Well, let's go then."

"How do we get past the guard?"

"Why you asking me? You're the guy who's worked here before."

I told the guard that I had blisters on my feet, and that I needed to buy bandages and antiseptic to clean them. He eyed me suspiciously, weighing whether or not it was worth it to disrespect a volunteer, and then reluctantly swung open the metal door.

"Make it quick," he said, scanning the darkened street. "Wait, where do you think you're going?" The guard held his arm across the doorway, barring Axel.

"I need him to show me where the pharmacy is," I said and pulled Axel beneath his arm before he could say no.

The street was empty, and we stuck to the shadows of the buildings in case a police patrol rolled around the corner. As we drew nearer to the Beast, I could just make out the shadows of about twenty people from the Viacrucis, including Shakira and el Chaparrito.

"What are you doing here?" I whispered. "The train's too dangerous. You'll all be caught."

"Get real, Levi," said Shakira. "Immigration is going to bust the shelter any day now. At least out here we can run." Everyone else nodded silently in agreement.

Then lights flashed in the distance.

"What the fuck is that?" yelled Axel, and, without waiting for the obvious answer, took off down the tracks. I instinctively followed after him.

"Don't run, you idiots," hissed Shakira. "They've been circling us for the last hour. But they haven't come any closer. If you run, you'll get their attention."

We froze and watched the immigration truck cruise lazily down the street, its lights swinging out across the open space of the train yard, like an anglerfish in the dark, luring in its prey. It slowed to a stop about fifty yards from us, its engine idling, but stayed where it was. After a short eternity, the engine growled and the truck rolled away. We all exhaled simultaneously. I turned to Shakira one more time and begged her to return, but she just wrapped her small arms around me and said goodbye. I gave el Chaparrito a parting handshake, and then Axel and I started to jog back toward the shelter. It was too dark to see the terrain properly. One moment I was leaping over a metal track, and the next I was neck-deep in a hole. I yelped in surprise and Axel reached his arm down to pull me out.

"I don't think I'm hurt," I said, running my hands over my legs to check for cuts. From around the corner came the roar of an engine, and then immigration's headlights were headed directly toward us. They must have heard me scream.

"Fuck," hollered Axel. "Fuckitty fuck fuck fuck."

We dashed across the street and into a nearby alleyway, running blindly, taking a left onto another street, then a right into a second alleyway, then another left, then hopped a fence. The lights were gone, then we turned a corner, and they were back again, and we ran and ran, and just before we reached the shelter gates, lungs burning and entirely out of breath, Axel reached into his pocket and slipped something into my hand. We banged on the metal door and pushed our way inside. The guard surveyed us, panting and pouring sweat, and asked suspiciously, "So what'd you buy from the pharmacy?"

I opened my hand. "Band-Aids," I said, holding them up to the guard, and then Axel swung his arm around my shoulder and steered me toward the men's dormitory, chuckling from sheer relief.

I WAS WALKING to the bathroom the next morning when I saw a pink figure bobbing along the train tracks. "Shakira," I called quietly, since most people were still sleeping. She came a few paces from the fence and smiled, just out of arm's reach, as if she thought I might try to pull her back inside. "What are you doing here?" I asked. "What happened to the train?"

"There was no train," she said. "False alarm. But there was an immigration raid at four in the morning. Three trucks came and started chasing us."

"Did they catch anyone?"

"I think mostly everyone got away. Look," she pointed to a small figure asleep on the ground. "There's el Chaparrito. He ran back to the shelter with everyone else."

"But not you."

"No, I hid in the bushes. I already told you, I'm not sticking around."

"Shakira, please," I said, but she was already walking back toward the tracks.

"Come visit me in Miami," she called, waving goodbye, and then she was gone, a pink dot skipping into the distance.

Just hours later, while waiting in line for breakfast, Armando Amante told me Shakira was dead. "The police just called to tell Solalinde," he said. "They found her body on the train tracks. They raped her. And her head was cut off. Decapitated."

"No," I said. "I just saw her a few hours ago. Shouldn't we check the body? I'll go. Let me go. It can't be her."

"Levi, you can't leave," said Armando. "The police could detain you as soon as you walk into the station."

"But we don't even know if it's her for sure."

"It was her. The body, they said it was wearing all pink."

"But there's all kinds of rumors in this place. And no one ever checks to make sure that they're real. Come on, man. Think about her family." I didn't know what Armando would think if I started to cry.

"I don't think Shakira had much family anymore, Levi."

"We've got to check."

"We can't."

"What do you mean we can't," I yelled. "I don't get it. First the police help us run a sting operation, and now they could deport us at any moment? We're trapped here like caged animals while gang members are murdering people right outside our walls? They need to do their jobs."

Armando had a strange expression on his face, like he was suddenly very angry, but when he spoke his voice was tender. "Who do you actually think killed her? You think it was just some random gang member? While Ixtepec is surrounded by the feds? It was them, Levi. It was the police. The gangs, the police, the cartels. Don't you see? They're the same thing. And they killed her. To send us a message. To show us what will happen to anyone else who tries to escape."

"What?"

"The police killed Shakira, Levi. And they want to kill us too."

Shakira's death lingered among us. It morphed and changed shape with rumor. The decapitation became a gunshot wound to the head. The rape became a trick gone wrong. She wasn't attacked, she was kidnapped. She resisted. She wasn't dead at all. She called from a town north. Her corpse became pliable and whatever anyone wanted it to be. I tried to talk with Beto, who had supposedly received the initial call from the police, but he brushed me aside. "Whatever it is, we're handling it," he said.

I never saw Shakira's body. In fact, I never saw the dead body of a single migrant in Mexico. During the Viacrucis, we'd been calling the Southern Border Program an undeclared war, with its armored vehicles and machine guns and military checkpoints. But this was not a war. In war, the dead are everywhere. You see them. You can touch them. But most migrants in southern Mexico don't die. They disappear. You watch them walk into the jungle or pass behind a train car, and then they never come back. You search for them in migrant shelters and bus terminals, in the hospitals and mortuaries, but they simply aren't there. Every so often, the government discovers a new mass grave. The bodies they find are the bodies of migrants, but they're never the ones you're looking for.

THE BITE ABOVE my left ankle started to ache. Three angry red rings formed around the fang marks, like a bullseye. Once, I stretched my leg towards my face to get a better look at it and gagged at the smell.

"I think it might be from a brown recluse," I told Axel.

"How do you know?"

"I don't. I just heard that they get red rings around the bite like this."

"Bro, if that's true, you're screwed."

"Thanks, man, very comforting."

Waiting out a siege, I came to learn, was less a terrifying process than mind numbing. You woke and you were still in the same place, stuck in the same shelter in the same tiny town. You sat in the shade, you walked in the sun. When there was water, you drank. When there was food, you ate. You stared through the chain link fence out into the world that no longer belonged to you. In Latin America, every Viacrucis reenactment ends with a crucifixion. It seemed that we were going to fill that role soon enough.

Strange as it may seem, I hadn't fully considered my own safety until that moment. Or maybe I hadn't allowed myself to. Months earlier, at my grant orientation, it was announced that any scholar caught protesting in Mexico would face deportation. I had joined the Viacrucis knowing that I was running some theoretical risk, but it felt entirely abstract and trivial compared to the overt fears of everyone else around me. If I was detained, I could lose a research grant. If anyone else was, they could lose their life. But now that the spider bite had swollen to the size of a baseball, I didn't want to acknowledge that my health might also be somewhat in jeopardy.

The only way to take my mind off things was to play soccer. After Shakira's disappearance, we played for hours while the police observed us from afar. I had just scored a goal when el Lobo kicked me right in the bite, a dirty play to trip me up, and I felt the rotten flesh explode beneath my sock.

"Bastard," I said, limping to the sidelines, "are you trying to kill me before the police do?"

"Calm down, gringo. The cops aren't going to kill you."

I peeled back my sock and a sour mixture of blood and pus gushed down my ankle. I didn't have bandages to salve it, or even any clean socks. The blood was orange and oily and smelled like rotting fish. Angry red lines flashed from the open hole and across my skin, a lightning trace of the venom or bacteria traveling through the veins. Each day the poison map spread higher up my leg. First my calf, then to the crook of my knee, then playing up my thigh, and finally shooting nearly up to my groin.

"Axel," I said, massaging my leg. "I think I need a doctor."

"Yeah dude. Your leg's been stinking for days now."

We discussed my options. I couldn't see a doctor in town. It was too risky. Immigration could get tipped off, and there'd be no escaping if they busted through the doors of the operating room while I had a scalpel digging around in my leg. Plus, the local clinics were infamously wretched. It wasn't guaranteed that they'd have anesthesia, or even properly sanitized equipment. I needed to go back to Mexico City.

"Yeah, that makes the most sense," said Axel.

"So you're not mad at me? For leaving?"

"Nah dude, you serious? That poison's gonna travel all the way up to your ding-a-ling. Get that shit fixed quick."

The bus station was about three quarters of a mile from Hermanos en el Camino, just beyond the train tracks of the Beast. Calling a cab was out of the question. Any taxi that pulled up to the shelter would be immediately stopped and searched by the police. I would have to sneak out on foot, but if I walked into the middle of a patrol, I was toast. To make matters more complicated, the last bus left in the late afternoon, so I wouldn't even have the cover of darkness. I tried to clean myself up as best I could, but it was useless. The busted plumbing meant that I couldn't adequately wash my clothes, or even myself for that matter. I looked in the mirror and had to smile at what a sad state I was in. "All I need is a Che Guevara shirt," I said to Axel. "To complete the dirty gringo look."

"Who's that?" he asked.

I packed my backpack: five t-shirts, two pairs of athletic shorts, three pairs of underwear, three pairs of socks, two notebooks, *The Savage Detectives*, by Roberto Bolaño—which I hadn't picked up once—my passport, the audio recorder, and 1,500 pesos in cash. I slipped Axel 500.

"Well, I guess this is it," I said.

"Keep an eye out for all the checkpoints you pass, bro. Text me the locations, in case we need them for later."

"I will."

"And hey, buddy, I'll miss you."

"I'll miss you too," I said.

The guard cracked the gate and poked his head out. "All clear," he said. "Once you leave, you're on your own. Don't expect me to open this door with the police chasing you down the street."

"I don't think I could run anyway," I said, rolling down my sock to show him the bite.

"Oh my god." He grabbed my shoulder. "Listen, you can't let them catch you. You can't. Do you understand? They'll just as soon let your leg rot off than take you to a hospital."

"Just what I needed to hear, thanks," I said, and stepped outside, the clink of the metal door behind me.

The street sat empty and quiet. The leaves of tropical trees purred in the breeze, and I hobbled underneath their protective shade for as long as I could, then stopped to collect myself once the train tracks were in sight. I'd have to cross them quickly, in full view of anyone surveilling the comings and goings of the town, but not so fast as to draw suspicion. I dragged my leg over the crisscross of iron tracks and hustled to the bus station. The air was scorching and my t-shirt was drenched in sweat. I bought a ticket with the last of my cash, so as to leave no digital record of being in Ixtepec. A solitary police truck rolled by, and I caught my breath, but it looped lazily around the tracks—just a couple local scrubs performing their normal routes, not the federales. I leaned against the wall and tried to appear nonchalant. When the bus arrived, it was already full of rural Oaxaqueños bound for the capital. I took my seat next to a small old woman, who instinctively shrank away from me and pulled a shawl over her head. I realized that I was even dirtier than I'd thought. Everything I had on—my cleanest clothes—was covered in swirls of dust and sweat, whole geographies of filth. I pressed my arms against my sides in an attempt to keep the stink in and wondered if anyone could smell the rot lurking under my sock.

Levi 4:47 PM On the bus
Levi 4:47 PM Kinda scared not gonna lie
Axel 4:48 PM Ok bro stay safe brother

Just miles outside of town, we hit the immigration blockade. The doors opened and two agents boarded, the bus swaying gently as their boots pressed their weight into the floor. The first officer greeted the driver casually, then stared directly down the aisle towards me. Our eyes met and I looked away quickly, but it was too late. His boots were already tapping briskly past the rows of cheap fabric seats. Could he tell I was with the Viacrucis? Was I now an enemy of the state? I clenched my fists and resolved to make a scene. I was going to yell and curse and fight. But then the officer was reaching past me and yanking down the shawl from the face of the old woman. He demanded her identification, and she slid some kind of plastic card from her breast pocket. Satisfied, the agent stepped off the bus, and we pulled back onto the highway.

Levi 5:12 PM Went through a checkpoint
Levi 5:12 PM but they didn't even inspect my docs or anything
Axel 5:13 PM Hells fuckin yeah keep rolling baby

We were stopped one more time, an hour farther down the road, and again I was passed over like I was invisible. We pulled into Mexico City in the early morning. On the bus, I had begun to feel sick. I chalked it up to a combination of exhaustion and guilt, and finally back in my apartment, I was so tired that I collapsed onto my mattress without even eating or bathing first.

When I woke up, I knew immediately that something was wrong. My hands and feet were swollen, and my fingers were so fat that I could barely grasp the doorknob to get out of my bedroom. I examined myself in the bathroom mirror and let out a low moan that sounded like the ululation of a wounded animal.

An engorged and grotesque tongue lolled out of my mouth. I wheezed and greedily sucked air down my rapidly constricting windpipe. Disoriented, I stumbled downstairs to the neighborhood off-license pharmacist, who took one look at me, squirted an unknown medicine down my throat, and sent me straight to the national hospital in the first taxi that passed by.

In the lobby of the emergency room, the medicine had done enough that my tongue stopped swelling, and I tried to explain to a nurse at reception that I'd been bitten by a brown recluse. But either my words were too slurred or I was using the wrong terminology, because the nurse had no clue what I was talking about. When I was finally called into the doctor's office, he didn't have any idea what I was saying either. "No, a spider bite," I repeated over and over while trying to steady my breathing. "A brown recluse." I felt like I was going crazy, hopelessly unable to explain a wound that no one else seemed to understand. It would not be the last time. But in the end, it was decided that an individualized diagnosis was not necessary to treat the symptom. Two medical students anesthetized my leg, sunk a scalpel deep into the flesh, and began scooping out the goop. Within minutes they were finished and handed me a bill to pay on my way out. I was terrified to open it. I had no insurance, and no money to pay for a procedure that, in the US, would have cost thousands of dollars. I considered attempting to sneak out of the hospital without paying, but when I opened the bill, the total was some two hundred pesos. Thirteen bucks.

Time inched along as I recovered and waited for news from the Viacrucis. The procedure had left a hole in my leg, and it was deep enough that it was hard to see exactly where it ended. I couldn't look at the soft, bloody flesh without feeling squeamish. I tried to read *The Savage Detectives* to pass the time, but for some reason I could never remember what I'd read the day before. Instead I occupied myself with trying to walk again. At first, I could only hobble down the block until the bite started to throb unbearably.

But each day I ambled a little farther, wandering into the posh neighborhood of la Condesa, then la Roma, or over to Bosque de Chapultepec to watch families and first dates coast across the lake on paddle boats, laughing in the sun, like everything was normal. Like we weren't in a country where the police were hunting migrants down.

Axel and I called each other every day. I decided not to tell him about the emergency room visit. It was trivial compared to still being trapped inside Hermanos.

"How are things down there?" I'd ask.

"Same old, same old, bro. Hot as fuck, bored as fuck, scared as fuck. And surrounded by motherfuckers."

After a while, I began to suspect that I was being followed. I'd spot strange men in the metro. Men who always entered one train car over from me, and who alighted at the same stop. Men who looked nondescript, like they were without a country or a name. Or who maybe had multiple countries and multiple names. But they never approached me. I was never stopped or questioned or pulled into a dark alley. They never even looked my way. Was I starting to go crazy? Who would want to follow me? The Mexican government? The US State Department? At night I would lock my door and jump every time the evening breeze fluttered through the window. Just months later, a photojournalist named Rubén Espinosa would be assassinated one neighborhood over for covering social protests in Mexico. Four women were also murdered in his apartment, but because they weren't journalists, or maybe because they weren't men, their names were not included in the initial reports. I searched for their names for days until they were finally published: Alejandra Negrete, Nadia Vera, Yesenia Quiroz, Mile Virginia Martín.

A mural appeared on the rooftop of the apartment next to mine. It was of a dismembered nude woman, her blood running down the wall. The way the mural was positioned, it was impossible to see from the street, or from any other vantage point except my living room window. It seemed to have somehow been painted just for me. I got drunk and stared at her and thought of Shakira. Within days, the mural was gone. Painted over like she was never there to begin with. If I hadn't taken a picture of her to send to Axel, I would have thought that I really was losing my mind.

Then one day Axel called me. "This is it, player. We bout to take the hit. Solalinde just told us. Tomorrow morning we face the police straight up, man-to-man."

CHAPTER 7

THE BATTLE OF IXTEPEC

HONESTLY, LEVI, IT'S good that you left when you did. Things got hot. Every day it seemed like immigration was getting closer and closer. And so Solalinde gathered us all around, and in that delicate little voice of his that you can barely hear, he said that it was time, that we had run outta food and water, and that there was no way we coulda stayed in the shelter no more. And of course that was music to my ears. We hadn't been doing nothing but baking in the sun and eating some crusty ass tortillas, so that got my engines revving. I was ready to bust loose.

Solalinde said he'd ordered four buses to drive us to Mexico City, but that the buses had been stopped by the police. They wouldn't let them pick us up in Ixtepec. So if we wanted to go to Mexico City, we'd have to march to them ourselves and get the police to back down. And honestly, the possibility of going face to face with the po-po was exciting. In some ways we wanted it, we wanted to be the people to stand up to them, doing what it took to survive. No pain, no gain, baby.

I grabbed my backpack and my cigarettes and we was out the door. When we started marching down the road, Solalinde sent Beto out ahead to do some reconnaissance on the whole situation. And suddenly he comes rushing back, yelling to the priest that there was a hell of a lot more cops than we'd thought. Over a hundred easy, he said. And not just immigration. There was feds there too. So we quickly hustled it to a nearby church to regroup, and Solalinde started making his phone calls again, and eventually a whole buncha guys I ain't never seen before

94

came sneaking in through the back door. I could tell they was Mexicans, even though they had covered their faces with bandanas. Just something about the way they walked. A lotta the guys came with weapons, the kinda weapons poor people has. Chains wrapped around their hands, or plain wooden boards that looked like they'd just been pulled off the side of somebody's house.

The Mexicans came and stood next to Solalinde. Then Irineo stood up next to them too, and he tried to talk first, saying something bout how we had to stick together, that it was now or never, or some other bullshit. But Solalinde cut him off quick, like, "Shut up you dumb bitch," except more polite, right, cause that's what I wanted to say, not how Solalinde talks. What Solalinde actually said was something like, "Quiet now Irineo, I'm speaking," with real politeness, cause he's always real polite with it, but underneath it's razor blades. Then Solalinde started to remind us that we was a peaceful march, a pilgrimage, and just cause we was about to face the cops didn't mean that we was gonna get violent.

And I said, "Man, how we supposed to be peaceful if they got a hundred bad boys out there waiting to beat the fuck outta us?"

And one of the guys in a bandana next to Solalinde said, "Don't you worry about that, my brother. Just wait and see."

Solalinde introduced them to us as the Teachers. I don't know why he called them that, but he did. "And the Teachers don't back down from shit," he said, except he didn't say that, that's just what I understood him to say.

Then we started chanting again and Solalinde led us back outside and down the road. When we saw the police in the distance, the Teachers told us to put all the women and children and the old people in the center, and then for all the men to link their arms around them in a big circle. To protect them, right? And then the Teachers formed another ring around our ring. Our bodies was their shields, and their bodies was our shields. The police was all in those blacked out uniforms with the batons and shit. Solalinde was walking out in front of us with his two bodyguards. He insisted on going out in front, even though the bodyguards said it was a bad idea. Honestly, I admired him for that. But just as he was walking up to the police line, tryna do his peaceful stuff, one of the Teachers came sprinting from the march and straight toward the police shields. He flew past Solalinde and fucking full-on drop kicked them bitches. And I thought, oh, I get it. We get to be peaceful cause the Teachers is backing us up physically. All the dirty work is hidden on the side, out of sight, and we get to say that we remained peaceful cause the Teachers wasn't never officially associated with us. I had to give it to Solalinde, man, he was a smart motherfucker.

Then it was on. The police smashed up against us and I was just tryna hold it tight, to keep my arms locked and not get hit in the face by a freaking baton. Solalinde was caught in the middle and got smashed immediately. The bodyguards dragged him out and he spent the rest of the time on the sidelines holding his head. Up in front the Teachers was doing they motherfucking thing, just drop-kicking the police shields and going nuts. They came for war, and not necessarily the one we was fighting, you know what I'm saying? Like you could tell they already had a history with the police, and not just any police, but like these police in specific. And then the police would return the kicks by beating us with batons and slamming their shields into our bodies and down on our feets. When somebody fell, it was our job to pick them up and make sure the police couldn't bust through the hole they left. This one migrant dude got caught between two police shields and they smashed him right in his neck, and he screamed and went to his knees and moaned, "I can't, I can't."

And we grabbed him and pulled him up and said, "You've got to, bro, don't you quit on us now."

Then behind us I heard a mama scream and I saw her little boy get knocked to the ground. People was trampling him in the confusion. I fought my way through and snatched him up and put him back in his mama's arms. He almost started to cry but then I told him the same thing I told the other guy—"Hold it together, don't you quit on me now"—and he wiped his eyes and held his mama's hand tight. My boy, my little man. I went back to the line once again and locked arms with

Charlie and Junior, and the Teachers was fighting like wild men. One Teacher went down, and then another filled his place, and then he went down too, and there was a hole in the line, so I rushed up. And just as I stuck my hand out to fill the hole, the police brought their shields down, and I saw my arm disappear in between the plexiglass and I heard something snap, and when I finally pulled my hand back, I couldn't move it. You ever been in a situation where it feels like you're looking at yourself from somewhere else? Like what's happening ain't actually happening to you? Like your body ain't your body? That's what it felt like. Like none of this was real. I just kept looking at my busted wrist and asking myself how the fuck I ever ended up here. And eventually I heard the head of immigration yelling that they'd had enough, that they should let us go, that it was over.

CHAPTER 8

RUFFRIDER QUEST

THE 2015 VIACRUCIS Migrante concluded in Mexico City. After the battle with the feds down in Ixtepec, everyone boarded the buses to the capital knowing that it was the end of the line. Many people were wounded: there were broken feet and hands, a fractured neck, and, by my judgment, many undiagnosed concussions and lacerations. Father Solalinde led a final procession—which was now more of a limp than a march—to the Basilica of Our Lady of Guadalupe, where it was said that the Virgin Mary had appeared in 1531, an apparition that signaled the fall of the Aztec empire of Tenochtitlán and the rise of what would eventually come to be known as Mexico. During the mass, I noticed that Solalinde positioned Axel to stand next to him. When it ended, the priest drove us straight to the National Human Rights Commission, an agency created especially to oversee the government's human rights violations. The priest intended to file a formal complaint against the National Institute of Migration and the federal police for the siege of the Viacrucis in Ixtepec and their subsequent beating of the marchers. Solalinde asked only a handful of people to accompany him for the commission hearing. Axel was one of them. It appeared that, after I left Hermanos, he went from being a skeptic of the Viacrucis to one of its key figures.

By the time the meeting concluded, it was early evening. A gymnasium in the south of the city had agreed to house the

Viacrucis for the time being, on the condition the migrants be held to a strict curfew so that they would not turn the neighbors against the gym. Anyone still outside after eight o'clock would be locked out for the night. Axel and I strolled to a nearby taco stand to talk about what had happened at the commission.

"It was like a big conference," he said. "They made me testify about getting beat. There was cameras recording and everything."

Later I would learn that part of Axel's testimony against immigration was broadcast on a public access channel, which was potentially dangerous. Activists had gone missing for less. Afterward, Solalinde told Axel that he did a good job, a very good job, and that the priest had chosen him because he knew he could speak well in front of the cameras.

"You and Solalinde seem to be becoming pretty close," I said.

"Ah, not really, buddy. I'm just tryna do what I need to do to get back home to my kids."

The mention of Axel's kids got me thinking. "Hey, I saw you added me on Facebook."

"Yeah buddy, Ruffrider Quest. Dope name, right?"

"Why don't you just use your real name?"

"Man, you know how it is out on the migrant trail. I don't want nobody knowing who I am."

We ordered tacos and waited at a cracking plastic table. I asked Axel whether he chose the name Ruffrider for any particular reason. I wondered if it was an allusion to the Rough Riders, Teddy Roosevelt's cavalry unit during the Spanish-American War, who'd volunteered to conquer Cuba and claim it under US dominion. Was he harkening back to that dark past and inverting it, as if his journey was somehow the opposite of the one that the Rough Riders took over a century ago?

"Did you just say the word 'harkening?' Man, you get too poetic with that kinda shit," said Axel. "It's just Ruffrider cause Axel rides rough. But you know what? My mom did used to work for the Roosevelts up in New York." The woman at the stand brought us our tacos, and Axel began ladling heaping spoonfuls of salsa verde onto his plate.

"Your mom was a maid for the Roosevelt family?" I asked, shocked. "Wait, which one? Teddy or FDR?"

"I dunno, man, whichever one used to be president." Axel shoved an entire taco into his mouth in one bite and immediately made a choking noise. "Oh shit," he whispered, his eyes watering. "Oh god, I just fucked up." He lurched beneath the table and put his head between his legs like he was going to retch. The other people at the taco stand eyed us curiously, wary of this odd couple causing a scene. "I thought that shit was guacamole," he moaned.

"That is very much not guacamole, my friend. That is the spiciest salsa on the menu."

"Oh my fuck, I'm gonna die. Oh deary me Jesusito de la verga." Someone nearby chuckled. "These people is crazy, Levi. Why they gotta do guacamole like that? What did guacamole ever do to them?"

"If you think you're in pain now," I said, swapping our plates so he could have my salsa-less tacos, "just wait until it comes out the other end."

I bought us each an horchata from the woman at the grill, who tittered when I explained why Axel had gone mute. "Would you look at that," she said, trying to make conversation, "that black guy is more gringo than you are."

I didn't like the joke, and I hoped Axel hadn't heard her. I brought the horchatas back to the table and changed the subject.

"Hey, I think I saw some pictures of your kids on your account."

"They're freaking beautiful ain't they?"

"Yeah man, your son looks just like you. But I was actually wondering—where were those photos taken?"

"What you mean? New York, obviously. Well, probably in New Jersey too."

"Oh, I guess some of the scenery just looked strange to me or something."

"Yeah man, you was mistaken."

It was getting close to the eight o'clock curfew. When we arrived back at the gymnasium, the door was already closed, and a man I'd never seen before was standing outside, his arms crossed like a bouncer.

"We need to get in," I said.

"No can do," he said. "It's 8:03."

"You've got to be kidding me."

The man didn't budge.

"Look, it's my fault he's late, alright?" I said, pointing to Axel. "It's okay, you can let him in. He was with me."

"And who exactly are you?" asked the man. It was only then that I realized he wasn't with the Viacrucis. The gymnasium must have hired him to keep an eye on the place. It seemed like there were always men guarding doors in Mexico. Poor men, usually, men who looked like they needed the work.

"I'm one of the organizers of the Viacrucis," I said, and then, attempting to put on a more authoritative voice, "so open the door, please."

The man sneered. "Door's not opening. For anybody."

"Don't worry about it, bro," said Axel. He was acting like he was unfazed, but I could tell he was upset.

"What do you mean don't worry about it?" I said, still glaring at the bouncer. "Where are you going to sleep?"

"I'll figure something out."

"Don't be ridiculous. You can't just sleep on the street."

"Dude, don't worry, it ain't even a big deal at this point. This is just Axel's life."

There was a pause between us that seemed to last a long time. "I mean, you could just come crash at my place," I said.

"Nah, brother, don't trip. You ain't gotta do that."

"Of course," I said. "It's my fault anyway. I kept you out too long. You can sleep on the couch. It'll be fine."

"Well, if you're offering for real, I won't say no."

We took the metro back to my neighborhood. I was suddenly very aware of how nice my apartment was. It was a cheap one bedroom and only sparsely furnished with things I'd bought secondhand, but it was still the most luxurious place Axel had slept in months. That thought embarrassed me for some reason, but then somehow also made me feel like I was doing the right thing, whatever that was, which in turn embarrassed me even more.

"Yo," said Axel with a twinkle in his eye, tapping the letter G that marked my apartment. "My man found the G Spot, you dirty dog."

While Axel showered, I made him a bed on the couch. He emerged from the bathroom dripping wet with a towel around his waist, and another one wrapped around his balding pate.

"I'm not even going to ask," I said.

"What? I like the way this towel feels on my scalp, player."

"Hey man, go wild. You deserve it."

I gave Axel a t-shirt and a clean pair of underwear, and he scrubbed the rest of his clothes in the sink. I reclined on the couch and pulled up Ruffrider Quest on my phone. All of the account's photos were gone. I was sure that they'd been there that afternoon, but now I couldn't access them. Sometime after dinner, Axel had blocked me. I was surprised at how hurt I felt. We'd been in the trenches together. I thought we shared a bond. I watched Axel from across the room. He was playing 50 Cent's "P.I.M.P." from his cell phone as he rinsed his clothes, bouncing along to the music in his underwear. He suddenly looked like a stranger again. Was it because I'd asked about his kids? What didn't he want me to see? I also realized that I was a little afraid. Within the parameters of the Viacrucis, I'd trusted Axel more than anyone. But we weren't with the Viacrucis anymore. We were alone.

I said that I was going to turn in. Axel asked if he could have the password to my laptop so he could message his wife.

"Sure," I said, trying to play it cool, but I could tell I hesitated for just a half second too long.

"What? You scared?" He was smirking, but in a way that wasn't clear if he thought something was actually funny.

"Scared? No way. Scared about what?"

"That I might steal your laptop and bounce in the middle of the night."

The thought had crossed my mind. But it was more than that. I'd never gotten a firm grasp on what Axel was doing when he disappeared to help Solalinde evade the police jammers. Part of me felt uneasy about letting him mess around on my computer, especially now that I knew there was something he wanted to keep from me. He'd theoretically have access to all my notes and photographs and private messages. But then again, I thought, none of that really mattered now. He'd be gone in a couple days.

"Nah, man," I said. "I trust you."

BECAUSE OF SOLALINDE'S negotiations, as well as Axel's testimony, the National Human Rights Commission announced that they would grant every Viacrucis member an amparo—a temporary emergency visa that allowed everyone to travel through the country legally for twenty days. Stay a day longer and you could be deported again. The message was clear: they wanted the entire mess out of their country as quickly as possible. We began to bleakly refer to the amparos as "la visa véte"—the fuck off visa.

Solalinde called one final meeting to distribute the amparos and gave a closing speech, which was brief and anticlimactic. Then that was it. The 2015 Viacrucis Migrante was officially over. Everyone was deflated, exhausted, and worried about getting out of the country before the deadline. Axel made plans with the Hondurans to leave for the border immediately.

"Dude," I said, "are you sure you have to leave so soon? If you'd like, you can stay with me for a while."

"Thank you, Levi, but I gotta go."

"I don't know, man, this all feels a little rushed to me. Let some of the other migrants go up to the border first and report back. So you have better information."

He looked me in the eyes. "Look, I don't know how to tell you this, but I got a call from my wife a couple nights ago. And she gave me a final option. Either get back and support the family within two weeks, or she's gonna find another man who can."

I didn't know what to say. "I'm sorry, dude."

"It ain't no thing, bro. There's a lot I haven't told you, cause honestly it ain't nice. Things between me and my wife have not always been the best, you feel me? But I gotta get back. If I wanna see my kids again, I gotta get back right this second."

"Yeah," I said. "I get it."

Before Axel left for the border, we met one last time at Avenida Benjamin Franklin, an eight-lane thoroughfare that separated the city's green, bourgeois center from the poorer, concrete neighborhoods to the south. Our goodbye was rushed. The last bus to Nuevo Laredo was leaving that afternoon, and Axel and the Hondurans were determined to catch it. Jimmy, Meme, and Charlie would hop off early—they had coyotes waiting for them in Reynosa. But Axel and the Robertos were broke, so they'd have to go it alone, relying on what Roberto Stanley could piece together from a crossing he made five years previous. They would wait on the Mexican side for a few days, stocking up on supplies and staking out the border for any weak points. They determined a list of expenses. Bus tickets, obviously, and three days' worth of food in Nuevo Laredo, plus enough canned goods and jugs of water to beat the Texas desert. An inner tube to carry their backpacks and Roberto Stanley, who couldn't swim, across the Rio Grande. A change of new, American-style clothes to blend in once they reached the outskirts of Laredo, Texas. And, most importantly, their bribes for Los Zetas to enter the US. Migrants who crossed without forking over the entry fee usually ended up in a bad way.

Later, I would receive news of a man who'd traveled with the Via-crucis, a Salvadoran guy poor as dirt, who didn't pay the cartel to cross. Police found his body on the dawn patrol, bobbing in some weeds on the Mexican side of the river. The dark ring around his neck indicated that he'd been strangled.

The total cost of the trip seemed doable, only about $300 per person. The Robertos got the money from family in the US. Axel asked me.

We met in Avenida Benjamin Franklin's grassy traffic island, with the city's commuters humming along either side of us on the warm asphalt. The sky was gray, and everything smelled like approaching rain and petroleum. I pressed the wad of bills into Axel's hand, and he stuffed them into his underwear. We hugged.

"We're gonna cross during the Mayweather-Pacquiao fight," he said.

"The boxing match?"

"Yeah man. Hopefully immigration will be distracted and we can run right through. Listen, could you do me a favor?"

"Of course, dude, anything."

"Could you text me updates? From the fight, I mean."

I laughed. "Really? Don't you think you'll be doing something a little more important?"

"Nah bro, it ain't about the fight. It's just to see if my phone will still work inside the States. If I get your texts, I'll know everything's all good. And if immigration catches me, the messages won't be about crossing the border. Less evidence." He paused. "Plus, it'd just be nice to know someone out there is thinking of me." He put his hand to his mouth and looked at the passing traffic. The cars' fumes were translucent, dancing clouds, the vapor of a substance that sat undisturbed for millions of years and then burned in an instant. "I'm just kinda scared, you feel me?"

I had a sudden urge to say, "I love you."

Instead I said, "I'll text you."

He turned and loped back through traffic to the entrance of Metro Patriotismo, where the Hondurans were waiting for him. Such a curious name for a metro station, I thought. Was it evoking Mexican patriotism specifically or just patriotism in general? But how could patriotism be general? I raised a hand in their direction, and they lifted theirs back in unison, a line of men without a country. Axel stood out among them, his arms gesticulating wildly about something. I tried to hold the moment in my mind, to remember it exactly as it was happening then. It was as if the world had placed a mystery in front of me and stolen it away again before I could grasp what any of it had meant. Then a semitruck dragged itself between us, spewing a charcoal billow that ate at the eyes and choked the throat, and by the time it had passed they were all gone, slipped into the belly of the city, headed north, always north.

CHAPTER 9

THE FIGHT OF THE CENTURY

THE PLAN WAS this: Floyd Mayweather was gonna fight Manny Pacquiao. They was calling it the Fight of the Century. And you know how much Mexicans fucking love boxing, right, and lots of border patrol guys consider themselves to be Mexican, so I was hoping they might get distracted tryna watch the fight. Just be like, "Forget these immigrants for a night," and turn the TV on at the station. Or at least try to listen to it on the radio when they're out on patrol or something. So I decided that as soon as Mayweather stepped in that ring, we would cross the river. That was my idea.

When we pulled up to Nuevo Laredo, it was pitch black. Don't even know what time it was. Just black. Roberto Stanley had already been there when he crossed several years ago, so he took us to a shelter he knew about. The streets was spooky, man. Prostitutes and crackheads and criminals everywhere. We couldn't tell if it was lumps of trash or people on the ground. We hustled to the shelter, and lemme tell you we was starving. But before they gave us breakfast, we had to sit through a speech for like one hour. Talking bout how if we cross the border, we're gonna get murdered. Before lunch, another speech. Before dinner, guess what, another speech. They try to brainwash you. They literally take pictures of who's been killed, who's been smashed, who's been shot, and they put them all right in front of your face while you eat, to try to get you to say, "Holy shit, what have I got myself into?" and call your embassy and ask for a ride back home.

Not me. I said to the Robertos, "Man, I did not come all the way here just to U-turn my ass back to Guatemala. Forget this shelter and forget these embassies. We out."

So then we didn't have nowhere to stay. But then Roberto Stanley said he could take care of it, and he walked into this broke ass motel. I don't know what he did, but when he came back he had convinced the owner to let us crash there for a discount. So we finally had a space to come up with the plan. I took Roberto Stanley to a cybercafé, and I did my thing and got a computer up and running. We started looking at the border, tryna jog his brain into action and remember where he crossed five years ago. But Roberto Stanley was real confused, and he couldn't figure out where he'd crossed previously. Finally, we found this train station in Texas on the map and he said, "Man, that's it. That's the train I rode to Houston." So we decided we was gonna run to the train station, then hide in one of the cars and ride it all the way through Texas. Imagine that. We couldn't ride the train in Mexico, but we could in the States. Like we was on some hobo bullshit.

We went to the store and bought supplies—cans of tuna fish, water, and clean clothes so we coulda blended in when we got to Laredo. I just got a basic shirt and jeans, nothing fancy. But Junior bought a soccer jersey even though I told him he was gonna attract attention, cause nobody in the States gives a shit about soccer. And cause Roberto Stanley couldn't swim, we hooked him up with an inner tube.

There was just one more thing we had to figure out: how to pay the falcons. Falcons are different than coyotes. They're the cartel guys who guard the border for Los Zetas. You gotta pay them to cross. You hire coyotes to take you across the border, to be a guide. And the cartels hire falcons to be the gatekeepers, to make sure you and the coyotes pay their taxes, so to speak. We wasn't gonna use a coyote, cause we didn't have enough money. But we still had to pay the falcon regardless. You see the difference? And if you don't pay, the falcons will kill you straight up, no questions asked. One second you're just walking, and the next second it's like they drop outta the sky and destroy you. That's why they call them falcons. So you gotta pay.

So I went to see Tico. Tico is a coyote, and everybody knows him cause he's always in the park. Like if you take a bus right now to Nuevo Laredo, you'll spot Tico there chilling. So I found Tico and I told him, "Listen man, I want to take the chance to cross, but I don't know how to pay the falcons."

And he just waved me away, like, "You're tryna do that yourself? You're stupid, man. If you go alone you'll get caught. There's a lotta drones, there's a lotta immigration. You gotta hire me to get you through."

"I'm broke, brother. All I got is a few bucks. But tell me how to pay the falcons and I'll give you a cut."

Then we was in business. "Let me make a phone call," he said, and rang Los Zetas up directly. "We have a bug on the run, three bugs"— that's what they call us migrants. Bichos, bugs.

Then he asked, "When you wanna do it? Evening or daytime?"

"Of course nighttime, buddy. In the dark."

"Alright, here's what you gotta do: Before you even approach the falcon, you call him up on your cell phone and say the password: India. Tell him that Tico sends you and you want to speak with la india. That's the code that proves you already paid for the take off. Cross the river, and the falcon will be waiting for you on the other side. Then you step up and face him like a man, and you repeat again that you know Tico and you want to speak with la india. Then he'll let you pass."

I gave Tico his cut and he gave me one last instruction. He took out a map and marked the territory where we was allowed to run through. We'd have one hour to cross. And if we got lost, or took too long, he said they was gonna kill us.

Levi 10:51 PM Hey dude, just texting like you asked
Levi 10:51 PM Might help me stay sane tonight at least
Levi 10:52 PM Mayweather just walked into in the ring
Levi 10:52 PM Godspeed bro

To get to the river we had to walk down this big ass hill, but first we got undressed and packed our clothes and food and phones in plastic bags so they wouldn't get wet. It's a long way to the water, just woods and loneliness. You gotta watch out cause you're not wearing any shoes, you're naked, and if you fall, your ass is gone. But the creepiest part was when we got to the bottom, the falcon didn't answer his phone. We didn't know if there was anybody waiting to meet us no more. Maybe Tico just ripped us off. So we climbed to the top of some trees, and we stayed there watching for a few minutes, just looking at the other side. But we couldn't see nothing. And I was praying that no other migrants would walk by, cause like, imagine seeing three butt-naked guys just hanging out on some tree branches together, right? Finally the only thing we saw—and we did see it, all three of us—was someone walking just inside the tree line. Time was running out, so we said, "Okay, that must be the falcon, so let's go to where we saw him walking. That must be the same section we're allowed in." And we jumped in the river.

Levi 10:58 PM first round
Levi 10:58 PM Mayweather's looking good
Levi 10:58 PM But Pacquiao is a little slow
Levi 10:59 PM they're just kinda dancing around each other

Since Roberto Stanley couldn't swim, I told him to put the inner tube around his waist and I would pull him. That way he could still walk and maintain balance. But instead he freaked out and sat down on the tube with his butt in the middle. Like if he was in a pool, not the fucking Rio Grande.

He was saying, "Axel, it's more steady, it's more steady." But it wasn't more steady. It was stupid as hell. And it was all up on me to pull his rickety ass. But at least we could put the bags in his lap. So I gave up and swung my arm around the inner tube and kicked off into the water. And the whole time Roberto Stanley was crying, like, "Axel, please don't let me die, man. Whatever you do don't kill me, man."

"Dude, I got you. Nobody's gonna let you die. Now please shut up or we're gonna get busted."

I realized Junior was gonna need some help too. On dry land he said he could swim, but now I was doubting it. Even when the water was shallow and we could walk, he was holding onto Roberto Stanley's hand so tight you woulda thought it was prom night. So I was pulling them both, making sure we stayed connected. At first, I used a lotta strength fighting the current. But then I realized—it's water. Water is gonna be my friend. Water helps you if you are familiar with water. All I needed to do was push them and follow the current. And for a while it worked. We made it halfway across.

But then the river dropped out. One second the water was at my hip and the next second I went under. My hand was just barely holding onto the tube, but my feets couldn't reach the bottom. I couldn't breathe. And that's when Roberto Stanley really started yelling. He saw us go under and he just started howling like a dog. And I kept tryna come up for air, but his ass was blocking the surface. I think I almost died. I promise you I almost suffocated underneath that man's ass. And then the current took us far away. By the time I got my head above water again we was flying down the river and Junior was nowhere to be found.

Eventually my feets touched the ground again, and I was like, okay, I gotta brake, I gotta brake. And I started pushing the inner tube to the rocks until finally I could grab one near the shore. But Junior was still back downstream. He saw us from far away and headed straight for the rock. But now he's flailing around, can't stop himself, and crashes into my back. And of course I lose grip again. Now I got two motherfuckers that I gotta keep alive, and both of them keep almost drowning me. So I wait until we hit another patch of rocks, and I wedged my leg in between them to stop us. It was painful to the max but if I didn't do it we'd be goners. And then I was like, "Stand up, fools, stand up quickly. It's shallow. You can walk."

I didn't have time to think about how it felt to step back in the States. The current had washed us far away from the starting point. Roberto Stanley didn't know which direction the train station was anymore. Fortunately, it was an extremely clear night. I don't know why but on the other side of the river it seemed brighter, and that ain't some kinda cheesy ass metaphor, that's just what it was. In the end we probably only spent like ten minutes in the water, but ten minutes is too much time in a boxing match. I was praying that nobody got KO-ed cause then border patrol woulda had to get back to work. We started getting dressed and everything was soaking wet—jeans, shoes, t-shirts, food, everything. I don't know if you know this but the Rio Grande is filled with shit, like literal doo-doo, so once stuff gets wet you can't really save it. We basically just left everything there except our phones and the clothes we put on. Then we started walking back upstream. Totally lost. But then the most amazing thing happened. We ran into this gravel road and suddenly Roberto Stanley was like, "Hey, wait, I recognize this. Follow me, follow me. I'm back on track." Everything came back to his mind. The gravel was white and glowed in the moonlight, so we stayed in the bushes for cover, hopping from bush to bush. And then, outta the blue, like ten other migrant dudes was in the bushes too. That's how the border is. Sometimes something ain't there and then it is. The migrants wasn't there and then they was. There was no time to be scared.

They were like, "Are you guys going up?"

"Hells yeah boy. Let's move." So they joined us.

Soon enough, we saw lights. A whole neighborhood, just sitting there all normal and quiet in the night, with rows of streetlights and porch lights and lights coming from the windows. We was so close. But the messed-up part was that there was a whole buncha open land between where we was and the neighborhood. It was just bare, no place to hide, and we had to run out in the open. And that's how the drone got us.

Levi 11:19 PM round five now

Levi 11:19 PM I'm freaking out not being able to talk to you

Levi 11:21 PM Mayweather's winning

Levi 11:21 PM but it's kinda lame to root for the american

Levi 11:21 PM given the circumstances

At first I wasn't sure if it was real or if I had imagined it. Just a small, dark ghost overhead, almost the same color as the sky, then it

was gone. Everything was silent for a minute and then all of a sudden two Tahoes came roaring outta the middle of the nowhere, just spitting up dust and flashing us out with their headlights. And then these guys hopped out and started chasing us on foot.

"It's immigration. Get the hell outta here."

Me and the Robertos peaced out from the other immigrant dudes. My lungs was burning, my adrenaline was pumping up, and my feets was hitting the earth. With each step my shoes squeaked from being soaked in the river, and I wondered even if we got away, maybe they coulda just followed the wet footprints straight to us. We found this building under construction. Some sort of gas station with busted chain link fences around it. We ran inside, found a dark corner, and hid behind the walls. I didn't hear nobody come in after us, so eventually I looked out a window, and I peeped the 5-0 in the distance. Everybody else from the other group was getting caught. And behind them was the neighborhood, still and quiet, with people just sitting there in the night watching their TVs like nothing was happening at all. We was so close. Probably just blocks from downtown, where there's freedom and safety and anonymousness. You can just be a regular guy there walking the streets and nobody's gonna mess with you. Then an immigration truck drove by and pulled up behind the gas station. We hadn't fooled them. We had to get outta there.

We busted our asses towards this small circle of trees near the neighborhood. The truck was right on top of us, flashing us out, like, boom, boom, boom with the headlights, revving the engine. But the lucky thing was that it was just this one guy cause the rest of them was busy arresting everyone else. This officer was left all alone, and he was scared to go into the woods cause he didn't know how many of us was in there. Like, it wasn't really more than just a few trees, but there was thick brush. Still, we knew at any minute we coulda got surrounded again. But then something crazy happened. All of a sudden, this dude appears from behind a tree next to us, just another random immigrant dude caught up in the raid. He just popped right from behind a tree like, "Boo bitch."

Man I almost doo-dooed my pants. I was like, "Who the fuck is you?"

"You boys brought the heat on me," he said. He looked real ghetto. Gold teeth and wife beater type dude. "Keep it quiet and we might get outta this."

So we kept it hush-hush for real, tryna wait it out. But the border patrol guy wasn't gonna leave. It was a standoff. And with each minute that passed Roberto Stanley was freaking out more and more. He dropped his self to the ground and started throwing leaves and dirt on his back for camouflage. And then of course Junior copied him.

"What are you idiots doing?" I whispered.

"Hiding from the drones," said Roberto Stanley. "I heard they can see the reflections from your eyes. Close your eyes, Junior."

The ghetto guy was getting impatient too. He was walking around all macho—I swear to god he was punching trees—talking about, "I should just step out and fuck this immigration motherfucker up." And then all of sudden, he made a break for it. He charges right at immigration and immediately gets tackled.

"Stop resisting or I'll blast your ass," yelled immigration. "Who was you with, how many were with you in there?"

That gave me an idea. I told the Robertos, "Look, there's only one way out. They don't know how many of us are in here, so I'm gonna take the heat. I'm the fastest runner. I'll go out, make him chase me, and run all the way back to Mexico. Then you two go the other way, hit the train, and when you get to Houston, don't forget about me."

"Okay, we won't." That's what they said. That they wouldn't forget.

Levi 11:31 PM Round eight just ended

Levi 11:31 PM Not looking good for pacman he's fading

I stepped out the woods real slow, so the officer would spot me. Sure enough he flashes his stupid flashlight and shouts in Spanish, "Pinche cabrón, párate allí."

So I was like, "Nah, not today, buddy," and started running. But I hadn't realized how tired I was. My legs was like jelly, I couldn't run like I thought I could, and I knew I was gonna get tackled. So I started speaking to him in English like, "Yo yo yo, man, hold up, calm down."

And he's like, "Get on the ground. I swear to god I'll put a bullet in your head, is that what you want me to do? I'll end your whole life."

That's exactly how he spoke to me. Like, using that police technique of yelling to make you feel like you ain't nothing. Like they're powerful and you're just an immigrant. But of course I understood that was just a technique, and I played him like a freaking fool. I laid down on the ground and let myself get busted. He jumped on top of me smiling and shit and jammed his knee into my spine. And I was like, "Yo man. I'm calm. You got me. Look, I speak English just like you. But you're a blessed man. You were born in the country—I'm just looking for a dream."

"Where the hell did you get that English from?" he said. "Get your ass up and talk to me for a second." So he dragged me to the front of the SUV where the ghetto guy was already handcuffed. He twisted some zip ties around my wrists, and he asks us in Spanish, "How many of you were in the woods?"

The other guy was like, "Four. It was the four of us."

What a snitch. I switched to English and said, "No no no, don't believe that guy. He's tryna trick you into staying here all night. It was just the two of us."

The officer was skeptical so he phoned it in to central command, right? Asking for back up. But nobody was coming. They was all busy with the other immigrants. So he pulled me to my feets and was like, "Are you gonna behave? Behave. I'm not gonna harm you. We're just gonna take you back to the station and then you're going back home."

"Okay man, cool. Not a problem."

"Tell me something though. Where have you been in the States? Your accent is crazy." I said yes and thank you and that I'd been in the States since I was one. I was being polite, killing him with kindness. He grabbed our zip ties and started dragging us to the side of the SUV to throw us in that jail cell they got installed in the back. But that got the ghetto guy yelling again about how he wasn't going back to prison.

So I whispered to him, "Listen bro, if you wanna get outta this, we're gonna have to run."

Well, that was all the permission he needed. Dude started acting like a straight fool. He was spitting and tryna headbutt the officer, like, "Cabrón, I swear to god I hope I don't see you in Mexico, cause Imma fucking kill you."

That got the border patrol guy pissed, which is exactly what I was hoping for, cause by then he'd forgotten all about the Robertos. I stayed calm and didn't move. And after the officer got the ghetto guy back under control, he was like, "Axel, man, thank you for being calm. Now I need you to do me a favor. I'm gonna take the zip ties off you so you can empty your pockets, but please don't be doing stupid shit like this guy, okay?"

And I just did what I was told, stayed real charming with it. I didn't have nothing in my pockets anyway, just my cell phone—which was probably broke now from crossing the river—and my amparo. But the officer was distracted by the ghetto dude. As soon as he saw my zip ties being took off, he went crazy again, slamming his head into the van window like a straight G. The immigration guy was yelling, "Sit your ass down." But the ghetto dude ain't listening, there's blood running down his face, and the po-po turns his back on me to restrain him. That was my opening. I started yelling, "Vamos a la verga, huh? Vamos a la verga, let's get the fuck outta here."

And the ghetto guy took off with the zip ties still on. The officer turned around and looked into my eyes, like he was betrayed, right, and then chases after the ghetto dude. And I only had, like, one particle of a second to make a decision—it was stay and get locked up forever, or bounce. So I bounced. I was running like a mofo back to Mexico. And the po-po sees what I'm doing and he changes directions and starts coming after me instead. But I'm already busted loose, jumping fences, weaving through long grass, hopping over rocks, whatever, man, just running, running, adrenaline flowing, pumping, rushed out, and how I outran him I'll never know, cause I was just inches ahead, booking it through the clearing, into the woods, and then he was gone, vanished, I *got away. Problem was, though, I was too busy running to think who else mighta been in the woods with me.*

Levi 11:43 PM last round
Levi 11:43 PM It's basically over mayweather's got it in the bag
Levi 11:44 PM hey when you see these please respond man
Levi 11:44 PM just want to know you're safe

I knew I was getting close to the river cause I could smell the water, right? Then I saw a shadow coming out the woods. I thought it must be immigration. That I was caught. I started to put my hands up in surrender but then the shadow went up on me, and I felt this boom to my skull. Then the front of my head got soaking wet. Something was dripping in my eyes. I didn't know then but it was my own blood. And then another boom.

Levi 11:45 PM this is brutal man pacquiao's against the ropes

It was like my head was getting swiped by freaking Freddy Krueger claws. I knew this wasn't no immigration, cause la migra ain't got baseball bats covered in fucking nails, dude, and all I'm thinking is that my only way outta here alive is the river. Then he hit me again, boom, and again, boom. Three, four times. Boom, boom. So hard I couldn't even make a sound.

Levi 11:45 PM he needs a miracle to save him now

Somehow I reached up and grabbed the bat and shoved it away and stood up again. He came after me swinging, and I covered my face with my arm. All I heard was a crack on my wrist, the one that was opposite from the one immigration smashed, and then my hand was just loose, flopping around like meat. All I could do was keep running until I was at the edge of the river. There was a five-foot drop into the current, and I let myself fall over the ledge and the water slipped over my head and everything was black.

Levi 11:46 PM that's the final bell it's over

I held my breath and tried to stay under for as long as I could, and when I came up, he wasn't behind me anymore. Whoever he was, he just stood at the ledge, scanning the water, but he couldn't see me. Then like two or three other guys with AK-47s came running outta the woods towards the first guy, shouting—and I will never forget this—"No lo mataste, pendejo? Why didn't you kill him, moron?" But by then it was too late, and even if they did see me, I was too far gone.

Levi 11:51 PM mayweather won by unanimous decision
Levi 11:51 PM hope you got to watch the end live with the robertos
Levi 12:32 AM hey bro im sure you're fine but message me when you can
Levi 12:35 AM just a little worried
Levi 12:47 AM going to bed soon
Levi 12:53 AM don't know if i'll get much sleep tho
Levi 6:19 AM axel?

I let the water take me. I just let it pull my body and, after I knew I had escaped those Zeta fuckers, I just lay on my back and looked at the stars and thought I could try to float all the way to the Gulf of Mexico or some shit. Ride the current to Jamaica. I started humming "Oh Bumbo Klaat" by Peter Tosh real soft to calm myself down. It was always my favorite at the block parties in Queens, and it helped me not think about how I had almost died and that maybe I was still gonna die. I don't know, maybe I was hallucinating. I was outta my mind. But then the water started to smell like doo-doo and chemicals, and I remembered what I was floating in. I started to worry that shit was gonna give me pink eye or crotch rot or something, so I drifted over to the side and tried to get out. But my left hand, that one that had got beat, it wasn't working. Like it was limp and I couldn't feel nothing.

When I finally got outta the river, I started to run. What else was I gonna do? There wasn't nothing around but flat, flat land. I think it was farms, but there wasn't much crops. I started busting it down this dusty ass road until the sun came up. There was almost no people around, and if a car came in the distance I'd jump in a ditch and lay there until it passed. Maybe drink some ditch water. Then I'd keep running. There wasn't any immigration. It was just flatness, emptiness, and it scared me cause it almost felt like I coulda been stuck there forever, just running forever.

I don't know when I passed out, but I woke up to a boot kicking me in the stomach. It was immigration. The dude kicked me again and rolled me over. I knew it was evening or morning cause the dirt kinda felt cool against my skin. I looked in the guy's eyes and he said, "Rise and shine. Time to go back home."

And I said, "I am home," and I don't remember if he was surprised that I spoke English, but he lifted me up by the arm and laid me down in the back of his SUV. He was older and had a mustache. I asked how did he find me, and he said it was a drone, that I probably woulda died all the way out there in the desert, but luckily the drone spotted my passed-out body, and so he got sent to pick me up. He drove me to a hospital I don't remember the name of, and they handcuffed me to the bed and stuck an IV in my arm. Then I went unconscious for a little while. When I woke up I was so mad that I had fell asleep, cause I just wanted to take it in, man. I was back in the States and I just wanted to sit there and feel it. The air conditioning and the way people talked and the architecture. Then the doctor came in the room, and I tried to tell him I got attacked by Los Zetas and that my left hand was all beat the hell up, but he told me I was just dehydrated and gave me two Tylenols and left.

At some point the immigration guy came back in the room and he looked all sorry. I told him about my kids and he looked down at the ground and said he felt bad cause he was a Christian, and then he asked if there was any American woman that I coulda called up on the spot and get married to right there in the hospital, so he didn't have to deport me. He really said that, I promise you. And I said no, people like me don't got no one like that, and then he said he was gonna have to call his supervisor in for the deportation proceedings. So that everything coulda been done 100 percent legal. I signed a buncha papers even though my eyes was having a hard time focusing on the words, and the supervisor told me I was gonna be banned from the States for five years. She said that if I got caught crossing again in the next five years it woulda been a felony and I'd go to federal prison.

Then I don't remember much else until they put me on the plane in handcuffs. It was like my whole life was starting over, like I was repeating the same shit over and over again, but also like something had changed. Like somehow in that moment the States wasn't my home no more. Like for the first time I didn't have a home. I don't know how to explain it.

PART II
THE MECHANIC

CHAPTER 10

TOO MUCH BLOOD

WE DIDN'T KNOW it at the time, but the 2015 Viacrucis Migrante changed migrant caravans forever. No priest—including and especially Father Solalinde—has ever led a real Viacrucis since. Whether because of direct threats from the government, or because priests simply sensed they were on thin ice, or some combination of the two, I do not know. But what I do know is that, after our Viacrucis Migrante, the Mexican state explicitly turned against migrant caravans. Without local priests to negotiate safe passage, there was no longer any tolerance for open demonstrations of defiance. The beating that the 2015 Viacrucis experienced outside of Ixtepec—the first of its kind, and incredibly shocking at the time—was the beginning of a new era of anti-caravan violence under the Program.

In response, migrant caravans transformed from relatively demure and inconsequential marches of a few hundred people into multitudinous, messy, and bloody affairs. Migrants began amassing by the thousands in countries like Honduras and Guatemala, rather than in Mexico itself, and then marching across Mexico's southern border, which was now guarded by hundreds of immigration agents and federal police armed for combat. It's unclear exactly how these new caravans were originally organized. My best guess is that migrants who had participated in previous caravans in Mexico decided to cut out the priests and take the reins themselves. Regardless, such large crowds also drew media coverage like never before. Suddenly, migrant caravans were catapulted from relative obscurity—at least in the global media—to being framed as an enemy of the modern nation-state intent on wrecking national sovereignty and international security.

In September 2015, only months after the Viacrucis Migrante concluded in Mexico City, a migrant caravan poured out of Syria toward western Europe, making headlines around the world. I don't know if the Syrian refugees were at all inspired by the previous caravans in Mexico, but Europe's reaction to them was largely the same as the United States'—wealthy European countries began paying Turkey to trap as many migrants as possible. The Southern Border Program became the blueprint for a new kind of international border security, one that externalized the borders of wealthy countries in order to prevent poor migrants from asking for asylum, as is their legal right under the 1951 Refugee Convention. And the 2015 Viacrucis Migrante became the counter-blueprint, the means of calling attention to the externalized borders that the West was erecting around the world.

General consensus was that Mexico was now under strict orders from the US to contain these migrant caravans or else run the risk of losing valuable trade agreements. Ironically, Mexico's national economic fate now lay not in the hands of its citizens but in those of undocumented migrants. In that deceptively small but incredibly significant way, the 2015 Viacrucis Migrante had a domino effect that would shape the course of Mexican history for a generation. From the public universities that educated the country's best minds, to the national hospitals that cared for the poor and infirm, the resources needed to keep it all running suddenly depended on how efficiently Mexican immigration could entrap, torment, and discard penniless refugees at the border. Then, in 2016, a new president would be elected in the US, bolstered by a wave of anti-immigrant sentiment. This president would wield a newfound hysteria around caravans to change the course of American history as well.

But, like I said, back then we didn't know any of that.

AXEL'S PHONE WAS no longer receiving texts. I checked to see if he had posted any updates on Ruffrider Quest, but there was nothing. I'd never experienced this kind of loss before, of being cut off from a person whose existence in the world was already so tenuous. It was like missing a ghost. If I fell out of touch with just about anyone else—if I lost their number or forgot their email—I'd almost certainly be able to find them eventually. But if I was ever going to speak to Axel again, he'd have to contact me first. If he was still alive.

I was spending most of my time at a makeshift migrant shelter in downtown Mexico City, which was run out of an abandoned office building to temporarily house Viacrucis members who wished to resettle in the capital rather than continue north. Ancient copy machines had been pushed into dusty corners, and blown fluorescent light bulbs dangled from the ceiling. To my surprise, the first time I visited, I ran into Ever. His brother Iván was taking the rest of the family to Monterrey, he said, but he'd decided to strike out on his own.

I asked who was in charge of the shelter.

"We all just call her la Abogada," said Ever. The Attorney. She was offering to help everyone apply for something called a "humanitarian visa," which apparently allowed migrants to reside legally in Mexico for one year. Later, I would learn that humanitarian visas—once an obscure and rarely-applied-for document in Mexico—were quickly becoming the fastest way for migrants to legalize themselves. In 2013, Mexico only granted 277 humanitarian visas total. In 2016, it granted 3,632, more than a thirteenfold increase, and it only went up from there. Their rapid expansion had to do with the Southern Border Program. In theory, humanitarian visas were reserved for foreigners who had been victims of extreme violence within Mexico. But with the advent of the Program, extreme violence was no longer unusual. Not only were migrants exponentially more likely to encounter such brutality, but it was also often inflicted by Mexican immigration and police officers. Essentially, Mexico had invented an immigration system in which many migrants could only legalize themselves through a process of physical suffering inflicted by state agents.

The Attorney believed that Ever, and all the other migrants on the Viacrucis, would qualify for humanitarian visas because of the beatings they received in Ixtepec. The next time I visited the shelter, Ever introduced us.

"Abogada," I said. "I'm Levi. I've heard so much about you."

While hanging out in the temporary shelter, I'd become privy to several rumors about the Attorney, mostly from Ever himself, and many of them contradictory. That she was Solalinde's right-hand woman. Or that she was even better connected than the priest, and in fact he was really working for her. Some said that she came from a secretive and insular family who had ruled Mexico City for centuries. Others that she was a new-money NAFTA heiress. She was alternatingly from Hermosillo, Cuernavaca, or Tlaxcala. She was a widow. She was a lesbian. Or maybe, in her youth, she'd been a model, but now she was a narco's wife. Others insisted that no one—no one—knew anything about her past at all.

The Attorney said Ever had told her about me as well; how I marched with the Viacrucis since the beginning and all that. She winked.

Despite the rumors, I knew immediately that the Attorney was part of Mexico City's insular elite. That much was obvious from her accent and handbag. When she spoke, she spoke as if she already knew you, almost as if she were trying to seduce you but without actually revealing anything about herself. Whether she was intentionally cultivating a bit of mystery or genuinely guarding something, I couldn't tell. She gave me her number and said to call if I ever needed anything. Then she excused herself and disappeared down one of the old office corridors. She never said her name.

Ever asked if he could use my phone. He hadn't spoken to his family since they left for Monterrey. I said that he should come back to my apartment instead. He could use my computer to video chat, and I could use the company. He ended up sleeping on my couch. A few days later, someone else from the shelter asked if he could call his family from my place as well. He also ended up crashing on the couch. That summer, while I waited day and night for any news from Axel, my little apartment quietly became a small migrant shelter of its own, with none of my neighbors any the wiser.

IN THE EVENINGS, I continued my long walks while waiting for news from Axel. I was passing through the Tacubaya neighborhood when it began to rain, the acidic rain of Mexico City that slips underneath your clothing and eats at your skin. I ducked into a metro station and looked for a train. But the metro—which was so much better organized than anything in the US—seemed to have transformed into a maze, a labyrinth I couldn't quite figure out how to navigate, and, bewildered, I hopped on the first train I found. It was just before midnight, and the car was mostly empty, save for a few prim couples minding their own business at one end and a huddled lump of a man at the other. The guy had been beaten to a pulp. His lip was split and a trail of bloody spittle hung from his chin. When our eyes met, he stood unsteadily and stumbled toward me.

"Help," he said, reaching out a hand. "They beat me up."

"Who beat you up?"

"The police. Outside. For being drunk."

It was clear that the man was inebriated, but he was also in a bad way. Every few seconds he'd hunch over, clutch his stomach, and moan. He could be bleeding internally, I thought. I pulled the man off the train just as a metro policeman was strolling by. He asked if the guy was giving me trouble. No, I responded. Actually, he needed medical attention, and could the officer please call an ambulance.

"Oh, there's nothing I can do about that," said the policeman, and sauntered away.

"Forget it," mumbled the man. "These bastards will never help me."

Then another cop approached and demanded that we leave the station immediately. "It's past midnight," he said. "We're closing."

"But you don't understand," I said, as he escorted us to an exit, "this man is in real pain. He says he's been beaten. We need to get him to a hospital."

"Not my problem," said the policeman, and slid the gate of the exit closed.

"He could die," I shouted.

"Have a good night," the policeman said.

Without warning, the thought entered my mind that, if I had a knife, I could reach through the bars of the gate and stab the cop in the chest. But I didn't have a knife. I looked up and was puzzled to see that we were standing outside Metro Tacubaya, the same station I'd entered. I couldn't understand how we'd ended up back there. A circle of taxis sat idling next to the metro entrance, watching us coolly. I offered to pay one of the drivers double to rush the beaten man to the closest emergency room, but he shook his head. "Too much blood," was all he said. All of the other drivers nodded silently in agreement.

"Just leave me be," said the man, limping across the street. "I'll be okay." It was only then that I realized he had an accent. His words were too slurred to be able to place where he was from, but he didn't sound Mexican.

"Wait," I called. "Where are you going?"

He waved me away, clambered over a rusty traffic barrier, and disappeared down a concrete embankment that ended in shadow. I called out for him again, but there was no answer. I walked home. Out of habit, I looked over my shoulder to check if I was being followed. But I was alone, as far as I could tell. If anyone really was shadowing me after the Viacrucis, they seemed to have lost interest. And yet, when I got to my neighborhood I began to run, to run as fast as I possibly could, and I didn't care that I felt my spider bite opening up again, or the blood soaking through my sock.

AFTER I LOCKED the door to my apartment, I saw that I had a friend request from an account called Axl Brooklyn HQ. I got a call seconds after I accepted.

"Brother, it's me."

"Oh my god, bro, you're alive."

"What bitch, you thought you could get rid of this old thundercat?"

"Dude, I'm so happy to hear your voice. I think I'm gonna cry."

"No time for that, bro. I'm back in Guatemala City. I got re-deported by those border patrol motherfuckers." He quickly ran through the whole story—the crossing, being cornered by immigration, and sacrificing himself so that the Robertos could make it across. Immigration had given him back his clothes, but they kept his phone, amparo, and pesos. That's why it'd taken him so long to call. He was living on a construction site in Guatemala City, inside the half-built skeleton of a high rise. Axel was worried that if he slept in the city center with the other recent deportees, the MS-13 gang member from the market would have recognized him and killed him for running away. The building's overseer was allowing him to hide out in the high rise in exchange for wiring the place with internet.

"Well, what's the plan?" I asked. "How long are you trying to stay?"

"Stay? I'm tryna get outta here as soon as possible, baby boy." He said that he was going to run on the same path through the jungle that he charted just weeks before with the Hondurans. In fact, he'd talked with the Robertos right before he called me. They made it to Houston.

"Because of you," I said.

"Because of me."

"Well, they can help you out, right? They owe you one. Hell, they owe you a million."

There was a hard silence on the other end of the line. "I asked," he said eventually, "but they said their expenses was a little bit tight at the moment."

"Bastards," I muttered, because I knew that's what he wanted to say.

"Roberto Junior did ask me for a favor though." Junior said that he couldn't send Axel any money, but his little brother, Lalo, was on his way north. He asked if Axel would mind linking up with him in Guatemala City, so that they could travel together and split expenses, which would hopefully be cheaper for the both of them. "What you think?" asked Axel.

"It could be nice to have a travel companion, right?"

"Yeah, I dunno, maybe. But I still ain't got money to move."

I had one hundred and thirteen dollars in my bank account. I knew because I'd just checked that morning, worried about how I was going to make it to the end of the month before my next grant deposit hit. I'd been feeding Ever and the other migrants whenever they crashed at my place, which wasn't cheap.

"Don't worry," I said, "I'll send you a hundred bucks now. That should at least get you back into Mexico. Just find someone who can withdraw it for you." Then I walked to Banco Azteca without a care in the world, because it didn't matter if I was broke, or if I had to eat exclusively beans for the next couple weeks, or even if I had to skip a meal every now and again. Axel was alive. Axel was alive and he was on his way back to Mexico City. Back to me.

CHAPTER 11

GODFORSAKEN CHAHUITES

"LEVI, CAN YOU hear m—" Axel's voice was cutting in and out. Each evening he'd call to give a quick update and then dive back into the jungle again with Lalo. They were in Tapachula, then Escuintla, Tonalá, Arriaga. The last time Axel called, he said that they were near Los Corazones, and that with any luck they'd be back at Hermanos en el Camino within a day.

"Brother, I busted—freaking knee. I was run—" The call cut out. "—freaking dark, and I tripped—" Silence. "—knee is all swollen—" More silence. "—can't run—fucking stuck, man, we're stuck—"

"Wait, I didn't get that. Where are you?" I closed my eyes and prayed he wasn't about to say what I thought he was about to say.

"—huites, man. Can you hear me? I'm stuck in fucking Chahuites—"

I cursed in my living room. "You've got to be kidding me."

"—dead ass—stranded right in the middle of the no—don't want Irineo to see—" There was more radio silence, garbled electronic noises pinging off satellites, then, "—come? Like can you come get me—fucked, bro, honestly—ain't moving, I'm—need you now—"

When the call eventually cut out, I collapsed on my couch and stared at the ceiling. From somewhere in the far-off distance came

131

the lone whistle of a camotero still out in the dark. I knew then that I had to decide, forever, between two things. It was either stay in Mexico City and throw Axel to the wolves, or go back to Chahuites—the one place in Mexico I'd sworn to never set foot in again—to help a man I'd met just a month ago. A man, I kept repeating to myself, I still barely knew. But a man who, from the moment I met him in godforsaken Chahuites, felt an awful lot like fate. "Alright then," I said to myself, "I'll go to hell."

WHEN I STEPPED off the bus, Axel was waiting astraddle a rumbling motorcycle. Behind him sat a young man, who I presumed to be his new travel companion, Lalo. Beside them on another motorcycle, holding an open can of Tecate, was a guy I'd never seen before.

"Hop on, bro," yelled Axel, motioning toward the man, who revved his engine and tossed the beer over his shoulder.

I barely had time to clamber on the back of the stranger's motorcycle before he took off, racing down the potholed dirt road after Axel. Chahuites was somehow even hotter than before. The wind that billowed around our clothes was thick and angry and almost indistinguishable from the heat of the engine humming between our legs. I felt something sizzle on my left calf, and I yelped and looked down to see that the man I was clinging to had a three-foot-long machete wedged into his belt. With each bump and jolt the blade sunk into my skin. The edge wasn't sharp enough to draw blood, but the metal was so hot it burned little red crescents into my leg.

We wove between rows of dilapidated houses and heaps of trash until we arrived at what appeared to be an abandoned shack on the outskirts of town. Beneath a coconut tree were a couple of old cars propped up on loose cinderblocks. We slowed to a stop and I dismounted. Without a word, my chauffer gave a thumbs up and sped off down the dirt road again.

Axel was grinning from ear to ear. "Bienvenido a la casa, my brother," he said, limping over to wrap me in a bear hug. It felt good to be back with him. He pointed to the teenager still straddling the other motorcycle. "Levi meet Lalo," he said in Spanish, playfully slapping the kid in the chest. "This big boy carried me on his back for hours after I busted my knee in the jungle. He saved my life."

Lalo smiled and massaged his sternum. His hands were hard and calloused. Axel told me that back in Honduras, Lalo had cut sugarcane since he was a child to help support his family. He was muscular, much taller than Axel, and his forearms were pockmarked with scars. You'd never know that he was still just a kid, I thought, except for his puppy dog grin.

"Dude, what's with the motorcycles?" I asked.

"Bro, if people saw a white dude walking around downtown, it'd cause a scene. And we don't want Irineo to find out you're here."

"And motorcycles are somehow more discreet?"

"Nah man, that guy you rode with, he's a smuggler. He uses the bikes to drive migrants down the back roads. Everybody around here knows him. So if anybody did see you, they probably woulda thought you was just one of his business transactions."

"How'd you get him to pick me up?"

Axel smirked. "He owed me a favor. I fixed his cell phone a couple weeks ago. Now c'mon, man, lemme show you the crib."

The crib was one room, with a tin roof propped several inches off the tops of the walls, which let the hot air out but the mosquitos in. The floor was exposed concrete, with puddles of what looked like congealed grease in the corners. A single bare mattress was pushed up against the far wall, and a threadbare blanket had been carefully stretched across its frame, like Axel had tried to tidy up before I arrived. The shack wasn't wired with electricity and had no windows, so it was dark inside even though it was midday. Instead, two extension cords snaked underneath the door from some unseen outside source. One was plugged into a dusty portable fan, which feebly provided the only ventilation in the room. The other was powering a 72-inch flat screen TV.

"Dude," I gaped, "is that an Xbox?"

Axel chuckled, clearly delighted at my shocked face. "A mechanic owns this place. It used to be his shop, but he doesn't use it much anymore. Too busy drinking these days, you know what I'm saying? So he turned it into his man cave. Our deal is that he lets us crash here, and I gotta help him fix cars on the days that he ain't drunk outta his mind."

"I feel like I'm in a dream," I said, plopping on the mattress as Lalo booted up *Grand Theft Auto*.

"Tell me about it," said Axel. "Oh shit be careful, bro. You gotta shake that blanket out. We got tons of scorpions in here."

THE NIGHT AXEL busted his knee, I called the Attorney to ask for help. Actually, I called Hermanos en el Camino first, but no one answered. So I called her next because I didn't know who else to turn to. It was only as the phone was ringing that I realized I still didn't know her name.

"Hello," I'd said. "Is this the Attorney?"

"Levi," she purred, "it's so nice to hear from you."

I quickly ran through everything I knew about Axel. That he'd been deported, that he was on his way back, that he'd busted his knee.

"Oh, yes, I remember Axel. Father Solalinde told me all about his . . . abilities. Where is he?"

"Chahuites."

"Oh heavens no," she'd exclaimed. "Where Irineo is? Well, we can't let that bastard get a hold of him, can we?"

The Attorney promised to pull some strings. When she rung me back a few days later, she said that she found someone willing to bring Axel and Lalo to Mexico City. His name was Don

Armando Vilchis, another activist she'd been introduced to by Father Solalinde, who called Don Armando an old friend. He agreed to not only transport Axel and Lalo to the capital but also to house them in a migrant shelter he ran in the area. The Attorney said that Don Armando would be heading down to Hermanos in the next few days to drop off some donations he'd recently collected at a fundraiser, and he agreed to scoop up Axel and Lalo, no problem. But then a few days came and went. Then weeks. Each time, Don Armando said that he was delayed by some unforeseen circumstance. By the time I arrived in Chahuites, it had been nearly a month since he first promised to come.

"I think the Attorney's annoyed with me," I told Axel. "Every time I call to ask about Don Armando she just says 'Patience, Levi, patience.'"

But it was impossible to be patient in the inferno of Chahuites. Mosquitos swirled around in thick clouds, and soon my limbs were covered in hundreds of itchy, red lumps. There was nothing to cook with in the shack, so we had to buy all of our food from tiendas or the few dingy watering holes in town, which was always risky with the threat of Irineo and immigration lurking around every corner. There was no fresh water, and we bathed using a bucket in the yard. The only bathroom was a crumbling brick outhouse, and the first time I used it, I'd already pulled my shorts around my ankles before I saw three fat, glistening scorpions crawling just inches from my feet.

Lalo spent most of the daylight hours playing *Grand Theft Auto* on the Xbox and texting a couple of local girls he'd inexplicably met while in hiding. Many of the young women in town had taken an interest in the tall, mysterious newcomer, and Lalo— bored to tears from being stuck inside with two "old guys," as he put it, who spoke in English all day—welcomed their curiosity. He kept three or four girlfriends and would disappear for hours with no warning, only to return with a mischievous smirk on his face. I mostly read—*The Art of Political Murder*, by Francisco

Goldman, and *Battles in the Desert*, by José Emilio Pacheco—and waited to hear back from the Attorney, who called infrequently and at strange hours, either very early or very late, as if the concept of sleep never crossed her mind.

Axel was busy hustling various computer gigs. Word of his services had spread throughout town, and he had a steady stream of work. In a place as remote as Chahuites, the nearest computer repair shop was hours away. When someone's phone or laptop broke, that was often the end of its lifespan. Any digital documents or photos died with the device. If you hadn't saved the number of a family member working on the other side of the border, you just might have lost touch with them indefinitely. But suddenly Axel showed up and started resurrecting electronics. I watched him gut three ancient computers and reassemble them into one living desktop. I saw him substitute toothpaste for thermal gel in a busted tablet, since that was all that was available. He did something with his shoelace I didn't understand, and a laptop's cooling fan spun back to life. Axel didn't just fix electronics, he marveled over them. To him, each mass-produced device was an individual work of art. Every mysterious malfunction, every symptomatic defect was a clue to be pursued, a sign that beckoned him toward an unknown that had revealed itself and could be tarried with. This was Axel's quiet genius, a truly astounding talent that no one else took the time to appreciate. Most were immediately put off by his general demeanor. Axel was a bizarre character who talked a little too loudly and much too crassly. When people looked at him, all they saw was a two-bit hustler angling for a scam. There was no doubt in my mind that this diagnosis was partly correct—Axel was hiding something, as I knew better than anyone—but only partly. Even on the Viacrucis, with supposedly open-minded activists and shelter staff, I was warned by more than one person not to trust Axel. When I asked why, no one could give me a straight answer. The responses boiled down to citations of an abstract "shifty nature," or his bad language, or his bald head, which he took to shaving—"shaved just like a gang member," someone remarked. The elephant in the room was that Axel was Afro-Latino, and when most people looked at him, that was all they noticed. But when I watched him gently reach his hands into the innards of a machine, I saw something else.

I was worried that word of Axel's small enterprise would get back to Irineo, but it was a risk he was willing to take to make a few pesos, and I couldn't blame him. Still, Axel didn't keep much of his income. Most went to the landlord, Jesús—a burly man, whose eyes always seemed slightly unfocused, even when he wasn't drunk, which was rare. He came around to play video games or collect his rent, and Axel would hand the money over diligently, almost earnestly, in a way that baffled me until one day an immigration truck rolled by, and Axel mentioned that Jesús had "reassured" him that as long as his time in the shack was profitable, there would be no need to inform anyone about his legal status.

The Southern Border Program had changed Chahuites since the last time I'd been there. Before the Viacrucis, migrants arrived in droves specifically because Chahuites was off the beaten path and away from the main immigration checkpoints. But la migra wised up, and now they frequently patrolled the town, stopping people on street corners and interrogating them. Talk of migrants being attacked and kidnapped in the jungle was even more prevalent than before, as were rumors about black market organ trafficking, though I was never able to confirm them. In response, Chahuites was quickly becoming a hotbed for small-time polleros, or human smugglers. Before the Program, a migrant could hire a smuggler to take them from one end of Mexico to the other. But now that there were so many checkpoints—and now that the gangs and cartels increasingly had a monopoly on this large-scale smuggling economy—a new kind of entrepreneurial smuggler emerged in southern Mexico. They specialized in ferrying migrants from one town to the next, sometimes no more than a few kilometers away. These new petty smugglers were usually men who had lived in poor towns like Chahuites their whole lives and knew the backroads that immigration didn't frequent, just like the man who drove me to the shack on his motorcycle. He'd actually offered to take Axel and Lalo to Hermanos, which was only a two-hour drive down the road, but demanded $500 a head. There were apparently no discounts for friends.

WE'D JUST FINISHED eating dinner one night when a heavy storm swept in from the Pacific. After we hustled home from the taco stand and dried off, Lalo flipped on the television, and Axel and I stepped back outside to call the Attorney, careful to press ourselves beneath the protective overhang of the tin roof. She didn't answer. Then Axel called his wife, who also didn't answer. Since his most recent deportation, she'd mostly stopped picking up. Axel lit a cigarette and we stared out into the darkness, slapping at mosquitos and watching the rain, which spun every which way in the howling wind.

"I haven't heard my kids' voices since the Viacrucis," he said numbly. "I talked to Monica a couple times, but she won't put them on the phone."

I didn't know what to say, so I said I was sorry. The palm trees swung wildly, and the tin roof shook like it might be sucked into the sky at any moment. Even in the storm, you could still hear the frogs and insects calling out into the night.

"Do you believe in God, Levi?" asked Axel, blowing cigarette smoke into the sheets of falling water. He reached his free hand out into the rain, as if to catch some of it, and I noticed it was trembling.

"Yeah," I said. "I do. Do you?"

"Nah. I don't think so, buddy. Not anymore. Not after all the shit I been through. I don't know why God woulda done something like this to me."

"I don't either."

"Ain't nobody listening."

"I'm listening."

"Yeah, Levi, but you ain't God." He threw his cigarette into the mud and walked back inside.

That night we had a fight over the bed. No matter what I did, Axel and Lalo insisted on sleeping on the floor. The mattress—disgusting, rotting, flea-infested, but also the best seat in the house—was given to me night after night. They also demanded that the lone fan, which was the only source of relief from the mosquitos and sweltering heat, be directly pointed at me all night long.

"Absolutely not," I said. "I'm not stealing your bed another night."

"Yes your ass is," said Axel, as he shook his blanket out for scorpions.

"No, dude. I refuse."

"You the guest, buddy. We're the migrants. We can sleep anywhere. But a delicate little cracker like you? You need it."

I lay there thinking about great unseen evils. About the global structures of conquest and colonization, and what it meant that two men were renouncing the only pleasures they had in the world so that I might be slightly more comfortable. All the small, unconscious sacrifices, the unspoken assumptions that of course the American traveler should have the best of things, even in the worst of places. It wasn't just that I didn't deserve it but that there was no way for me to refuse. The mattress became a constant reminder that we were not equal, no matter how much I might have pretended to be so. Axel was right. I wasn't a god. And yet everywhere I went, I was treated as something otherworldly, some minor deity, a US citizen with a US passport, thanked merely for my presence, for being there, for witnessing, for gazing upon them.

ONE MORNING, BEFORE sunrise, the Attorney called and said that Don Armando would pick up Axel and Lalo sometime that day, though when exactly she couldn't say. She instructed us to sit in Chahuites's main square, so that we could hop into his van as soon as he arrived.

"Don't make him go looking for you," she said. "He'll sooner leave than exert any extra energy."

We sat in the shade of a convenience store, where we were less exposed both to the sun and immigration. I bought us Cokes and cigarettes, and we settled into the long wait. Chahuites was suffocating and silent. Every once in a while, a lone figure would shuffle by—a stray dog who looked us in the eyes or a man carrying a machete who didn't. To pass the time, we conducted interviews. It was a habit that we were used to by then. When Axel didn't have a computer gig, and there was nothing else to do in the shack, I'd pull out my notebook or recorder, and we'd begin to talk. I'd ask Axel questions for hours and hours, and he would respond. The questions sometimes had no real point except to keep the conversation going, and his answers weren't always answers but rather long, drawn-out stories about his past, stories that had no real conclusion or climax, just events that blurred into other events or nonevents until I asked a clarifying question, and then it would start all over again, a back-and-forth, like I was hunting for something, and he was either trying to find it for me or to keep me from finding it, but what exactly that thing was neither of us seemed to be certain.

All I knew was that something wasn't making sense. I wanted to know why Axel had blocked me from seeing his Ruffrider Quest account. And why in his new account, Axl Brooklyn HQ, photos were conspicuously absent. There were also little moments when Axel seemed to have ascertained knowledge about me that I could have sworn I hadn't revealed. For instance, he once referenced a conversation I'd had with my girlfriend Atlee. During the Viacrucis, Axel had added her on social media as well, and when she asked if I knew who Ruffrider Quest was, I shot off a quick message without thinking: "hes just a migrant im working with."

"Just a migrant?" Axel had cackled the next time he'd seen me. "I'm just a migrant to you?"

I didn't understand what he meant at first, and, confused, I changed the subject. It was only days later that I remembered my message to Atlee, but by then so much time had passed that I wondered if I was just being paranoid. In Chahuites, however, the questions I'd previously pushed to the back of my mind kept forcing their way to the front. Watching Axel fix computers had been equal parts thrilling and unsettling. It made me rethink exactly what Axel had accomplished when he thwarted the police jammers and why he so impressed Father Solalinde. In the heat of the moment, I hadn't asked questions. I was just relieved that Axel found a solution. But how? How on earth did a man like Axel know how to outfox a federal police unit? And what else did he know?

As my mind wandered, Axel began reminiscing about high school. "Player, if you woulda knew Axel back then, you woulda knew that Axel could kick it with anyone—black, white, Spanish. Everybody knew Axel and everybody liked Axel. I was even friends with the exchange student from China. He didn't speak English, but he understood that hanging out with Axel was a good time." It was also in high school, he said, that he found the one space where he could truly be himself—the robotics club. The club's supervising teacher recruited him to help build robots because he saw something in him, some potential, a gift, a thing that other teachers missed when they looked at Axel or heard him speak.

"What was his name?" I asked.

"Ah, shit, it's been so long now, I don't even remember."

"You don't remember the name of the one teacher you actually liked?"

"Nah bro, I guess not." Suddenly there was an edge to Axel's voice. "And I can guarantee that he don't remember me either."

There was something about that that irritated me. "To be honest, dude," I said, "I don't get it."

"Get what?"

"You. These stories you're telling me. Look, I don't mean to be rude, but some of these things just aren't adding up. Like when you told me that you traveled to London in high school? I actually looked into that, and there's just no way that you could have traveled from the US to the UK and back on a Guatemalan passport alone. You'd need a visa."

"You saying I'm lying, bro?"

"Hey, you were the one who said that after you were deported to Guatemala, they didn't recognize you as a citizen. So how would you have had a passport as a teenager?"

"Leave it alone, Levi."

I was starting to get heated. "Leave it alone? Dude, look around. I'm in the middle of the nowhere for you. Would anyone else do that? If you were so popular in high school, why aren't any of your friends helping you? Or your parents? Why am I the only one here?"

Axel was silent. I could tell that I'd hurt him.

"I'm sorry, man," I backtracked. "I'm just scared. Back when you crossed the border, and I didn't hear from you, I was freaking out. I thought that maybe, like, I don't know, maybe you'd died."

"Fuck, bro."

"It's a terrible thing to say, but it's the truth. I was losing my mind. But you didn't die. And the day that you called me from Guatemala City was one of the happiest days of my life. Because I care about you, man. I really care. But come on. I know something else is going on. I've seen what you can do with computers out here with no tools or resources or anything. You can't tell me that you just learned all this stuff for fun."

Axel squinted into the sun. "Look, Levi, I ain't sure how to say this. But I've had to do things in my life. Things that I dunno if you'd understand."

"Well, you're right about that. I don't understand. I don't understand how back in Hermanos you managed to take down a police jammer single-handedly. And I don't understand Solalinde being all buddy-buddy with you afterward. What does he know about you?"

Axel started to speak, but I cut him off.

"Dude, I know I'm always pestering you with questions, and asking you all this intrusive stuff about your life, but now you listen to what I have to say for once. You're right. I don't know what it's like to be deported, or what it's like to run through Mexico. But I marched next to you. I've been sending you money that I don't have so that you can travel. And I came all the way back to this hell on earth for you. So I want to know what the deal is. What happened back in Hermanos that day?"

Axel looked me in the eyes. "Alright, Levi. The truth is, bro, sometimes I'm forced to do things."

"What kinds of things?"

"Things that is not exactly legit." He shifted in his seat. "Illegal things."

In that moment, it felt like the world narrowed and all I could see was Axel. The relentless heat, the endless dust, the insufferable town of Chahuites, all of it melted away, and the only thing I could feel was my heart pounding in my chest.

"Ah, screw it," he said, and a big smile cracked across his face. "You caught me, motherfucker. I'm a hacker."

CHAPTER 12

THE POWER OF TECHNOLOGY

NOW I AIN'T saying I'm the best hacker in the world or nothing. Or even that I'm that good. Back in the States, cybersecurity is tight these days, you feel me, and a player can only do so much. Plus, people in the States is always expecting an attack, so they protect themselves more. But I ain't the worst hacker in the world either, and a person with my skill set, a person who knows the things I know, in a country like Mexico? Well, now we talking business, baby. The security systems in Mexico is all, like, from the 1990s or some shit, and for a guy like me, who actually grew up messing around with computers during that time period, it's the easiest thing in the world to break into. That I can do in my sleep, you understand what I'm saying?

People always think hackers are, like, some kinda smart ass brainiac geniuses or something. But that ain't the truth. The truth is that a hacker could honestly be a dumbass motherfucker. Being smart ain't the most important thing that's required. It's something else. That's why I think hacking is a gift. Some people are just born with it, I believe. It's like you can see things that for anybody else wouldn't have made sense. It's a language, a living thing, a world. It's a passion. It's love. It's like an urge inside, this desire to break into things that someone else tells you not to, or that you can't, or that you shouldn't. Like some desire to penetrate the system. To come back again and again and again and again, just to see if you can go a little further than before.

And that's why, at the same time, a hacker is just the humblest guy who can do magic with a system. And by humble I don't just mean the normal English definition, I mean humble like "humilde" in Spanish, which kinda means something like poor, low class, invisible, the don't-nobody-care-about-you and don't-nobody-pay-attention-to-you kinda humble. Cause hackers ain't the English kinda humble. We're cocky as shit. Hacking is our place to shine, baby. Maybe you don't see me in the real world, maybe you look right past this old bald thundercat, but that's my advantage on computers. It's kinda like a dare. If you come up and tell me, "Yo, I got the hardest, most sophisticated software on the market and there's no way you can break it," then you best believe I'm gonna sit down and take the time to analyze the whole system and find the weakest spot. Just to prove you wrong.

Ah, shit. Forgive me, man. I don't know if I'm even making sense. I'm getting into my bullshit again. And when you get Axel on his bullshit, he's gonna be on that bullshit for a while, you feel me? I guess what poetry is for you, Levi, hacking is for me. But, actually, now that I think about it, it's way more than poetry to me, cause I can do things with hacking that I couldn't never do with my own body. And really, hacking is kinda more like history than poetry. Why? Cause it's you sitting in front of the system and saying, "Okay, I see you. When were you created? How did they make you? From when did they begin?" There's gotta be an end and a beginning to every single system and every single security measure. It's got a history. It was written by somebody, and that somebody wanted to keep you out. So you have to analyze every little detail about the system you're hacking, cause the cyber security avoids being hacked by making its code so blurry and complicated, from the beginning to the end, that you'd never have any idea what was up or down. But once you decipher that, their ass is yours. And that's when the magic begins.

Here's my history: I first got into computers cause of my uncle. He brought home this secondhand computer when I was eight. I remember just looking at it and my eight-year-old brain was like, "Oh my goodness, where the hell did you get this fascinating device?" I was hooked. And when he was outta the house, I'd sneak into his room and mess around on it. Then one day I accidentally found his porn collection in a folder. And it was the first time I'd seen a naked girl besides my mom, and then that really got me fascinated, you feel me? Little Axel realized the power of technology in that moment.

As I got older, my uncle used to take me to drive around Port Washington with him late at night before the garbage pickup. And we'd dig through the trash, looking for electronics. Bro, you woulda never believed the shit rich people throws away. I got my first Atari and Sega Genesis outta the trash. And my first desktop too. If a computer was broken, my uncle showed me how to fix it up and get it running again. Like how to replace the keyboard or solder the USB drive or do some basic coding. But my first real hack—like, my first offensive attack, if you wanna call it like that—was in high school against this dude named Carlos. Carlos was a bully, like a legit bastard asshole, and he was a couple grades above me. Big dude with big muscles and a big attitude, you feel me? He was the kinda guy who woulda literally pushed you up into a locker whenever he got the chance, just like in the movies. He'd hit you in the face just for the attention. Except he didn't pick on me for no reason. I was dancing with his girl. Oops. Honestly, I didn't even know she was his girl. It was just a dance at a random house party, no biggie. But then Carlos walked in and freaked the fuck out. He pulled out a gun and started chasing my ass. I ran outside and down the street, zigzagging like a motherfucker, thinking I was running for my life, you know what I'm saying? And the whole time I can hear the pop-pop-pop of the gun as he's shooting at me, and people yelling from the front yard. It was only later that I learned it was just a BB gun, not a real gun, but I didn't know it at the time. At the time I thought I was gonna die.

After I got away I called up some of my friends. There was Tina, who was black. Linda, who was white. And Ricardo, who was Spanish like me, except he was legal. We called ourselves the Geek Squad. So I called the Geek Squad up and I was like, "Yo, Carlos just tried to shoot me. Let's get his ass."

And they was immediately down with it. Tina was like, "What are we gonna do?"

And I was like, "He's always bragging about having money. Let's hack into his bank account."

Now, none of us had never done a hack like that before. We was just some friends who liked to mess around on computers. But that night we crossed into new territory. I won't bother you with the details, but, back then, online bank accounts didn't have hardly none of the security that they got now. And after so many hours, so late at night, all of a sudden Ricardo was like, "We're in, baby."

We was sitting there, just amazed at what we was seeing, something so secret and private. And then we saw that he had, like, five thousand dollars. And we started slapping each other silly. Five grand, five Gs, five big ass stacks. That was a helluva lotta money for kids like us. But what we decided to do was, we knew we couldn't just take it all. Cause that woulda been real suspicious. So we figured we'd take half. Back then, most people still didn't have online banking, right? So we thought maybe he wouldn't even notice for a while, and by then it'd be too late. He'd get confused, think he got drunk at the club and blew the money on bitches or something, who knows.

So that's what we did.

And once we got that money, honey, we went to Atlantic City. Took the dolla dolla bills straight to the ocean and had a little fun. I bought some shoes. Tina bought a dress. Ricardo went to the casino. But most of the time we just spent the day chilling on the beach. Drinking Cherry Cokes and living in the moment. It was one of the best days of my life.

After that everything was hacking to me. The only place I wanted to be was in front of a computer. It was my escape, man, cause things was getting crazy at my house. My mom and step-pops ended up kicking me outta my room so they coulda rented it for extra money. Otherwise we was gonna get evicted, they said. So I had to sleep in the living room. But there was already one immigrant guy who paid to crash on the couch, and another guy who sometimes slept in the dining room. So

I tried to fall asleep underneath the coffee table, but my stepdad was always having these dudes over to drink and play cards and I couldn't get to sleep. And then I noticed that every once in a while one of them would disappear back into my mom's bedroom. So I started acting all tough about it, yelling something like, "Yo you dirty ass bastards, get the fuck away from my moms."

And then one of the dudes slapped the bejeezus outta me immediately. Straight across the face. I'm seeing stars, my tongue's slobbering outta my head, and my stepdad just looks at me, like, "Well, don't act like you don't deserve it."

So after that I mostly didn't crash at my place no more. Sometimes a friend would sneak me into their room. Or sometimes, especially in the winter, I'd check to see if somebody's car in the neighborhood was unlocked, and I'd pass out in the back seat. But most of the time I couldn't find nowhere safe so I'd just walk the streets, walk the streets, walk the streets. One foot in front of the other, you know what I'm saying? Like I was training to walk across Mexico my whole life. And then I'd sleep in school. Or skip school and sleep in the park. And then I started to fail my classes, and then I just thought, fuck it, who cares, and I dropped out. So I'm sorry I lied to you, Levi, when I said I had a high school diploma. And an associate's. I ain't got none of that shit. I'm just a dropout. But I tried to make the best of it. I realized that— since I was already out at night anyways—I could dig through the trash like me and my uncle used to do, get a buncha busted old devices, and then fix them up to sell on the street. At first, it wasn't a lotta money or nothing like that, but over years and years I taught myself how to do things that most people never woulda thought of with computers. Then I found Kali Linux, the most beautiful software I coulda ever imagined. With Kali Linux, you get the tools to penetrate way more systems, and all of a sudden I could hack so many more things than I ever coulda done before.

That's one of the reasons that Solalinde wanted to hire me. Once I realized that the police was jamming the signal, I went straight to Beto and told him that I needed the most badass computer that they

148

had in the shelter. And just by pure luckiness, there was this volunteer there named el Colocho who already had Kali Linux on a bootable USB drive. I guess that from time to time he liked hacking too or something, I don't know. But I got it up and running and figured out the jammer. And after Father Solalinde saw me work my magic, and el Colocho was there confirming to him that I was the real deal, he sat me down, and in that soft, gentle voice he has—a voice that sounds like he knows someone else might be tryna listen—he asked me what else I could do. And I don't know why I answered him honestly, cause whenever I speak honest I always get freaking screwed, but I guess I thought he was a priest and I coulda trusted him. So I told him I was a hacker. And then he got serious, even more serious than he normally seems, and he whispered that he had lots of enemies, especially enemies in the government. People who was always tryna hurt him. And that he needed someone like me. Someone that coulda kept him safe from outside attacks, and someone who coulda been more aggressive and find out who wanted to do damage. Someone who could monitor the situation, you feel me? And then he asked if I might be that someone.

And I said, "In this country? No biggie, padre. Just gimme a name and I'll show you what I can do."

And he said that specific names wasn't necessary right now, but that after all this Viacrucis nonsense was over, and the little problem we were having with the police had been resolved—that's what he called it, a "little problem," like it was a headache or a fly or some shit—that I should stay behind and live with him in the shelter. But that before we went any further, he had to know that we trusted each other. Trusted each other to the max, 110 percent.

And I didn't know what to say, but I knew that I wasn't gonna stick around Hermanos forever wasting my life. So I said, "Uh, I'm sorry, Father, I gotta get back to my kids in the States."

But he wouldn't take no for an answer. "Just think about it," he kept saying. "Just think about it. We can help you apply for asylum here. You could work legally. You could have a good life. You wouldn't have to risk your life crossing the border, living in fear."

And so I said, okay, that I'd think about it, and Solalinde smiled a little bit and patted me on the shoulder and then he got up and said that he had to take a phone call and left. And for the rest of the Viacrucis it was like I was his new best friend. I was always right up in the front of the march next to him, always running little errands for him.

"Oh, Axel, can you fetch us some water?"

"Oh, Axelillo, what do you think about this situation?"

"Hey Axel, I need you to come testify against the police."

And the whole time I just nodded and smiled and kept my mouth shut, and then as soon as the Viacrucis ended and I got that amparo in my hand, I bounced. I didn't tell Solalinde goodbye or nothing. And that's why I think I've been stuck in Chahuites for forever. Cause the Attorney has been telling Solalinde I'm stuck here. Fuck, I'm right down the road from him. He can control an entire freaking SWAT team at the touch of a button but he can't send someone to pick me up? I ain't got no proof, but I think he's letting me suffer, maybe. For not helping him out. For rejecting him. Or maybe he thinks that I'm also tryna hack him now or something. I dunno. But I ain't done none of that bullshit.

But it is what I did to you, Levi. I hacked you, bro. And I'm sorry for that, but I had to know. I had to be sure that you was who you said you was. Or at least that you wasn't what you seemed like. Cause look at it from my position: What are the chances that you get deported and then all of a sudden you run into some crazy ass white guy who's actually living with migrants and asks you all about your life? That's fishy, bro. That's weird. So you remember when we first met and I was asking you all those questions? Like where you was born, where you went to school, what your parents' names was, and all that? What did you think that was about, bro? I was getting intel for passwords. And then I phished you, and the night I stayed at your place I also installed a keylogger on your computer and did a little background check. I got into your Facebook, I got into your email, and, yeah, I did your bank account too. I just wanted to see if there was any sketchy transactions going in and out. I was looking for a confirmation that you was who you said you was, that you wasn't some weird CIA motherfucker or some shit. I *coulda tried to take your money, but I didn't. I put everything back just like I found it. I saw that you had a little bit more money than you had told me you had, but not much more. For the most part you was telling the truth. Basically you're just a broke ass motherfucker like me, but with a passport. And that's when I kinda started to trust you.*

CHAPTER 13

HOT SPOTS

DON ARMANDO NEVER showed. When the sun went down, we walked home. In the dark, the town's brightly painted buildings were muted and moody. The fading hand-painted advertisements for Coca-Cola and local radio stations looked like ancient hieroglyphs, and the shadows emphasized how scuffed and chipped the paint was, timeless in a way, as if these structures had existed long before the conquistadors ever arrived. We didn't speak. I wasn't angry, exactly. Part of me didn't blame Axel for hacking me, and yet it also felt strange not to blame him. I felt exposed but also relieved, like something had been reciprocated. He was prying into my life like I was prying into his. We shared a secret. And yet the secret did make me more cautious. Just as soon as everything with Axel seemed to have an explanation, I only had more questions. I understood his need to anonymize himself, of course. But the other, seemingly smaller lies were the ones that were the most confusing. Lying about traveling to London, for instance, didn't seem to do much to protect his identity. It was just bizarre. So why did he do it?

Not long after, Axel was in the middle of fixing a laptop when he received a mysterious phone call late in the night, in which he conversed in cryptic sentences, as if the person on the other end of the line was speaking in code.

He hung up and rolled his eyes. "Honestly bro, Irineo and immigration ain't even my biggest concerns. That was the mayor."

"The mayor of Chahuites?"

"Yeah man. Dude is a nutty bastard."

"What did he want?"

"Well, a little while back I fixed some fancy guy's laptop, right? And it turns out he was the mayor's assistant or some shit. Next thing I know, I got the mayor calling me on my phone day and night, asking me how much do I really know about computers, and if I can hack this other guy who's running against him in the election."

If the mayor knew about Axel, then surely other powerful people in the area were starting to as well. This kind of skill could put him in great danger. "What'd you say?" I asked.

"Obviously I said yes."

I tried to hide my shock. "What do you mean yes? You're hacking his political opponent?"

"Nah, man, of course I ain't gonna hack for that bastard. I ain't getting involved in that bullshit."

"Then why'd you say yes?"

Axel massaged his temples. "Levi, just cause I ain't gonna do it, it don't mean that I can say no, you feel me? If a guy like me rejects someone that powerful on the spot, how do you think he's gonna take it? He's gonna take it like a big 'Fuck you,' that's how he's gonna take it. And then he'll kick our broke asses outta town. A guy like me has always gotta say yes first, then decide what I'm actually gonna do later."

I wondered what that meant for us, and how many times Axel had said yes to my interviews while still trying to hold me at arm's length. "And what are you actually gonna do?"

"Stall like a motherfucker," he said, squeezing a smidge of toothpaste into some unseen corner of the laptop, "with a smile on my face."

It was clear that Axel and Lalo were not going to stay under-cover much longer, and my presence wasn't doing them any favors either. Jesús the landlord would swing by at odd hours, usually to show me off to his friends and mooch beer money. Then his friends started turning up on their own, also for beer money. The shack was becoming the hottest spot in all of Chahuites. Axel and I agreed that it was time for me to leave. So I boarded a bus to Mexico City and prayed that Don Armando would keep his word.

AFTER NEARLY TWO months of waiting, one day the Attorney in-structed Axel and Lalo to walk to Irineo's shelter to be picked up. When they arrived, Don Armando wasn't there, but Father Solalinde was. The priest said that Don Armando was busy un-loading donations in Hermanos, so he came to give them a lift to the shelter instead. Irineo tagged along as well. His demeanor was light and happy, as if he wasn't at all surprised to see them.

"You never woulda believed it," Axel told me later. "This motherfucker was acting like he was our best freaking buddy. Like we ain't been hiding from his ass for months."

In the SUV, Father Solalinde stayed quiet. If he still bore any lingering resentment against Axel for rejecting him, Axel couldn't tell. Instead, Irineo filled the silence with idle chatter. He asked Lalo where he was from. Then he ran his fingers up the back of Lalo's calf when no one was looking. Lalo stayed quiet, uncertain of what to do.

When they arrived at Hermanos, Don Armando was busy unloading boxes of donations from his van. He was a large man, likely in his early sixties, with a salt-and-pepper beard. He clapped Axel on the back like they were old friends. "So you're the bas-tard that woman's been nagging me about for all this time?" he chuckled.

It was too late for the twelve-hour drive back to Mexico City, so they spent the night in the shelter. Strangely, Irineo didn't spend the night in the volunteer quarters, like he had during the

Viacrucis, but instead opted to sleep next to Lalo in the migrant common area.

"I couldn't sleep the entire night," Lalo told me later. "All night long he was touching me, spooning me, running his fingers up and down my arm."

Lalo went on to tell me that the next morning, over breakfast in the cafeteria, Irineo told Don Armando that there was no need to take Lalo back to Mexico City. "I can take care of him in Chahuites," he said.

"No," said Axel immediately because Lalo was too shocked to speak. "We travel together. Period."

"I wasn't asking you," said Irineo. "It's Don Armando's decision, not yours."

Don Armando continued to chew his food, seemingly unperturbed.

Axel called the Attorney, who then called Don Armando. "Remember," she said to him over the phone, "I'm paying you to bring two migrants up to Mexico City, not one. If Lalo doesn't come, I want my money back."

That changed Don Armando's tune, and Lalo stayed with him.

Don Armando packed the van, which legally sat seven, with fourteen people. Axel and Lalo were crammed into the storage compartment behind the back seat. Around seven o'clock in the evening, I got a call from a number I didn't recognize. It was Axel. He said he was at a gas station an hour and a half south of the city.

"Dude, he just left us in the middle of the nowhere."

"What? Why?"

"He said he was tired and he didn't feel like dealing with traffic no more. So he just opened the door and kicked us out on the highway."

When I finally found them, it was almost one in the morning. They looked even more starved and disheveled than they had in Chahuites. Their faces were gaunt, and their cheekbones protruded so sharply it was like an invisible hand had reached inside their heads and warped the pottery of their skulls. As we made our way back to my apartment, I noticed that they were both walking strangely, with ginger steps that were almost bow-legged. When we arrived at my front door, Axel touched my arm and whispered, "Listen brother, you got some extra clothes we can borrow?"

I shrugged. "Sure. What for?"

It was only then that, in the confines of the small, stale stairwell, that I smelled it. "Dude, it don't make me feel like a man to tell you this, but we doo-dooed ourselves."

During the drive, Don Armando had refused to let anyone out of the vehicle for fear that they would draw unwanted attention. After hours in the van, Axel and Lalo defecated on themselves and then were forced to sit in it for hours longer. By the time I found them, it had dried all over their legs and pants. I just hadn't seen it in the dim streetlight.

"It wasn't just us," said Axel as I coaxed a thin but relatively steady stream of water from my janky shower head. "There was a pregnant lady with us and she pissed herself like four times cause that motherfucker wouldn't pull over."

I left Axel and Lalo to shower while I disposed of their clothes in the trash cans downstairs. Afterward, they stepped from the bathroom timidly, their skin rubbed red and raw, as if they'd kept scrubbing long after they were clean. It was strange to see them standing there, in my clothing. Axel was wearing one of my old t-shirts that had "Camden County High School Varsity Tennis" emblazoned across the chest, and I imagined what it would have been like to go to school together. We could have passed each other in the hallway a hundred times, and I never would have known how different his life was from mine, or that, despite it all, the world could still throw us together.

"Bro we're fucking starving. You got any food?"

I swung open the fridge. "Well boys, we got eggs, beans, and tortillas. Oh, and salsa of course."

"Jesus Christ," Axel huffed, reaching into the fridge for the carton of eggs. "You're turning into a freaking Mexican on me."

DURING DINNER, I asked if Axel had run into Armando Amante while he was in Hermanos.

"Nah man, he wasn't around. And we never saw him once the entire time we was in Chahuites."

It seemed that Armando Amante's falling out with Irineo during the Viacrucis was permanent.

"And dude," said Axel, "Hermanos ain't the same shelter no more, bro. It's changed." He said that, at first, he couldn't put a finger on exactly what it was. Then he spoke to a young man in the shelter who remembered him from the Viacrucis, a Honduran named Memo, who'd been at Hermanos for months waiting on the results of a humanitarian visa application. Axel asked why everything at the shelter felt so different.

"He said that Beto had started selling a buncha the stuff in Hermanos on the low-low and keeping the money. Like the sleeping mats and donations and stuff."

And that wasn't the worst of it. Memo said that while Beto was fighting the gangs and cartels in public, behind the scenes they'd struck a deal, allowing a certain number of gang members into the shelter to recruit migrants to smuggle drugs.

"Does Solalinde know about this?" I asked.

"Memo says Solalinde's never there. He's always gone. So he never knows what the hell is happening. But bro, it gets even dirtier."

Memo accused Beto of having sex with women in the shelter. He promised them all kinds of things—visas, first picks of shelter donations, better sleeping arrangements—if he could sleep with them. "Memo said that Beto even keeps their panties after they have sex," Axel said, "and hangs them above his bed."

"You've got to be kidding me," I said. "That can't be true. He can't be that indiscreet."

"Hey, I'm just telling you what Memo told me."

After we went to bed, I thought I heard Axel talking on his phone, but when I peeked into the living room, he was asleep on the ground, muttering about things I couldn't quite understand.

IN THE MORNING, I called the Attorney and told her that Don Armando had abandoned Axel and Lalo on the outskirts of Mexico City.

"Oh Levi," she sighed. "What on earth was that man thinking?" She did sound genuinely disturbed and promised to find Axel and Lalo new accommodations as quickly as possible. "In the meantime," she asked, "can they stay with you?"

But finding decent accommodations for migrants in Mexico City proved to be no easy feat. Every month I heard a new story from a Central American about being turned away as soon as a potential landlord heard their accent. The racism in the capital was very real, and as the weeks dragged on, the Attorney maintained that she still hadn't found anyone willing to rent to migrants.

Then my girlfriend Atlee arrived. While I was in Mexico, she'd been completing a master's degree, and I convinced her to move down after finishing her coursework. I promised her a serene respite where she could write her thesis in peace. Instead, she found a tiny apartment crammed with three grown men, all of whom were slowly starting to lose their minds in such close quarters. I'd told Atlee about Axel, of course, though I downplayed some of our more harrowing exploits on the Viacrucis so as not to worry her. Now his eccentricities—and their influence upon me—were on full display.

"You've even started to wave your arms like him," Atlee observed, poking fun at us.

She took it all in stride, however, and organized several touristic outings, worried that I had not been giving Lalo a sufficient cultural education in the great Latin American metropolis.

"My dude," said Axel, "you don't know how lucky you are to have a woman like that."

In the evenings, Lalo—who had quickly grown weary of Mexican high culture and the seemingly endless number of plaques on seventeenth-century nuns that it entailed—insisted on introducing us to the low by surveying Eddie Murphy's entire oeuvre. Night after night, while waiting for the Attorney's call, we'd watch *Beverly Hills Cop* and *Dr. Dolittle* and *Norbit* over plates of rice and beans until Lalo's eyes began to droop. Then Atlee would slip a pillow under his head and retreat into our bedroom to plug away at her thesis. Axel and I would relocate up to the roof to discuss his next move. These days, he was even more jittery than when we first met. His limbs would occasionally jerk this way or that, as if pulled by invisible strings, and our conversations were becoming increasingly circular and disorienting.

How long would he stay in Mexico City? Who knew, but with this five-year ban from the US, it might be smart to cool his jets for a little while.

But what did that mean about seeing his kids? Again, who knew, which was maybe why he should just say fuck it and bounce to the border again.

But what if he got caught, since now with the ban he could face prison time? Well, that's why he was thinking about staying in Mexico for now, he'd say, a cigarette's red ember dancing erratically between his trembling fingers.

Finally, the Attorney called.

"Look," she said, after we put her on speakerphone, "before you say anything, just hear me out. I've found something, and right now, something is better than nothing." She paused for a moment, as if to allow those words to sink to profound depths. "I've spoken with Don Armando, and he's agreed to let Axel and Lalo stay in his shelter long-term."

"What?" I said, before I could stop myself.

"Chicos, I know it's not ideal"—she was always calling us boys, as if Axel wasn't just a few years younger than her—"but Don Armando has apologized for what he did. He says it was a simple miscommunication, that's all. I've agreed to pay for Axel and Lalo's food each month if he can give them a nice place to sleep and help them apply for humanitarian visas. So there it is. That's the best I can offer for now."

That evening we mulled the idea over eggs and beans.

"Fuck it," said Axel. "Let's give it a shot."

I frowned. "I'm just not sure going back to the guy who left you stranded on the side of the road is a great idea." Atlee agreed.

But Axel was firm. "The chance of getting a visa is worth it."

Lalo nodded and shoveled a spoonful of beans into his mouth.

"Besides," said Axel, raising a hand to count the ways, "I been deported, beat up by the po-po, chased by immigration, beat up again by narcos, re-deported, and then busted my knee in the middle of the fucking nowhere Chahuites. Whatever's next, it can't be much worser than that, right?"

CHAPTER 14

DOGS AND WOLVES

Axel 11:47 PM brother u r not gunna believ this
Axel 11:47 PM This place aint a shelter bro
Axel 11:48 PM Its a ducking auto shop
Axel 11:48 PM fucking
Levi 12:11 AM what ??
Axel 12:14 AM its a fucking mechanic place bro
Axel 12:14 AM he got us sleeping out door
Axel 12:15 AM in some broked down cars

Don Armando's "shelter" was, in fact, worse than we could have imagined. It was an open-air auto shop, enclosed by twelve-foot chain link fences topped with barbed wire. Like a prison. No one was ever allowed to leave, and at night the gates were locked with heavy deadbolts. Nor was the shop in Mexico City, like Don Armando had led us to believe, but two hours away in Metepec, a suburb of a city called Toluca. Despite Toluca being one of the coldest places in all of Mexico, with temperatures regularly dropping below freezing at night, there was no heat, hot water, or indoor accommodations. There was a single bathroom, which had no light and was covered in a slick mold. Everyone slept in dilapidated cars, which were propped up on cinderblocks and didn't even have functioning batteries. Upon arrival, Axel and Lalo were assigned a beaten-up yellow Volkswagen van. The seats had been removed and a bare mattress was wedged in the back. To keep warm, they burrowed under heaps of old blankets and towels, many of which were stained with oil and grease.

During the day, Don Armando forced everyone to work on the cars. If they didn't work, they didn't eat. None of them were paid. "He says our payment is a roof over our heads," said Axel on the phone. "And I'm like, man, what roof? Every day it's wake up, work our asses off, go to sleep. They treat us like dogs, man. I swear to god it's like we're his fucking dogs."

I was horrified. Axel and Lalo had been given over to a wolf, and I had a hand in it. I immediately called the Attorney, but she didn't pick up. So I called again, and again. Nothing. She was avoiding me. When I finally tracked her down, she was with two other migrants, a husband and wife, outside an immigration office in Polanco, one of the fanciest neighborhoods in Mexico City. The couple had also ridden in Don Armando's van, and he'd also abandoned them on the side of the road. But unlike Axel and Lalo, they got lucky and were granted long-term quarters at a shelter in Mexico City because they were married. The Attorney was helping them apply for humanitarian visas.

"Axel says they're trapped inside," I said, before we finished kissing cheeks. "It's not even a shelter, apparently, it's just an auto shop. Did you know about this?"

"No, Levi," she sighed. "Remember, I don't know Don Armando either. I've only been in this world for a few months now. Father Solalinde said that Don Armando ran a shelter, and I believed him. He said that Hermanos sends migrants to Don Armando all the time."

"Axel says that there's no food or beds. They have to sleep in the cars."

"I know, he's texting me as well."

"Well, what are we going to do? We've got to get them out."

"Yes, Axel—I mean, Levi. Yes, Levi." She'd mixed up our names. She was flustered. The Attorney took off her sunglasses.

162

With them on she seemed eternally glamorous and unruffled, like a movie star easing into middle age, but when they were off, I could see dark bags under her eyes. "I need you to be patient."

"Patient?" I said. "Axel might as well have been kidnapped."

"Think of it this way." She rubbed a microfiber cloth across the dark lenses and then slipped them back on. "What's happening in Don Armando's shelter is awful. We're talking imprisonment. Slavery. Serious stuff. Now, I might be able to go down there tomorrow and make something up to get Axel and Lalo back. Maybe I could say that I've found them a room in Mexico City. But even if Don Armando lets them walk out the door, what happens to the rest of the people trapped in his shop? They don't have anyone waiting for them on the outside, and I doubt Don Armando would let his precious little servants leave without a fight."

I hadn't thought of that.

"Every day Axel is inside that shop," continued the Attorney, "is a day that he can gather evidence. Every single thing he sees or hears or is forced to do, he can document. If we went to Father Solalinde and caused a fuss right now, who do you think he'd believe? Us or Don Armando, his childhood friend?"

"You think he'd cover for Don Armando?"

"I don't know, Levi. But what I do know is that in situations like this, you don't ask questions you don't already have the answers to. Axel also told me about what he witnessed in Hermanos and everything that Beto is supposedly up to. Whatever's going on down there, it's not good. And look," she nodded to the Honduran couple sitting quietly at a table nearby. "I've agreed to help these people apply for visas. But I'm new to this game. We're wasting time in this waiting room because I have to play by the rules. I don't have the right connections yet. But Don Armando has contacts in the Senate. He can get anyone a visa he wants, and he's promised them to Axel and Lalo. If they can hang on long enough, and make him happy enough, they could become legalized. Then they'll be free to go wherever they want. But in the meantime, I need them to stay and collect information against Don Armando. Because, believe me, if we're making accusations against someone as well connected as him, we're going to need all the evidence we can get. So we wait. We bide our time."

I buried my face in my hands. "I don't like this. It's too dangerous."

"Dangerous, indeed," said the Attorney, running her fingers through her perfect hair. "Welcome to Mexico."

AT THE END of the workday, Don Armando would dig several canned goods out of a box of donations and distribute them among the migrants to cook in the shop. There was rarely any consideration for the complementarity of food they were forced to eat—tins of black beans and pineapple one night, cream of corn and preserved mushrooms the next—and it was often not nearly enough to fill their stomachs. In an attempt to win everyone better rations, Axel offered to fix an old laptop that was lying around the shop. That evening, Don Armando brought a whole chicken for dinner. Then he pulled Axel aside.

"How good are you with computers, honestly?" he asked.

"What was I supposed to say?" Axel recounted over the phone. "I'm starving, so I was like, man, I know everything about computers. You just tell me what you want me to do."

"I want you to hack somebody," Don Armando responded, without batting an eye.

"Who?" Axel asked.

"The priest," Don Armando replied. "Solalinde."

Not long after, Don Armando arranged for the priest to visit the auto shop. According to Axel, it was clearly not Solalinde's first time at the "shelter." "He didn't even blink when he saw us locked up like this," he said. "It was just business as usual."

While Don Armando distracted Solalinde by chatting him up about various potential fundraisers and donation drives in the greater Mexico City area, Axel asked if he could borrow the priest's phone to make a call. Solalinde handed it to him absentmindedly.

"I walked around the corner," said Axel, "and then I cloned his WhatsApp account onto one of Don Armando's phones, so that any messages that Solalinde sent or received, Don Armando woulda gotten them on his device too." Axel also managed to phish the priest and gain access to his email account. Don Armando was now fully apprised of everyone Solalinde was in contact with at all times.

After the hack, Axel excitedly sent an electronic record to the Attorney. Surely, he thought, it would be enough evidence to prove to Solalinde that Don Armando wasn't trustworthy. But the Attorney still wasn't satisfied. It would be even more shocking, she said, if they were actually able to collect some of the priest's juiciest conversations, private correspondences that he didn't want to get out into the world.

"I'm starting to think that she just wants me to spy on Solalinde too," said Axel. "Like a blackmail kinda situation."

To make matters worse, Don Armando began toting Axel around to fundraisers in the Mexico City and Toluca area as a kind of walking testimony to his charity. Axel would be forced to take the stage and sing Don Armando's praises. Without the man in front of them, Axel would say to the audience, he might be locked up by immigration right now, or maybe dead in a ditch. No one in the entire country was doing more to help migrants, except for the esteemed Father Alejandro Solalinde, who was Don Armando's confidant and close friend. Then Axel would ask, if anyone felt so moved, that they please make a donation to keep the shelter running. Cash, clothing, food, and electronics were most welcome. If Axel did well, Don Armando would swing by Burger King or allow him to keep any item of clothing he wanted from the donation bin. Extolling Don Armando's virtues night after night was understandably taking a toll. Axel's knee had mostly healed, and he began entertaining the idea of trying to return to

New York. "Just imagining my kids up there without their daddy makes my head wanna explode," he said over the phone.

One night, in a fit of desperation, Axel managed to squeeze his slim frame through a gap in one of the gates. He thought about escaping, but Lalo's broad shoulders couldn't fit, so he stayed. Not long after, Axel's phone went dark. Every text I sent went unread. Every call went straight to voicemail. For two days there was radio silence. I texted the Attorney, but she hadn't heard from him either. I was worried he skipped town. Or, worse, that he'd attempted to make a break for it and been caught. Then, on the third night, Axel finally called.

"What's popping, my brother." His voice was hushed and muffled.

"Dude, where have you been? I'm losing my mind over here trying to get ahold of you."

"Bro, Don Armando's wife came busting up in here, all pissed off, saying we was just a buncha lazy immigrants who wasn't pulling their weight, and then stole our phones. And you know what the craziest thing is? I think she was lying. I think she got scared. I think she learned about Don Armando making me hack all these important people, and she freaked out. Took away our phones, took away my laptop, she won't even let me in Don Armando's office no more."

"How'd you get your phone back?"

"Man, Don Armando gave it back to me. He said we just had to wait it out a couple days until she calmed down."

"That's insane," I seethed. "They can't just cut off your contact with the outside world every time they have a fight with each other. I didn't know what had happened to you. I didn't know if you had tried to escape, or if immigration came, or . . ."

Axel cackled. "Or what? They killed me?"

"The thought crossed my mind."

"Things is getting hot. Too motherfucking hot. At this point I've seen too much and done too much for him to just let me go."

It was early October. My grant was set to expire in a few weeks, and not long after that my visa would be up as well. To hell with the Attorney and all her talk about patience and strategy. It was her strategizing that had gotten Axel into this mess in the first place. Now I needed to get him out.

"Well," I said, "I guess it's time for a jail break."

BEFORE I LEFT for Metepec, I received a text from Axel's mother, who still lived in New York. We occasionally corresponded when she sent Axel money and needed me to withdraw it for him. The sum was always exceedingly small and only arrived after much begging on Axel's part.

"He made his bed the moment he started seeing that awful woman," she'd told me once, referring to Monica. "Now he has to lay his broke ass in it."

So I did my best not to pry when it came to finances. But on this day, Axel's mother messaged to say that she'd made a mistake. She'd just sent me another small sum of money, but at the last minute, Axel had called to say that she should send it to someone else in Guatemala instead. "For the kids," she said. She asked if I could forward the money on to a woman whose first name I didn't recognize, but who had the same last name as Monica. I couldn't believe it. Previously, I'd enjoyed texting with Axel's mom. She'd send me old pictures of Axel when he was a child, pictures with backgrounds that seemed to confirm that he really did grow up in New York. She also occasionally sent me photos of herself just to say hello—which I'd found was a relatively common custom of migrants and former migrants—and they too seemed to indicate that she lived in New York, just as Axel had said.

But now things weren't adding up again. I spent the rest of the day reading and rereading the text. Confronting Axel directly was a lose-lose. Either it was all a misunderstanding on my part and his kids really were in the US—in which case Axel would be wounded that I didn't trust him—or I'd just caught him in a lie.

And not just any lie. Axel's singular goal had always been to re-turn to his children. He was risking his life every day to get back to them. Or so it seemed. Had his mother just revealed that they were actually in Guatemala? Had he left Guatemala in order to support them? But why lie about that? Clearly because he'd aban-doned them, I thought. But no, that couldn't be possible. I'd seen Axel carry babies for miles during the Viacrucis and spend the only money he had in the world on diapers and baby formula for them. My head was spinning. No, I thought, it couldn't be true. Since the moment I met Axel, the only thing that made him light up besides computers was his children. They were his whole world, the sole reason to continue fighting.

I decided to sit on the text for a while. The last thing Axel needed was me nit-picking at the most intimate aspects of his life while he was being held prisoner. And the last thing I needed, though I couldn't quite admit it to myself at the time, was to carry around the knowledge that the man who'd been sleeping in my apartment still wasn't the person he was claiming to be.

CHAPTER 15

THE AMERICAN AXEL

I FOUND OUT I wasn't legal cause of a girl. The love of my life, Jen Russo. We was in the same grade in school, right, but she was in a different class. Like, she was in the A building with the smart kids and I was in the B building. She was white and I wasn't. She was rich and I wasn't. But I was in love with her from the jump.

We met when we was fifteen, and we used to do everything together. We went to the mall together. We went to prom together. And we lost our virginity together. She was everything to me, man. I felt like I coulda told her anything, even the messed-up things that I started noticing in my own house. Like that my stepdad didn't ever really wanna be my father, and my mom was never sticking up for me and all that. We'd stay up late at night talking and even though her life was, like, completely different from mine, she'd listen, you feel me? She showed me love like no one else ever has since. Jen's daddy was, like, some kinda retired cop and her mother was a flight attendant. Compared to my family, they had a helluva lotta money. Her dad even owned land in upstate New York, where he had a couple horses. At first, Jen's family kinda tolerated me. I'd come over and kick it, and her parents would invite me to stay for dinner, right? They was polite and all that. But after a while, daddy started to realize I was hanging around his daughter a little too much. And that me and her mighta been doing a little too much, you feel me? Jen started saying that, when I wasn't there, he'd talk about me behind my back. Saying that Italian girls shouldn't be dating Spanish guys and shit. Daddy was tryna break us apart. He thought I wasn't gonna amount to nothing, that I was too broke for his precious little girl, and so I said, "Axel, you gotta get yourself a job, baby boy. Show daddy that you can hustle up a little money."

So me and Jen applied to work together at this electronics store called *Nobody Beats the Wiz*. You're probably too young to remember it, cause it's outta business now, but back in the day it was the spot. We both interviewed and we both got the job. The only thing was I needed to give them my social security number so I coulda got paid, right?

So I went back to my mom and said, "Yo moms, I got this fine ass job, you got my birth certificate?"

And she was like, "Kid, you better chill out with that nonsense. That's something we ain't talking bout."

So, believe it or not, that's how I learned I was illegal. Like, I knew that I was from Guatemala, but I didn't know I was what I really was, you feel me? And I couldn't tell Jen the truth. She started asking what was taking so long for me to start work, but I couldn't tell her. I just couldn't do it. It felt like I had been lying to her this whole time bout the person I was, the person she loved, like somehow I'd tricked her.

So eventually I was just like, "Jen, chill out. I got a better job, I'm working somewhere else now."

Which of course wasn't true. I was just living it fake and Jen could tell. After that, things wasn't the same, and eventually her family moved down to Florida and she went with them and that was it. Daddy got his way and Axel was outta the picture. I went through a lotta hardcore shit after that. I was just tryna hustle life, right? When I realized I wasn't legal, I also started to understand that my life was gonna be restricted. I watched all my friends from high school applying to college and jobs and getting excited for life, but for me it was just the underground and under-the-table and undercover. You feel me? It was like I was disappearing and couldn't do nothing to stop it, but also like I needed to make myself disappear to survive. I don't even know if that makes sense to you, Levi, but that's what it felt like.

The one thing I did know for sure was that I had to make money. So at first, and I'm ashamed to say it, I figured out how to skim credit cards. I did it cause I needed to eat, man, and cause I lived right next to the one place in the world where you're guaranteed to find some rich, dumbass motherfuckers who can afford to lose a little moolah: Manhattan. I identified the ATMs outside all the fancy stores, like Macy's, Prada, Gucci, and all those bullshit brands, right? And then I worked my magic. There's people there, bro, who you woulda never believed how much money they got in their banks. More money than me and you coulda ever dreamed of. People who don't even realize when a couple hundred dollars goes missing. I almost couldn't believe that those people even existed. So those was the people I would target. The rich people, not the poor people. They wouldn't miss it, and it was safer for me. I'd only hit their account one time, and then I'd go buy a cellphone or a laptop or something like that, something that I could easily sell for cash on the streets, and then I'd ditch the account. Then rinse and repeat, you feel me?

But still, bro, after a while, living like that, it gets to you. You start thinking bout being caught and going to jail. You don't feel good about yourself, you feel ashamed, and so I said, "Axel, I don't know how it's gonna happen, player, but things gotta change."

I moved around between Long Island and Queens and Brooklyn and the Bronx tryna hustle up work. I was washing dishes at a Mexican restaurant, but that wouldn't pay the bills. So I'd go mop floors in an office. Still wouldn't pay the bills. For a while, I was working construction and living in the back of a trailer with another worker, a Puerto Rican guy from the Bronx, just to save on rent. But guess what? That still ain't paying the bills. And what you don't understand is that, once you're illegal, it's like other illegal things is attracted to you. You're illegal, and you're working with lots of other illegal people, and then, like, all these other kinds of strange things start popping up. And strange people. Strange people offering you money to do things that ain't exactly illegal but maybe don't feel fully legal either. Deliver this package for me and I'll give you fifty bucks no questions asked kinda jobs. And you never know what's in the box. Maybe it's just important documents, or a present for the guy's daughter, or maybe it's drugs or a gun or a chopped off head. But you gotta do it, you gotta hustle on the side, cause otherwise you ain't got no money. You feel me?

But one day things changed. I applied for a job, like a legit job, to be a software engineer at a company. Now I had applied to jobs like this a whole buncha times in the past, right, and usually they'd just deny me on the spot when I couldn't produce a social security number. But this time was different. They needed someone immediately, so they hired me first and told me just to turn in all my documents later. And, oh my god, that was my lucky break. Cause this job was for debt collection. The company called people who had credit card debt, and it tried to make them pay up, right?

Well, that was perfect for me, cause all of a sudden I had access to all these debtors' files. Like, I didn't have direct access, but I quickly figured out how to hack into parts of the system that I wasn't supposed to have access to. I had names, dates of birth, social security numbers, driver's licenses, everything. And so I started to pull information from people that sorta looked, like, kinda similar to me, but they were born in the US, right? Like an American Axel. And that's how I played the system for a while. I'd find an identity and pretend to be the American Axel for like six months. Then I'd quit that job, get another identity, and then apply to work somewhere else. That way there was less chance of getting caught. I figured it benefitted both of us, me and the American Axel, even if he never knew nothing bout the arrangement. Cause I could work and get paid, and with every paycheck I got, a certain percentage was automatically taken out to pay back his debt. Garnished wages, you know what I'm saying? So he was getting out of debt and I was getting rent money.

But eventually I stopped doing that too. Security at these debt collection companies was getting tighter, and I was worried I was gonna get caught. And there ain't no way that you can explain that assuming someone else's identity coulda actually been helping them, you feel me?

So I stopped. But I still kept hacking. I had this badass computer that I built back in Port Washington. Half of it was just from stuff I dug outta the trash. When I had some free time, I would get on there and hack for fun. It was just to mess around. Not to hurt nobody or take nothing. Just to see if I could still do it, just to see if I could get inside someone else's system. And you woulda never believed how many other people are out there, in the shadows and the dark. So many people you woulda never seen unless you know where to look. And once you find them, once they understand that you see them, they disappear again.

CHAPTER 16

THE AUTO SHOP

IT WAS SURPRISINGLY easy to get into Don Armando's shop. In fact, he invited me himself.

"Screw it," I said to Axel, after a night of concocting wild strategies over the phone, each breakout scenario more elaborate and fantastical than the last. "I'm just going to call him."

"Please, Levi, come," Don Armando said, and his voice sounded genuinely hospitable, as if he were trying to convince an old friend to visit. "Anyone who's been a guest of Father Solalinde's is a guest of mine."

"Do you think it's some kind of trap?" I asked Axel afterward.

"Dude, you ain't gonna believe this, but I think he's actually convinced himself that he's legit doing us a favor. Plus, he loves the idea of a white guy from the States showing up. He probably thinks he can get money outta you."

"So he's crazy."

"Totally batshit, my brother."

I arranged to meet Don Armando in la Doctores, a Mexico City neighborhood filled with mechanics shops. I found him in an oily garage that simply advertised "Used Car Parts." Don Armando shook my hand, purchased several unidentifiable cylinders with cash, and then walked me to his car, a vintage VW Beetle with chipping paint. He didn't stop talking the entire drive to Metepec. The topic of conversation, I learned quickly, was always himself. He claimed to have worked as a bodyguard in his youth and to have protected some very important people, including several Mexican senators, some of whom helped him bypass the normal immigration bureaucracy. He said that he and Father Solalinde had been childhood friends, and that the priest still sent him dozens of migrants to take care of every year. If that was true, I thought, then it meant that Hermanos en el Camino—supposedly one of the most prestigious humanitarian organizations in all of Latin America—was shuttling incredibly vulnerable people through Mexico with essentially no supervision and then declining to follow up on where they were or how they were faring.

Eventually, Don Armando's recitation of his resume was interrupted by a phone call. It was his son, Armando Jr., who sounded frantic. Immigration was outside of the garage, claiming that someone had called in an anonymous tip that it was a human trafficking front. They were demanding to take a look around.

"Absolutely not," barked Don Armando. "Keep those fuckers out until I get there. And tell the migrants to stay out of sight."

He gunned the engine, weaving in and out of traffic on the highway. I searched in vain for something to grasp onto, but everything in the car looked like it would break off at the slightest touch. Fortunately, minutes later, Armando Jr. called back to say the situation was under control. He'd told immigration that he wasn't unlocking the door until his father got home, and, sensing a stalemate, the agents left.

"Those sons of bitches," Don Armando crowed. "Always trying to pull a fast one over on me. But it never works."

It was dark by the time we arrived at his house. Don Armando invited me inside for a Coke, which I didn't particularly want, since Axel was finally just a few blocks away, but I accepted because I sensed that one did not tell Don Armando no without suffering some kind of future retribution. He escorted me upstairs to his study, which was packed floor to ceiling with large donation boxes labeled with phrases like "men's clothes" or "canned goods" or "electronics."

A woman burst into the study. "These bastards," she seethed. "Pardon my language, darling, I do believe in God, but we've sacrificed our whole lives for these migrants and look at what it's gotten us." The woman had one of the most grating voices I'd ever heard in my life, like teeth scraped across a chalkboard. Don Armando didn't introduce us, so I assumed that she was his wife, Doña Vilchis.

Minutes later, a young man burst through the door. "These bastards," he hollered. "They were crawling all over the outside of the shop. But I kept them out. Tell him, mom." Armando Jr. He was stocky and had dark hair, and everything he said, he said with a smirk, as if even he didn't quite believe it. We were approximately the same age, and it was soon clear that he hoped to be my friend.

"I think it was the neighbor," said Armando Jr. He quickly recounted how a man who lived a few doors down—"a xenophobe," sighed Don Armando—had come around last week, threatening to call the cops because of the people living in the shop.

"Are you sure you want to go in there, dear?" Doña Vilchis asked me. "I wouldn't want you in the shop if immigration came back. Plus, these migrants aren't normal. They can be dangerous. You could stay with Armando Jr. instead."

Armando Jr. nodded eagerly. I thanked them both but insisted that my anthropological research required that I live with the people I worked with, even if the circumstances were less than ideal.

"What an absurd idea," mused Doña Vilchis.

"Of course you think it's absurd," said Don Armando, standing from his desk. "You couldn't last a minute without your nice, comfy mattress. But I'm the same as you, Levi. We are men of the people. Whenever I go to Hermanos, they try to give me a bed, but I insist on sleeping on the ground with the migrants."

Don Armando escorted me a couple blocks down the dimly lit neighborhood street, until we reached an old garage on the corner. He unlocked the gate and slid it ever so slightly ajar, so that I only had enough room to squeeze through. Once I was on the other side, he pulled it closed again.

"Wait," I said, "are you locking me in too?"

"Of course," he said with an apologetic smile. "After immigration showed up today, you can't be too careful. And besides, if I don't, the migrants will get out and run all over the street. You understand, I'm sure." Then he turned and strolled back toward his house, whistling as he went.

The garage was black and packed with cars. An unmistakable bald head popped out from the shadows. "Waddup, my brother."

Axel and Lalo showed me around. The shop was bifurcated by a cinder block wall. The front half was the portion the customers saw. It was slightly more orderly, and Axel said that migrants were only allowed in it during working hours. The back, which was obscured, was where they lived. It was just as crammed with cars, many of which looked like they'd been rusting in the same spot for decades. Between the heaps of junk were also a small color television and a greasy two-burner cooktop with a single pan.

"That's where Don Armando's wife brings the slop for her little piggies," said Axel.

In the bottom of the pan were a few remaining scraps from that night's dinner. I grimaced. "Is that canned corn and tuna fish?"

It was even worse than I'd imagined. I asked if now was a good time to tell everyone about our plans to break out, but Axel shook his head no and gestured almost imperceptibly toward a man sitting in the gloom of the shop. He had white hair and wore a cowboy hat. The man wasn't a migrant, said Axel, but a homeless, alcoholic Mexican. Don Armando had allowed him to sleep in the garage for as long as anyone could remember. "And in return he snitches about anything fishy going down. Who's not working, who's talking shit, things like that." The man's name was Ernesto.

I heard the gate in the front of the shop slide open and closed again. Axel held a finger to his lips and pointed over my shoulder to a thin two-story building that abutted the front of the auto shop. A light turned on in a second story window. "That's where Armando Jr. lives. If we make too much noise at night, he bitches at us."

A bitingly cold drizzle began to fall, so we retreated to Axel and Lalo's van. We whispered for a while longer about the likelihood of immigration returning—perhaps in a few days, when they'd had a chance to regroup, or even in the middle of the night, to catch us unawares—and then, faced with the impenetrable uncertainty of that great fear, we fell quiet. I could tell that Axel had fallen asleep by the soft noises he made under his pile of dirty blankets. But I couldn't decipher what language he was speaking. He mumbled something that might have been "pizza" in English, or "pisa" in Spanish. He said "Asia" or "hacia." "Floor" or "flor."

I became stuck in a shallow kind of dream loop, neither quite awake nor asleep, in which the gates to the shop were suddenly battered open and swarms of immigration agents—dressed just like the SWAT team in Hermanos—poured inside. Twice I leapt up, swung open the van's heavy door, and stumbled barefoot onto the icy concrete floor of the shop before the fog of the dream faded away and I was left standing in an eerie and silent blackness. I wondered if nightmares were contagious, if somehow Axel's dreams had slipped out of his head and into mine, or vice versa. Then Axel would murmur to please close the door, that it was freezing outside, and I would clamber into the van and drift back into the visions of men coming to kidnap us from a man who already had.

AFTER THE NEAR miss with immigration, Don Armando ran the place like a prison camp. Everyone was to be working at all times.

This included me as well. My first morning in the shop, Don Armando laid out the used parts I saw him purchase in Mexico City and instructed me to help another man install them in a Volkswagen Jetta. I laughed. I'd never worked on a car in my life, I said.

But Don Armando was not joking. "Everyone works here," he said sternly. "Everyone."

Though the garage didn't seem to be a particularly bustling enterprise, with our slave labor Don Armando was likely doing pretty well for himself. But you wouldn't know it from the way he and his wife complained. Doña Vilchis—who all the migrants simply referred to as "la Chimoltrufia," the name of an infamously obnoxious television character in Mexico with a similarly horrid voice, and which has no English equivalent but is approximated by "the Shrew"—would arrive every morning at the stroke of six and begin banging on the windows of the cars. Her antics were so theatrically evil as to be nearly beyond belief.

"Get up you miscreants," she'd squawk. "You lazy, ungrateful, money-grubbing slackers."

Then I'd roll out of bed, my hair a mess, and she'd chirp, her voice sickly sweet, "Oh good morning, darling. Did you sleep well? Here, I've brought you some coffee from the house."

The Shrew had a particular contempt for Axel. She almost never called him by his name, instead referring to him as "el negro" or "el negrito."

"Darling, I just don't understand why you choose to sleep with el negrito here," she'd say. "You have to be careful. I wouldn't leave anything valuable around him, that's for sure."

At first, I chalked it up to a base racism latent in all that she did. Which, of course, it was. But then I noticed that the Shrew never called me by my name either. It was always darling this and darling that. The reason became apparent when, one day, she absentmindedly called me "Axel." "I can't remember any of these strange names," she huffed after I corrected her. From then on, we were exclusively "negrito" and "darling."

My hope was that the longer I stayed, the more the cracks in Don Armando's security would begin to appear. There were times, for instance, that initially seemed opportune for a getaway, such as when Don Armando had to unlock the gates to pull cars in and out of the shop. But the problem was that we couldn't flee without being seen. And though there was still some lingering worry about an immigration raid, the Vilchis family was not shy about switching teams if they got so much as a whiff of rebellion.

"Don't even think about trying to leave," Armando Jr. had said not long after Axel and Lalo arrived. "Immigration is everywhere, and all it will take is one call from me or my dad and they'll catch you."

Another reason everyone continued to live in the shop was that there was, at least initially, a real hope Don Armando could land them humanitarian visas. Under the Program, asylum requests in Mexico had skyrocketed, and migrants sometimes had to wait years before receiving a verdict. Don Armando thrived where this bureaucracy failed, and he managed to carve out a small but lucrative kingdom by branding himself as one of the few individuals who supposedly understood how to grease the gears of an otherwise malfunctioning immigration machinery—which official to bribe or which sympathetic politician to appeal to when one's application hit a snag. Wherever things broke down, Don Armando saw an opportunity, and his mechanic's shop was just as much a space to fix visas as it was to fix cars. But in order to have Don Armando advocate on your behalf, you needed to please him. For Axel, that meant hacking day after day.

"You're not gonna believe this," he said as he climbed into the van late one night. "This dude just made me hack the freaking Attorney."

Don Armando wanted Axel to hack the Attorney in order to investigate her finances, basically to see if she was pulling the same scam he was. The most lucrative aspect of Axel's hacks, for instance, lay in finding how much money certain politicians had available at the moment—whether through government funding or campaign fundraisers—and then hitting up the ones flush with cash. And Don Armando did not want competition. He also wanted Axel to spy on the Attorney's correspondence with Solalinde, to see if she was successfully ingratiating herself with the priest, and he did not like what he saw. The Attorney and Solalinde corresponded frequently. Migrants who might have once been sent to Don Armando—like the Honduran couple I met in Polanco—were now being sent to her. She was cutting into his business.

"This fucking bitch," Don Armando muttered to himself when Axel showed him her messages with the priest, "needs to know her place."

While Axel was busy spying for Don Armando, I was preoccupied with another spy—Ernesto. The snitch was a complication I hadn't anticipated. With him always lurking around the shop, there was no way to openly organize the breakout. Instead, Axel and I would invite one or two people to meet us in the yellow van and feel them out. The first person we talked to was Memo, the migrant Axel had met in Hermanos, who had arrived at the auto shop around the same time as Axel and Lalo. Memo was Honduran, approximately twenty-five years old, and had been waiting on a humanitarian visa for months. He'd asked Hermanos to transfer him to Don Armando himself after hearing that the mechanic could supposedly speed up the process. But the visa still hadn't come, and Memo was getting restless. When we told him that we wanted to escape, he—much to our confusion—hopped out of the van and disappeared, only to return momentarily with a small backpack.

"Let's go," he said. "I'm ready." He'd been keeping a getaway bag for just such an occasion, and he was disappointed when we clarified that we didn't intend to break out that very second.

In the end, tired of waiting around for visas that never seemed to come, about ten other people said that they wanted to leave

Don Armando's auto shop with us. We just had to wait for the right opportunity to present itself.

IN THE EVENINGS, after filling our styrofoam bowls with gruel, Lalo or Memo would fiddle with the antenna of the television until a grainy fútbol match appeared on the screen. Axel never watched soccer. Instead, he'd squeeze himself between one car or another and text on his phone.

"Who you talking to?" I asked one night.

"Oh, just my moms."

I felt my stomach knot. "You know, I was texting with her recently, and she said something." I could see Axel's muscles tense, but he kept his eyes on his phone.

"Yeah?"

"Yeah. She said your kids were back in Guatemala."

He stared at the ground for a long time. Then he said that I was right, that his ex and his kids weren't in the US anymore. He said that up until a couple weeks ago, he really had believed that they were in the States. He hadn't spoken to Monica in almost a month. He couldn't get through—no texts, calls, nothing. When she finally responded, she was short. "She said she took my babies back to Guatemala, and not to contact her anymore. That was it."

At some point, Monica had found another man to support her children, just like she promised she would if Axel didn't come home. Axel knew the man, he said. He was Guatemalan and had a visa to travel back and forth to the US, just like Monica. Apparently, he'd convinced her to return to Guatemala City, where they could live rent-free in a big house that his family owned. Monica told Axel not to come looking for her. She said she'd moved on, and that his children were someone else's now.

I tried to watch Axel's movements, to analyze the cadence and delivery of his words. He seemed genuinely distraught, but was that because his children had been ripped from his grasp or because the white guy dumb enough to give him money had finally figured out the grift?

"You can see," I said, "how from my perspective this story is a little hard to swallow, right? That the very moment I find out that your kids actually aren't in the US, you have the perfect excuse about why that is?"

Axel froze for a moment, and I realized that my words had come out more callous than I'd intended. His eyes started to tear up.

"You gotta believe me, brother." His voice cracked. "I didn't know. I swear to god I didn't know nothing."

"I saw those pictures on your old account, you know. Ruffrider Quest. And it didn't look like your kids were in New York. It looked like they were in Guatemala."

Axel's face darkened. "Man, just cause I didn't tell you, that don't make it less true. My kids was my whole life. The only reason you know about any of this is cause the second I found out that they was in Guatemala, I told my moms to take that money and send it to them, not me. And now I gotta figure out if I should still try to get back to the States, or if I should just say fuck it and bounce to Guatemala. I don't know what to do, bro." He wilted to the ground and wrapped his arms around his knees. His body was quivering. "But whatever, man, this ain't your problem. If you wanna leave, just leave. Nothing's keeping you here."

I blew air into my cold hands and tried to think. It was too much information to process. I was angry, but angry at what exactly? At Axel? But what if he wasn't lying, as unlikely as that seemed? Was I angry at myself for trusting him? Or was I angry for doubting him, a guy with no family and no friends? It felt cruel to hold him up to the light like this.

"Maybe this is selfish of me," I said, standing above him, "but I don't think you should go back." If it really was true, I reasoned, if Monica really did tell him to stay away, then there wasn't much he could do. Even if he managed to find them in a city of a million people, then what? Get in a fight with the boyfriend? Kidnap the children? How would he raise them, where would they go?

"I know man, but sometimes, being stuck here, I just go nuts."

"Look, just stay here for now. If it's money she wants, then going back to Guatemala isn't going to solve anything."

"I don't think you understand, bro. Every time I start to think about it, I lose my fucking mind."

"You'll be just as broke in Guatemala as you are in Mexico."

"Sometimes I think I'm actually going crazy for real."

"But if we can get you back to the States, and you can make money again, then Monica will get back in touch."

"Do you think I'm a bad dad?"

"What? No, man, no. I don't think that."

"Well I'm starting think it. My kids are so little, they ain't even gonna remember my name, man. Not even my name."

THINGS WITH DON Armando were becoming complicated. "What are you writing in that notebook all the time?" he asked one afternoon.

"Oh, you know," I replied, trying to sound vague and uninteresting, "we anthropologists are always taking notes. Most of it doesn't make much sense, really, even to me."

Don Armando grunted and turned back to the computer. After a bit, he asked if I'd mind picking up some hamburgers down the street for lunch. I thought letting me out of the shop was a sign of trust, but when I returned, my backpack was open. Nothing was missing, but some of the pages of my notebook were ever so lightly smudged with grease, as if someone with dirty hands had quickly riffled through its contents.

That night, Don Armando didn't bring any dinner.

"He can't honestly expect us to go to bed without eating again," I said.

Memo shrugged.

"No way." I tested the chains wrapped around the gate on the side of the shop. "I can definitely squeeze through here. I'm getting us some food."

"Wait up, bro," said Axel, following behind me. "If you go, I go."

I searched for a late-night spot on my phone and found a Little Caesars. We walked with our heads down and stuck to the shadows in case immigration happened to roll by. But other than a few passing cars, there was no one else out at such a late hour. Eventually the buildings dwindled and a flat expanse opened up on either side of the road—farmland that was slowly being paved into industrial sprawl. In the stillness we could hear what sounded like thousands of frogs, which filled the empty plains with a throaty moan. The Little Caesars shone like a beacon in the distance, a bright new building in the middle of the nowhere. I paid for six pizzas and we waited in the lobby, which was filled with the familiar, borderless scent of stale butter. Axel was strangely quiet.

"Something wrong?" I asked.

"It's just, I ain't been in a Little Caesars since New York." He shook his head, and I could see that his eyes were wet. "Ah shit, bro, I'm crying like a bitch. But it feels like home, almost like I'm back, just hanging out with a friend."

We took the pizzas outside and sat on the curb. I opened one of the boxes and handed Axel a slice. Then I fished another out for myself and held it aloft until Axel touched his slice to mine, like a toast. "To real New York pizza," I said.

I watched him as he chewed and paced along the road. Every once in a while, a car would drive by, and its headlights would backlight Axel's wiry body, coiled like a delicate spring, a ballet dancer trapped inside a wind-up music box. The wind from the traffic caught at his oversized jacket, which flapped loosely around his thin frame, and it was like I'd never seen anyone so beautiful and haunting in my life. Somehow, in that desolate urban periphery, I glimpsed the overwhelming forces that Axel and I had found ourselves up against. Incessant specters that exceeded all names were there with us in the monstrous night, and I knew that Axel and I would not beat them on our own. But we could still face them together, no matter my uncertainties about his past or my fears about what I might learn in the future. So that's what I decided to do. Then we walked silently back to the shop and passed out the pizza to much fanfare, and everyone ate until they were full.

We thought about hiding the pizza boxes the next morning, but we all agreed that it would be good for Don Armando to see them, especially since Ernesto was almost certainly going to snitch on us anyway, even though he'd also partaken. My hope was that Don Armando would feel ashamed that I had to feed everyone, and that he'd start bringing more food, which turned out to be an incredibly stupid thing to hope.

"What's this?" he said, pointing to the stack of orange cardboard.

"Pizza," I said, crossing my arms.

Don Armando's eyes flashed. "You left the shop?"

"I was hungry. You didn't give us any dinner."

"I told you they're not allowed to leave the shop. Immigration is out to get me."

"They didn't leave," I said. "I left on my own. What? Is that not allowed either?"

Don Armando's gaze bore into me. "Well, it looks like you all ate well last night. I'm guessing you're still too full for breakfast." He turned and walked into his office. From then on, the mechanic was much colder with me, and our interactions became an intense set of social negotiations, in which all manner of insipid and terse cordialities were exchanged, but beneath the pretense it felt as if we were circling each other, probing, feeling for points of weakness.

It was time to finalize an exit strategy.

THE OPPORTUNITY TO escape presented itself in the strangest of ways. Whatever animosity Don Armando might have been fostering against me, Armando Jr. had not received the memo. Nearly every night he sidled down from his lofty perch in the apartment and invited me up for a drink. Maybe he could ask some ladies to join us if I was into that kind of thing. I would politely decline. No rest for the weary anthropologist and all that. Armando Jr. would shrug and slide the door of the van closed again. But it got me thinking. Armando Jr. showed an interest in me because I was essentially a new toy, a shiny American trinket to show off to his friends, who were a small posse of party boys with matching gelled hair and gold chains. At night electronic music would thump from his apartment, and occasionally dark shapes of girls in tight polyester dresses would glide past the windows. Perhaps, I thought, it was time to accept his invitation.

The next time Armando Jr. invited me up to his place, I stalled. I'd love to come, I said, but I was just too dirty at the moment. I didn't have any nice clothes. What if he gave me a few days to go to Mexico City, freshen up, and then return for the rager of a lifetime? Armando Jr. was thrilled. After we set a date, Axel and I called the Attorney and informed her of the impending breakout. No matter how difficult it was, we needed her to find housing. There was no point in everyone escaping only to be homeless in Mexico City. The Attorney started to protest, but we cut her off. We weren't asking anymore. Life in the shop had become untenable and we were leaving. She had no choice but to reluctantly agree, and we had no choice but to hope that she would actually follow through.

Finally, when an apartment was secured and Axel and the other migrants were ready, I would return to the auto shop well dressed and clean shaven, and get Armando Jr. as inebriated as possible, as quickly as possible. Then, sometime before the last bus left the station, I'd find a way to steal his keys, unlock the gate, and we'd all make a break for it while he was still seeing double.

Axel and the rest of the gang, however, would have to survive Don Armando's wrath until I returned.

MY LAST NIGHT in the shop, Axel and I lay awake in the soft glow of our cell phones, listening to the sound of rain tap gently against the van.

"I'm going to get you out of here," I said, "but you have to promise me something."

"My brother, you already know that one day I'm gonna pay you back all the money I owe you."

"No dude, don't be ridiculous. That's not what I'm talking about." I took a deep breath. "Listen, I still don't know what to think about your kids being in Guatemala. But, really, whether you've been telling me the truth or not doesn't matter right now. What matters is that you won't go back to look for them."

I could see Axel's neck tense. "What the fuck, Levi."

"I know how it sounds, but I need you to promise me. Look man, you're not even recognized as a citizen. And a couple months ago a gang member there threatened to kill you. Remember that?"

"Levi, if you was a father, you wouldn't never of asked me something as horrible as that."

The van was silent for a while, except for the sound of Lalo's faint snoring. I thought about Axel's children. I thought about meeting them one day, many years later, after they'd grown up without their father, and explaining what I'd asked of him, what I'd decided for them without their knowledge or permission.

"Do you think you're gonna miss it?" asked Axel suddenly, his voice soft and low.

"Miss what?"

"Mexico."

"Yeah I suppose so. I will miss some things." I gestured toward the leaking roof. "I won't miss this, though."

"The thing is, bro, if I was you, and I had all the benefits that you have, I think I could miss this country."

"Will you miss it?"

"Me miss Mexico? Hells fucking no. But I'll tell you one thing. This is gonna be the last time I do this shit. The last fucking time. I'm too old, Levi. My body can't handle this no more. So the next time I cross the border, that's gonna be it."

I didn't want to ask what it would mean, then, if he got caught.

"But that's good that you think you'll miss it," he continued, and his voice sounded sleepy. "It's good to wanna miss things. Instead of wanting to not miss them."

Then he pulled a blanket over his head, and the van was quiet, and the wind blew the rain over the mountain range and across the valley, just like it had for eons, long before the idea of Mexico existed. I didn't think Axel was really asking if I was going to miss Mexico. I think he was asking, in his own way, if I was going to miss him.

"I'm sorry dude, but I need you to promise."

"Fine, Levi."

"You won't go back?"

"I won't go back."

CHAPTER 17

THE BREAKOUT

I BEEN THINKING, Levi. About the truth and all the things I told you bout myself. For starters, my real name ain't Axel Kirschner. Apparently, my biological dad really was a German dude, or at least that's what my mom always told me, but she never gave me his name. She didn't even know the guy's name, he raped her, how was she supposed to know anything about him, you feel me? I just thought that you was another journalist or activist or something passing through, and so I started to tell you what I told all the other journalists and activists: bullshit. You can even search for me online, and you'll find other interviews I did with some Mexican journalists that ain't true. Just these random reporters who would show up to migrant shelters for, like, a weekend and start tryna get quotes from everyone bout our suffering and our poverty and how sad it was to be a migrant. So I'd tell one guy this, and another lady that. That's what a lotta migrants do when we're traveling. Me and the Hondurans, we used to have this game, right? Whenever a journalist approached us, we used to see who coulda come up with the most ridiculous, fantastical story. Jimmy said once that he was so poor he had to eat his own dog. And Meme used to tell everyone that he was hired to kill Miss Honduras, and that he had buried her body in the jungle himself. Actually, now that I think about it, I never did hear Meme tell that story to journalists, only to other migrants. He always swore that story was true. But, I mean, I traveled with Meme.

I trusted that dumbass to watch my back. So it couldn't be true. He couldn't really be a killer, could he?

Then again, I dunno, maybe he could. Cause that's what I'm tryna explain. You just don't know with people. Or yourself. You kinda get used to telling these stories. Maybe you tell it to a journalist or whoever first, but later on you gotta tell it to Don Armando or another activist, and of course all the migrants in the shelter hear it too. And then suddenly you become the thing you made up. The guy who ate his dog. The guy who went to London for a field trip. All the confusing stories is kinda like protection. It's harder for people to know who you really is, and that way they can't hurt you as easy.

But, at the same time, Levi, I need you to stop fact-checking me every single second, you feel me? Sometimes you just gotta shut the fuck up and trust me. Honestly man, like, your questions can start making me even question myself. Cause sometimes the lies ain't exactly lies either. For instance, when you grow up in a family that don't never celebrate your birthday, it's hard to remember if something happened when you was fifteen or eighteen. And if your moms was always tryna hide stuff from you, bout where you was from, or who was your real dad, or what she had to do for work, you wouldn't always know what was actually the truth in the first place. My whole life I ain't been able to tell people what I really am, that I don't got documents. So I had to make up, like, entire histories about myself that ain't exactly true. Cause when people at school or on the job ask you about yourself, sometimes you know you gotta tell them something, so you just answer. You say the first thing that pops into your brain, right? And then you repeat it. And that answer ain't true, but it's true as you can make it. You know what I'm saying?

But it gets even crazier, cause it ain't like I just wanted to tell you the truth but didn't know how. It's like sometimes the lies can actually be more real. Not in a stupid way, like something a poet would say, no offense, but like in a real way. Like me telling you that I got an associate's degree was a lie, but only cause that's what I woulda really done if I was allowed to get an associate's degree, you feel me? Like I coulda lied to you about anything, told you all kinds of crazy shit, but instead I lied about the person I wished I was. Someone who coulda traveled and got an education and been a good dad. The person I ain't allowed to be. And it's like, maybe if you believe that lie, I—a person who ain't never been nothing to nobody—can kinda become that thing you think I am, you know what I'm saying?

BEING BACK IN Mexico City felt like a dream. Atlee and I spent our days in public museums and quaint cafés, places that suddenly put me on edge in ways that I couldn't quite comprehend. In the evenings, we attended social functions with other Fulbright scholars. A party was thrown on the top floor of a high rise in la Condesa. It had a rooftop pool that no one swam in. The host, whose whole identity seemed to be that he had graduated from Harvard, introduced us to his wealthy Mexican friends. Some worked for branches of US and European corporations. Some didn't work at all.

One of them asked what I did, and I said that I traveled with Central Americans to document the abuses and crimes that happened on the migrant trail.

"I imagine it's hard to document them all," he said with a smile, "since they commit so many."

One day Ever called to say goodbye. The Attorney had done it, he said. She landed him a humanitarian visa. But he decided Mexico City wasn't for him after all. It was still impossible to find a job as a migrant, even with a visa, so he was headed to Monterrey to live with his family. I was always welcome to visit, he said, and then we hung up.

But whatever goodwill I might have felt toward the Attorney for helping Ever was immediately dashed by her continual foot-dragging about finding an apartment. I had to postpone my rendezvous with Armando Jr. several times because she still hadn't found anything, which I sensed was her way of reminding us who was actually in charge. Whenever I asked her about potential neighborhoods—neighborhoods that I knew were cheap and full of sleazy landlords who rented to any number of marginal characters, even migrants—she wasn't able to place them on a map. It was becoming increasingly clear that most of the Attorney's life consisted of flitting from one glamorous enclave to another. Whereas Don Armando was in the activist game for the money, the Attorney was in it for the social prestige. She rarely left the insulated cloisters of wealth scattered across Mexico City and was otherwise at a loss outside the little emerald archipelagos that glittered across the concrete lakebed.

In the meantime, Don Armando was still trotting Axel from church to church and fundraiser to fundraiser, as if he was afraid to leave him alone in the shop for even a moment. When they were in the garage, the mechanic made sure that Axel spent every available second hacking. His paranoia seemed to know no bounds, and he cursed at Axel if he didn't get the information he wanted fast enough. Every activist or politician he landed a meeting with, he made sure Axel hacked. Axel was careful to take screenshots and send them to the Attorney.

Finally, I decided that there was simply no more time to waste. I dressed in the nicest clothes I had—slacks, a button-down shirt, and a pair of old leather loafers. I gelled my hair in a way that I hoped resembled the greasy locks of Armando Jr.'s posse, took one glance in the mirror, and concluded that I looked like an absolute idiot. Perfect.

On the bus ride to Metepec, I caught myself clenching and unclenching my fists. When we arrived at the station, I bought twelve one-way tickets to Mexico City, and slid them carefully into my pocket. Axel and I agreed that, after the breakout, I should board the first bus that arrived alone, in order to scout for immigration checkpoints on the way back to Mexico City. Since the Program, checkpoints occasionally materialized on the thoroughfares south of the capital to catch migrants traveling north. Once I gave the all clear, they would take the next bus.

The soles of my shoes clicked along the pavement as I wound my way through the neighborhood to Don Armando's garage. I'd timed my arrival for twilight, when the mechanic normally closed shop. He was burrowed into the innards of a van, like a rat among his trash. He spotted me from a distance and waved me over.

"Levi," he said, wiping his hands on his pants. "I was just about to lock up."

I'd been worried that, given his particularly foul outbursts with Axel as of late, Don Armando would be suspicious of my arrival. But, if anything, it seemed to put him at ease. Maybe he believed my return was a sign that Armando Jr. and I were becoming friends, and that I approved of his enterprise. I didn't see Axel anywhere.

"You're a little early," said Don Armando. "Junior is still at soccer practice."

"That's fine," I said, feigning nonchalance. "I'm in no rush."

I helped Don Armando pack up his tools. "Just wait here," he said, sliding the gate closed behind him. "Junior should be back any minute." Then he was gone.

The garage, so still and hushed just moments ago, broke into a flurry of commotion. Axel appeared from the far recesses of the shop, already changing into a wrinkled pinstripe shirt. We'd agreed that everyone should dress in the nicest clothes they could find. In the event that immigration boarded their bus, everyone would look slightly more respectable, not like migrants on the run. Memo jammed his feet into impeccably polished black loafers. Lalo tucked a collared shirt into his jeans. I suddenly felt the same sensation I'd had just before the sting operation in Hermanos, like I was in a play, each of us dressing for roles that had already been set out before us by mysterious forces. Then everyone retreated to their respective vehicles, waiting in the darkened wings for the scene to begin. The only person seemingly unmoved by the drama was Ernesto the snitch. He was glued to the television, immersed in a soccer match.

The lock to the gate clicked open. Armando Jr. stood in the entrance in a sweaty soccer jersey, his body framed by the negative space of the open gate. He spotted me and grinned from ear to ear.

"Armando," I heard myself say as we embraced. "What's up, man? You ready to party?"

We made small talk for a few minutes, me apologizing profusely for taking so long to come back, and him telling me about all the things I'd missed out on, all the crazy times I should have been there for.

"Hey, man, I'm here now," I said. "Let's get this thing started."

"Absolutely," said Armando Jr., climbing the stairs to his apartment. "Just let me shower quick." Behind him, the gate remained ajar. He'd forgotten to lock it. In a flash, I realized that I needed to keep his attention on me, to stop him from turning around and realizing his mistake.

"Dude," I said, gazing up at him and rubbing my hands together theatrically. "Did you score that coke we talked about?"

"You know it," he chuckled. My Juliet was on the balcony of the staircase now, digging into his pockets for the key. For some reason, he still hadn't invited me upstairs. It was more than I could have hoped for. The best laid plans of mice and migrants were nothing compared to luck. If Armando Jr. stepped into the shower, we could bypass the partying entirely and make a break for it right then and there.

"And the ladies?" I called up to him, my hands running over imaginary curves.

Armando Jr. loved that. "You're fucking crazy, Levi," he guffawed from his perch. "Just give me a few minutes. Then you can come up."

"No problem, man." I felt my body lean nonchalantly against the hood of the car, as if I wasn't ready to burst. "I'll be here."

The door closed. I held my breath, unable to move. Then soft light broke through the curtain of the bathroom window, and I could hear the water running.

"Now," I whispered as loudly as I dared. "Now's our chance. Go, go, go."

All of the car doors flew open. I pulled the gate slightly more ajar, until it began to squeak, and everyone hustled out single file. I glanced back at Ernesto. He still hadn't turned away from the television.

"Don't worry," said Axel, "I made sure he started drinking early today. Motherfucker's absolutely hammered outta his mind."

"I could kiss you," I said, and we sprinted down the darkening street, like two tiny revolutionaries or criminals or detectives, charging into an immense unknown.

CHAPTER 18

FREER IN MEXICO

AT THE STATION, I passed out the tickets and then boarded the first bus as planned, in order to scout for immigration checkpoints. Everyone else would have to wait another fifteen minutes out in the open before the next one arrived. If Don Armando got wind of what was going down, everything would fall to pieces.

Levi 7:37 PM all clear so far
Levi 7:41 PM oh crap blue lights ahead
Levi 7:41 PM Slowing down, don't know why
Axel 7:41 PM FUCK
Levi 7:42 PM still can't see what it is
Levi 7:43 PM completely stopped now not moving at all
Levi 7:45 PM just an accident
Levi 7:45 PM All clear
Axel 7:46 PM omfg bro
Axel 7:46 PM don't scare me like that
Levi 7:47 PM still no don armando?
Axel 7:49 PM Not yet but its creepy out here bro
Axel 7:49 PM Feel like ppl is watchin us
Axel 7:51 PM ON THE BUS BROTHER WE MADE IT PLAYA
Axel 7:51 PM !!!!!!!!!!!!!!!!!!!!!!!!!!!!!!!!!!!!!!!

There were no immigration checkpoints on the highway. When the buses pulled into Mexico City, Axel dropped to his knees and kissed the pavement. "I'm free," he yelled, as the flow of commuters parted around the man lying prostrate on the ground and came back together again. "I'm free."

THE ATTORNEY STILL hadn't located permanent lodgings for anyone. At first, a Catholic convent agreed to host the migrants for a time. The convent was a solitary, removed place where people in danger of being hunted down, usually by the government, could safely sequester themselves. One resident had checked in after being shot by immigration. He said he had a case pending against the National Institute of Migration for attempted murder. Then he lifted his shirt and instructed Axel to remove the gauze taped to his back. Below his right shoulder blade were two dark circles where the bullets had entered. They were not quite holes and not quite scabs. Just a dark flesh, or a bright absence of flesh, depending on how you looked at them, though Axel could barely stomach the sight of them at all. When the man turned or shifted his weight, the bullet holes rippled and pulled at his skin, like two minuscule planets sent off course by some unseen source of gravity.

The man asked if Axel was also hiding from the government.

No, said Axel. He was hiding from an activist.

What kind of activist?

For migrants.

Imagínate, said the man. Go figure.

Soon after, the Attorney said that Don Armando had sent men to hunt us down. How she'd received this news she didn't say.

"What, like hitmen?" Axel asked.

"Maybe," she responded, "maybe not. Maybe just to track you, to find out where you are and keep an eye on you. But, yes, maybe like hitmen." She didn't know how many of them there were or how long they'd be looking for us. In the meantime, she said, it was probably best if we stayed out of sight.

Axel and Lalo remained in the convent. I decided to skip town and take Ever up on his invitation to visit Monterrey. The city was near the Texas border, in an arenaceous stretch of land that felt like everything in sight—the buildings, the people, the landscape itself—was being gathered up into a great heap and waiting to be pulverized. Ever, Iván, and the rest of the Hernández family lived on the far outskirts of the city, literally where the last bit of development—a shoddy and derelict housing project—stared resolutely into the desert. It was housing, claimed Iván, for the Lego factory down the street, which wasn't so much a factory as a sweatshop, and—depending on how hard the workers worked or whose dick they sucked—they could purchase one of the homes from the corporation at supposedly below-market mortgage rates.

"Or," he smirked, "you can just move into one of the abandoned ones for free."

And so they had. The entire family—all nine of them—lived in an abandoned two-bedroom, one bath townhouse. The place originally had no doors, windows, kitchen, or electricity. Iván and his younger brother Marcos dragged windows and doors from the dump, knocked together a rudimentary kitchen, and figured out how to syphon juice from the electrical grid. What they hadn't realized, however, was that the pipes in the bathroom weren't hooked up properly, and shortly after they'd settled in, the toilet literally exploded. They were now in the process of moving to the townhouse next door, which they'd ensured had a well-plumbed commode.

Another teenager from the Viacrucis named Dónovan had moved in across the street. He'd followed Ever's sister Celia to Monterrey, but they broke up somewhere along the way. Now Dónovan passed his time hanging with a group of neighborhood teenagers, all of whom were poor and Mexican. Some of the teenagers were part of the youth group at the local evangelical church. Others had formed a breakdancing troupe that performed downtown for tips, which they blew on alcohol and cheap weed. Dónovan participated in both.

Ever, for his part, seemed distant. The Attorney had told him that, in theory, he would be able to work legally with his humanitarian visa, but in practice that proved to be false. Most companies had never seen a humanitarian visa before, and, wary that it was some kind of new Central American scam, were rejecting migrants wholesale. Ever had applied for and been rejected from about a dozen low-level office jobs in Monterrey, even though he'd previously held similar positions in Honduras.

"This place is suffocating me," he said one evening. We were standing in the middle of the street. Dónovan and several other teenagers circled around us on bicycles, popping wheelies and freestyle rapping. It seemed that Ever lived in a completely different world from everyone else in the neighborhood. During the day, as Iván and Marcos hauled wood and banged hammers and mixed concrete—and as I clumsily assisted as best I could—Ever usually listened to Rihanna on the stereo or cooked with his mother in the kitchen. I could tell that things were tense between the brothers. "Iván and I had a big fight a few days before you came," said Ever, nimbly sidestepping Dónovan as he swerved toward us.

"What about?" I asked.

"Oh, you know, about everything and nothing. About living here. About not finding work. About being poor."

"Better than being in the United States though," shouted one of the teenagers. He skidded to a stop beside us and looked me up and down. "You're American," he observed. "What do you think? All my uncles have been to the US, and they say that Mexico is freer."

"Freer?" I repeated.

"Yeah, they say that here in Mexico, you can drive your car however you want. You can go as fast as you want, you can run over curbs or drive drunk, and the police don't care at all."

"Hm," I said.

"And in Mexico," continued the kid, "you can be out in the streets as late as you want, just like us right now. You can hang out and smoke and have fun and nobody cares. But my uncles say that in the US, the cops will arrest you in a second for that. That's why my uncles got deported. Because they didn't understand that in the US you aren't supposed to act like you're free."

"Well, I don't feel very free here either," said Ever, rubbing his arms. "It's getting chilly. I'm going back inside."

WHILE I WAS in Monterrey, I received a call from the Attorney. Solalinde had agreed to meet with her the next day, she said. He was in Mexico City on some kind of errand. It was time to hit Don Armando where it hurt and expose all of the shady business happening in the auto shop.

"Can you come?" she asked.

I told her no, I was out of town, but that I was happy to help any way I could from afar. This did not please the Attorney. Her voice became formal and distant. She asked if I could at least send her all the evidence I gathered against Don Armando—all the copies of all the hacks he forced Axel to complete. I said that I didn't understand. I didn't have any copies of the hacks. Axel had been sending them to her all along, not to me.

This was, apparently, the wrong answer. "I don't have time for this," she snapped. "Do you understand how busy I've been, Levi, how many people I'm in communication with all the time? I can't keep track of everything Axel texts me. Listen, I'm getting another call, I've got to go. It's a shame you can't come tomorrow, Levi. You shouldn't be missing this, you know."

I was about to say that there was nothing I could do, that no one had warned me that a meeting with Solalinde was in the works, and that in fact the Attorney was the very person who said leaving Mexico City until things cooled off was a sound idea. But before I could say any of that, she hung up.

I called Axel. "Dude," I said, incredulous, "what was that all about?"

"Bro, she realized she fucked up. She looks dumb as shit for not saving all the stuff I sent her. So she's taking it out on us. She yelled at me today for the same exact thing, saying that I shoulda figured out a way to keep a backup. I wanted to be like, 'Bitch, you was the backup.'"

Axel had risked his life for months to collect evidence against Don Armando, and the Attorney had apparently lost it all.

I tried to assist as best as I could. There were still my pictures and interviews from the shop, and there were more than enough migrants hiding in the convent who could testify directly to Father Solalinde about their imprisonment. The hacking was obviously shocking, I thought, but surely enslaving people was more than enough to bring Don Armando down. I sent Axel an electronic file with everything I had and waited.

The next day, Axel called me after the meeting. "Man, you are not gonna believe this bullshit."

"What happened? Was Solalinde pissed?"

"Oh yeah, but not in the way you woulda expected. He was pissed at us."

Axel recounted the incident in full. They met Solalinde in a diner. The Attorney opened the meeting by showing the priest the various photos of the auto shop, an auto shop that was clearly not a shelter like Don Armando had promised, but a grim place, a terrible place, a place filled with angst and melancholia. She showed him my pictures of the grotesque food and the broken-down cars where people had to sleep. And, fortunately, she managed to scrounge up at least a few of the files that Axel had sent her, files that proved he was forced to hack government officials on Don Armando's behalf. Then it was Axel's turn to talk, to reaffirm everything the Attorney had already said, and to state that he was sorry, terribly sorry, Father, but Don Armando had even forced him to hack the priest as well, to spy on his private correspondence.

Axel said that Father Solalinde sat through the whole presentation, listening to each testimony unblinkingly as the waitresses moseyed past to refill cups of coffee. Then, when everyone had said their piece, the priest cleared his throat.

"I don't want to hear another word," Axel said that the priest whispered. "You don't understand how delicate this situation is. So make it disappear, or I will."

Then Solalinde folded up his napkin, excused himself, and walked out the door.

Several weeks later, Solalinde asked the Attorney to meet him in another diner. This time no migrants were invited. When she showed up, Solalinde, Beto, Don Armando, and a Mexican politician—who the Attorney believed was related to the mechanic—were waiting for her. The Attorney refused to reveal exactly what was said in that meeting, but afterward, she told us to forget any remaining notions we had about exposing Don Armando.

If there was any upside to Solalinde quashing the Attorney's revolt, it was that the mechanic apparently no longer felt threatened, and the Attorney said that he called off the men who were searching for us. With the immediate danger now past, the convent asked everyone to move out. The Attorney eventually agreed to pay the rent for an apartment in Copilco, a working-class neighborhood not far from UNAM, Mexico's most prestigious university. The apartment had two bedrooms and was on the third floor of a family home. On one of the kitchen walls, in fading black marker, the lyrics to "Happy Birthday" were scrawled in Korean. The landlord couldn't remember how it had gotten there.

I helped Axel hang a cheap Diego Rivera print next to it. The painting was untitled. Just two small nameless girls, bent beneath a mountain of calla lilies.

The landlady, who lived on the bottom two floors with her adult son, turned out to be the local bruja. People from around the neighborhood came when they wanted to cure an illness or cast a spell. Her inner sanctum was on the second floor, directly beneath Axel's bedroom, and he could hear her sacrificing chickens late into the night in front of an altar, the centerpiece of which was a life-size statue of Santa Muerte. Her son, who readily admitted to Axel that he was in hiding, had become an early convert after running with some narcos in Sinaloa.

"I escaped the cartel," he told Axel, while rolling up his shirt sleeve to reveal a skull that glared from underneath a black shawl. "But I still believe in la Santa."

"What happens if the cartel finds out you're here?" Axel asked.

"Oh, they'll probably kill everyone in the house," said the son casually.

After the breakout, most of the migrants didn't stick around. Soon, only Axel, Lalo, and Memo remained in the apartment. The Attorney quickly replaced the vacancies with four teenage minors from El Salvador. Father Solalinde sent them. They'd been living in Hermanos en el Camino, and the priest almost granted them to Don Armando, "but instead he called me," the Attorney said. It seemed that her silence was paying off.

As my days in Mexico dwindled, Axel and I discussed our limited options. I was moving to Washington, DC, with Atlee to be closer to her family. Axel would stay in Mexico City for the time being, where he at least had stable shelter and could hopefully land the odd job while waiting for his papers to come through. The Attorney had promised to take over the humanitarian visa applications for Axel and Lalo, along with the other four teenagers. Axel and I would work on either side of the border until we could afford a coyote. It was a kind of mutual purgatory, a previously agreed upon limbo, but also the most practical strategy. Given Axel's five-year ban from the US, the next logical step was simply to wait.

"You ever lived in DC before?" Axel asked.

"No," I said. "Have you?"

"Yeah. I kicked it there for a minute once."

"Did you like it?"

"Not really," was all he said. "I got too much New York in me."

I'd begun to notice a decline in Axel's demeanor. Our return to Mexico City hadn't been the liberating remedy I'd hoped it would be. In fact, Axel seemed more forlorn and on edge than ever. He jumped at every little sound in the street and, when safely back inside, stared off in contemplative silence for long stretches of time.

One night, Axel called me in a panic. "Bro, you gotta get down here quick. I dunno what the fuck is going on, but we bout to lose our goddamn minds."

"Calm down, dude, just tell me what's happening."

"All these freaking freaks out here is worshipping death itself."

Neither Axel, nor any of the five teenage boys he was now in charge of, had ever heard of Day of the Dead. That evening, they stepped outside for tacos and, as if in a nightmare, were surrounded by ghastly, skeletal figures. They promptly barricaded themselves in their apartment, certain they were now at the center of the apocalypse. With the phone on speaker, I tried to explain that they weren't in danger. Día de los Muertos was mostly a southern Mexican tradition, and for many in Mexico City the holiday was more about having a big party than anything else. "After everything you've been through, this is what scares you?" I laughed. "Just go have fun."

"Nope nope nope," came the immediate refusal. "Axel don't fuck with that death shit."

Axel's unwillingness to leave the apartment gave me an ominous feeling. Whenever we were apart I was overcome by an alien solitude, and yet now, in our last days together, I felt the same.

The quick-witted, sharp-tongued migrant I'd first met in Cha-huites had lost some of his spark, and no matter what I did, I couldn't seem to reignite it. There was no one else who could help Axel—no therapist or friends or government officials we could call. We were alone.

My last night in Mexico, the Attorney invited me out to eat with Axel and the boys, who followed him around almost as if he were their father or a schoolteacher leading them on an explor-atory field trip. We ate dinner in a shabby restaurant and discussed the Attorney's latest crusade. A woman named Nestora Salgado, she said between bites of queso fundido, was being held in a fed-eral prison in Mexico City. She was a freedom fighter, a guerrilla who had led an uprising against the cartels and corrupt officials in the state of Guerrero. But the federal government didn't like that one bit, said the Attorney, so they arrested Nestora. The Attorney was working on her release. She regularly visited Nestora in prison and also drove to Guerrero to meet with her family, to bring them supplies and news from the capitol. The Attorney said that, actu-ally, she was headed back to Guerrero in a few weeks, and could use a chauffeur, since driving long distances didn't suit her. Maybe she'd bring Axel along.

PACKING UP THE apartment didn't take long. What little furniture Atlee and I had—a table, two chairs, a microwave, a couch—went to Axel. Then it was time to go. Axel and Lalo accompanied us to the airport. The drive was quiet. The city was gray and contempla-tive. Apartment buildings loomed over the highway, their facades covered in the soot of never-ending traffic. It began to rain. The downpour warped the view from the taxi windows, and, for a moment, with the apartments stacked on top of one another, they looked like Aztec pyramids. I peered up at their peaks and imag-ined the rooftop maids' quarters were sacrificial sanctums where victims were still killed and discarded in the name of prosperity.

We parked at the airport terminal and pulled our suitcases from the trunk. I paid the driver double and asked him to take Axel and Lalo back to Copilco. Then we hugged. Axel's arms felt weak around me, thin and frail.

"I love you, bro," he said.

"I love you too."

"Don't you forget about this old thundercat."

Then I was on the plane, and the plane was in the sky, and Mexico was gone.

PART III
THE ATTORNEY

CHAPTER 19

THE MARTIAN

I ENDED UP in DC *when I was like sixteen or seventeen or something. I had got kicked outta the house again. Plus, the school was hassling me every single day. Saying I was always late, that I was missing too much class, and that they was gonna expel me. And I never coulda explained to them that I was absent cause I was sleeping in the park, cause I was hungry, cause my step-pops was beating me up again. Cause if I did, then Schreiber High probably woulda called child protective services, and I wasn't tryna get everybody deported. So instead I decided, hey, DC is the capital of this country, and I hear there's a lotta Central Americans there. Let's leave these New York problems behind and go see what's popping down south, you feel me?*

It was the first time I was outside of New York on my own, and, looking out the train window, everything seemed so big and open and possible. I got off the train at Union Station and went straight to the air and space museum. It felt like the rockets there was speaking to me. I always loved space. If they ever want a volunteer for Mars, blast me up baby. Get me off this planet. I was ready for a new one, even back then. I stayed at the museum until it closed, just staring up at the rockets, and then I was out on the streets again. I had the same problem as always: I didn't have no money. So I figured I'd do what I always did, which was to walk for as long as I could, walk all through the night, and then when I couldn't walk no more I'd find a quiet park to sleep in. It was cold cause it was still spring, and I didn't have a jacket, so I was walking fast tryna keep myself warm. All the bars and restaurants had already closed when I walked past this dude. He was a white guy, maybe about thirty or something, I don't know, I wasn't good at telling older people's ages back then. He had blond hair. I do remember that, his super blond hair, and just as I walked by him our eyes met and he stopped and looked me up and down and said, "Aren't you cold?"

I said yeah I was freezing but I was good. And he kinda just stood there and asked me again, like, for real, "Aren't you cold?" And then he asked where was my parents.

And I don't know why, I just started telling him everything like I trusted him. I told him I was from New York and I had got kicked outta my house and I dropped outta high school. I told him that I just arrived in DC and that I saw the air and space museum, which was cool, but now I didn't have no place to crash, so I was just walking. Then he took off his jacket and put it around my shoulders and said that I could kick it at his place tonight. I thought it was kinda weird to help a stranger like that, but maybe it coulda been weird in a nice way, like some DC hospitality or something, and honestly I was starting to get freaked out about being alone in a city I knew nothing about. So I said okay, thank you, and we went back to his place. I remember his apartment was real small, like a studio, basically just a bathroom and a bed and a big pile of clothes on the floor. There was dirty clothes everywhere. But it was off the streets, and I'd slept in a lot of worser places. So I pushed the clothes out the way and laid down and closed my eyes. Then I opened them again and he was standing there just smiling and said I shouldn't sleep on the floor, that I could share the bed with him.

I said okay, cause I didn't know what else to say, and then I added that I was gonna keep my clothes on. I remember being scared to say it, but also feeling proud after I did. I kinda felt a little more grown, like I knew how to take care of myself after all.

The blond guy just laughed and said of course, no problem, and climbed into the other side of the bed. When I woke up he was unbuckling my belt. And he pulled my pants down and I couldn't say a word. And then I could feel my underwear sliding down, but my muscles was *frozen like ice and I was just looking at the ceiling and he said to relax. Relax, relax, relax. And when he was finished I asked if I had to do him now, and he said not if I didn't want to, so I just closed my eyes and tried to go back to sleep and early in the morning I grabbed my shoes and bounced.*

I went back to the museums but this time I went to the one for natural history, the one with the big stumps of petrified wood out front. I was like, "Petrified motherfucking wood, you gotta be kidding me. That's too real right now." I went inside and stared at the extinct woolly mammoths and the extinct velociraptors, and I tried to only think about being extinct, about how crazy it is that some things don't exist no more. I spent the night wandering the streets again, but this time I didn't stop for nobody. Then I said, "Axel, you can't live like this, baby boy, roaming the street, white dudes raping you and shit. Start hustling, buddy." And so I headed to this neighborhood called Mount Pleasant, where I heard all the immigrants moved after the wars in Central America, and I saw a liquor shop that said Help Wanted in the window. The owners was this older couple, and I told them I was looking for a job. They asked how old I was, and I said eighteen. The lady looked at me like she doubted it but didn't say nothing else, and I spent the whole day cleaning and sweeping and scrubbing without even speaking about pay or compensation. At the end of the night they asked me where I lived, and I said nowhere. And then they said that I could make a bed in the storage room if I wanted, and that I could pay my rent by working in the store during the day.

I worked there for six months, and the owners were always so nice to me, but at the end of it I still hadn't made no money. So one day I decided it was time to go back to New York, and I never went to DC again.

CHAPTER 20

A PHONE FOR NESTORA SALGADO

IN WASHINGTON, DC, Atlee and I moved into a basement apartment near Mount Pleasant and split the rent with a roommate. I found a job at an immigration nonprofit as a "program assistant," which was basically the same as an immigration paralegal but with less pay. I took the job because it was the only one I was offered. Fulbright scholars in DC were a dime a dozen, and, in late 2015, none of the research institutions in the city seemed to have heard of migrant caravans. It certainly sounded like a strange phenomenon, they said, but a minor one, not worthy of study. I decided to change course and try my hand as a freelance journalist, but most of the outlets I pitched to responded similarly.

"I'm sorry," apologized one editor, "you sound very knowledgeable about all this, but I just don't think the American public is going to care about migrant caravans."

So I took the job as a lowly program assistant. My office was in one of the squat, nondescript DC buildings that looked exactly like the boxy suits who worked in them. It was centrally nestled among the city's top law firms and just a stone's throw away from the White House and the *Washington Post*—about as far removed from the migrant trail as anyone could possibly get. Suddenly I was wearing button downs and loafers—the same ones I wore to break Axel out of Don Armando's shop—to work every day. I tied my mane of hair back into a neat bun, then cut it short after someone heckled me for it from their apartment balcony and pelted me with raw eggs. I felt entirely out of place in the world, and it seemed like everyone else could tell. But I didn't complain about any of that to Axel. Compared to him, I was lucky to have a job at all. And at least, I thought, I could use my time in DC to study US immigration law and relay what I learned back to him.

"Who knows," I said over the phone, "maybe I'll find some kind of loophole and we can get you documents."

Things in Mexico City were not going well. The Attorney had successfully won humanitarian visas for Ever and several other migrants within a month or two, but Axel and Lalo's applications remained in perpetual limbo.

"I have been told," the Attorney advised us, "that Don Armando is behind the delay. His people at the Institute have made the applications disappear."

I didn't know how much credence to give this theory at first, but over the course of several months, I knew of three migrants who applied for and were granted humanitarian visas, while Axel and Lalo were continuously turned away. Either their applications had been lost in a pile of paperwork, or someone was intentionally holding up the process. Without the visas, the only work Axel and the boys could find was in a local warehouse. They were paid approximately four dollars a day, not even enough to feed themselves. I sent money when I could, but between the skyrocketing DC rent and my student loan payments, I was barely getting by myself. To make more money, Axel began to fix cell phones and computers in his time off, but it still wasn't enough to feed the six people living in the apartment.

"I feel responsible for these kids, bro," he said. "I can't just let them starve."

When Axel asked the Attorney for more money, she proposed a mutually beneficial solution. It seemed pointless to let his computer skills go to waste. If Axel started working for her, she would make sure that the rent was paid and that there was food in the fridge.

"What does she mean 'working'?" I asked over the phone.

"Hacking, of course," said Axel. "But also other things. She wants me to be her driver, and to help her with her meetings around town. Like be her sidekick."

Axel and I, in two capital cities separated by two thousand miles, were now both attorneys' assistants. One day, the Attorney told Axel that they were leaving for Guerrero. She was going to meet with Nestora Salgado's family, and he was going to drive her. She instructed him to arrive at her house by five o'clock in the morning so they could hit the road early. As Axel drove, the Attorney told him more about Nestora.

She was born in the small town of Olinalá but left at the age of nineteen to work in the US. While she was away, the cartels determined that Guerrero's land was perfect for poppy cultivation, which was then processed into heroin. By the time Nestora returned to her homeland at the age of forty-one, it was a much more dangerous place than when she'd grown up. As heroin production boomed and the cartels warred for position, the violence regularly spilled into Olinalá. Determined to take her town back, Nestora quickly became a commander of the community police force, called the CRAC-PC, which in reality was more like a militia than a normal police force, and more like a bunch of untrained men with guns than a militia. But according to the Attorney, Nestora was a brilliant military commander, and she soon whipped the militia into shape and pushed the cartels out of town. Then she did the same in the next town over, and then the next, and the next, until Nestora was helping command a large swath of Guerrero autonomously. But in 2013, Nestora was kidnapped by the Mexican government and was now being held in a maximum-security prison for women. It was a wrongful imprisonment, said the Attorney. That's why she said "kidnapped" and not "arrested." Nestora had every right to rebel against the narco state, the Attorney believed, and so she was leading the campaign for her release. She was also acting as one of Nestora's personal messengers, passing sensitive information back and forth between militia leaders in Olinalá and Nestora's prison cell.

When the Attorney and Axel pulled up to Olinalá, they were stopped by armed men in ski masks. It was the CRAC-PC. The Attorney identified herself and said she was there to meet with Nestora's family. The men wordlessly stepped aside and waved them through. While the Attorney was in the meeting, Axel waited by the car. Every so often, a man or a boy in a balaclava would march by carrying a rifle. That night, they slept in Nestora Salgado's house, which her family still occupied and which was filled, said Axel, with olinalá boxes, a beautifully ornate lacquerware that was famously the town's namesake. Its tocayo. The next day, the Attorney ordered Axel to drive her to the nearest supermarket. They packed her car with groceries and then donated them to the militia to distribute among the townspeople.

Even for Axel, the whole trip was surreal. "Bro there's dudes with guns everywhere," he told me over the phone as he strolled through town. "They're doing military demonstrations and everything. You best believe I took some badass selfies."

I was just as shocked as Axel. I'd grown accustomed to migrant activists like Irineo and Don Armando inflating their resumes. But the Attorney clearly had much better connections than either of them. Which was, frankly, terrifying. Within the span of a few months, Axel went from being a lowly deportee who knew essentially nothing about Mexico to being dragged into an armed revolt against the federal government. What would happen if cartel forces started a firefight in town? Where would Axel run? I didn't trust the Attorney to risk her life to protect his. But I also wasn't making enough money to pay Axel's rent instead.

On the third day, after several more meetings, Axel drove the Attorney back to Mexico City. She reclined in her seat and said that she had received instructions from Nestora's family. They were tired of only communicating with Nestora through messengers. They needed someone to smuggle a phone into her prison cell. The Attorney peered at Axel through her sunglasses. "I told them that I might know someone who was up to the job," she said.

AFTER YOU LEFT, bro, I ain't gonna lie, it felt like the whole fucking world closed up a little bit. At least when you was here, I had someone around who I coulda talked to. It was like wherever we was, we was somewhere together. And then you got on that plane and I was back in the middle of the nowhere, all by myself. I'm stuck up in this bitch with these five teenage boys and they're driving me absolutely nuts, chasing girls and skipping work and eating all the food in the fridge. And every night I can hear chickens getting freaking sacrificed right beneath my bed by a real-life witch, and the only other person in the world I can talk to is the Attorney. And bro, you ain't never gonna believe the shit she got me into this time. Not long after we got back from Guerrero, she pulled up in her SUV and told me to get in, that we was gonna visit Nestora at the women's prison. Apparently, Nestora was all over the news by that point, cause the Mexican government wasn't granting her calls with her lawyers like they shoulda been, and activists was pissed off about it. Like, the only times she coulda talked to them was when they came to visit her in person, which was a big hassle. At first, I thought the Attorney actually was Nestora's attorney, cause that's the way she always acted, right? But sooner or later I realized that wasn't the case. The Attorney's job was to help organize activists on the outside, to hold protests and fundraisers, and to visit Nestora in jail, so that she could pass messages on to her family and to her real legal team.

Anyway, as we was driving to the prison, the Attorney said I needed to scout for how to sneak a phone inside. And I said of course, no problem, cause that's my job, to always say of course and no problem to the Attorney, no questions asked. When we arrived, the first thing I noticed was that the security wasn't very sophisticated—just a single metal detector, not an x-ray scanner, and that the prison guards didn't seem like they even wanted to be there. The second thing I noticed was that none of our phones was working. They musta had a jammer in the prison, so even if you had managed to get a phone inside, the jammer woulda blocked all your calls. And the third thing I noticed was that there was cameras in the hallways, but not in the cells themselves.

When we got to Nestora's cell, the Attorney introduced me, and Nestora said hello, but then she never spoke to me again. She was wearing one of those khaki jumpsuits that all the inmates wear. Her and the Attorney talked about the conditions in the prison and the messages she wanted the Attorney to spread out to the world. And even though she was being denied calls, I could tell that Nestora was still getting well fed. Like she had a big ass watermelon inside her cell that someone else had brought. None of the other inmates were allowed to have that kinda stuff. Nestora had, like, fancy fruit privileges or some shit, you know what I'm saying, and later on for her birthday the prison even let us bring her a cake. So that got old Axel thinking.

When we left the prison, the Attorney asked what I needed and handed me a stack of cash. The first thing I did was go out and look for a phone. And not just any phone. The perfect phone had to be old, made mostly of plastic, and its logic board—which is like the heart and the brain of a phone—had to be small enough to shove up my asshole. In the end I got this old flip phone called StarTAC. Then I bought a compatible SIM card and an external Wi-Fi signal detector, which has the capability of finding all the Wi-Fi signals within a given range, as well as jammers, and it tells you what frequencies they're working on and how powerful they are.

Then we drove back to the prison a few days later. The Attorney went inside to talk to Nestora, and I stayed in the SUV and tried to locate the jammer signal. My hunch was right. The prison's jammer was new. And cause of that, it blocked the frequency that all current digital devices operate on, like smartphones and shit. But really old phones like the StarTAC ain't digital, they're analog and operate on a different frequency, and it didn't look like the jammer was blocking analog. So I got outta the SUV and started walking along the prison walls, and sure enough the StarTAC worked perfectly.

The night before we went back to the prison for the third time, I went over to the Attorney's house, this big fancy ass place where she lives with her husband and two daughters. And after dinner, I told her to bring me a watermelon, a razor blade, super glue, and green nail polish. Then I cut a small hole in the watermelon and disassembled the StarTAC. I took out the battery and SIM card and logic board and put them to the side, and then I put all the plastic parts of the phone in a little baggie and slid them inside the watermelon. Then I superglued it back together and painted over the cut with the green nail polish, and you basically coulda never told that the watermelon had been messed with in the first place.

Then the Attorney said there was one more thing I had to do. She wanted me to clone the SIM card of Nestora's phone. That way, any call or text that went in or out, any correspondence that Nestora had, the Attorney woulda got a copy. So she'd always be in the loop, right, and to know what Nestora wanted and how she could give it to her first before anybody else. The whole thing was like a big gamble on the Attorney's part. She wanted to grant Nestora whatever she needed in the moment to get outta prison, so that, if Nestora was ever actually released, she'd owe the Attorney a buncha favors in the future. So the Attorney was invested in making sure that her gamble paid off no matter what, you feel me?

When we pulled back up to the prison, the Attorney handed me a box of condoms and a jar of vaseline, and I walked to a restaurant across the street. I went in the bathroom and squished the battery and SIM card and logic board into a condom and tied it all up tight. Then I pulled down my jeans and underwear, and squatted over the dirty floor, and started playing with that shit just tryna make it go in. Lemme tell you, I never felt so sad and worthless in my life. I looked at myself in the mirror, with my drawers around my ankles and a phone sticking halfway out my ass, and believe it or not I thought about my babies. My baby *boy and baby girl. And how I ain't talked to them in who knows how long. All I could think about was how, if I ever see them again, they ain't gonna be how I remember them. How they already probably looked different than they looked when I got deported. How they're gonna be taller. How my little girl might not even remember that I'm her daddy at all. And I had to look in the mirror and tell myself to get it together, Axel, that I was just doing what I had to do to survive, and that was it.*

When I finally managed to get wide open and place everything inside all strategic, I pulled my jeans back up and walked out kinda bow-legged, just keeping it clenched tight. The Attorney gave me a cowboy belt, the kind with a giant buckle on the front with like an eagle on a nopal or some other Mexican shit, so that it would intentionally set off the metal detector and draw suspicion away from my booty hole. And that's exactly what happened. The metal detector went off and I just pointed to the belt buckle and the guard shrugged and let me pass through. Then I busted it straight for the bathroom with the watermelon still in my hands.

I pulled my jeans down little by little, real careful, right, so I wouldn't disturb anything too suddenly. And then I started pushing. And I was like oh my god, it's stuck, I'm gonna have to shit it out. What a way to blow your cover, just shit all over your own clothes. But luckily that didn't happen. The package came out, and I rinsed the doo-doo off in the sink and then took all the parts out and flushed the condom down the toilet. Then I put the phone together quick and stuffed it back into the watermelon and walked out the bathroom and toward Nestora's cell.

I gave Nestora the watermelon and she went into the back corner of her cell, where she was sure no cameras could see. Then she called her daughter, who was in the States, and everything worked perfect. Then she talked to her other daughter and her husband, and that worked perfect too. And when we got back home, a copy of all her calls was waiting on the Attorney's computer.

CHAPTER 21

THE RIGHT KIND OF TRAUMATIZED

BEING A PROGRAM assistant was, undoubtedly, the worst job I had ever done in my life. Nearly every day, I would scan our list of potential "clients"—as I was instructed to call them—hoping to see the name of someone I recognized. Ever's younger brother Marcos, maybe, or Dónovan. But none of the kids from the Viacrucis ever came across my desk. Most of the clients I met with were teenagers and living in the DC area with an aunt or cousin or brother. Some had no one at all and were wards of the state. They ranged in age from seventeen to just a few months old. Most of the babies had been born while their mothers, all of whom were also minors, were crossing Mexico.

My organization was one of several nonprofits that offered pro bono representation for immigrants in the DC area, which were all more or less interchangeable in practice, and, in fact, were at times literally so, as staff bounced from one organization to another, then back again, as they chased slightly higher salaries on the nonprofit ladder. As the lowest rung of that ladder, my job was to conduct "intakes," which were preliminary interviews with unaccompanied minors, kids who had traveled to the US alone and been detained by border patrol. If their immigration case met our criteria, we would either take their case ourselves or find them pro bono representation.

"Immigrant children," I was instructed to repeat, "are five times more likely to be deported if they don't have representation. That's where we come in."

The statement wasn't false, exactly, but it was true only because program assistants like me were directed to keep an eye out for straightforward cases, especially no brainers that anyone could win, and to reject the children whose cases seemed too strange or complicated. This was the point of the intakes: to act as a sieve of children. To determine, through a round of questioning, which youths we would usher into American society, and which we would leave behind. Compared to the interviews I conducted in Mexico, the intakes were shallow, one-dimensional affairs. They lasted only an hour, and, after establishing the basic information, my job was to determine what kind of "relief" the kid in front of my desk might qualify for—the kinds of documents potentially available to them. We specialized in helping immigrant children apply for two kinds of documents: asylum or SIJS. Asylum cases were commonplace, but they were often laborious battles that lasted years in court. Under the Obama administration, approval rates for Central Americans were abysmally low—on average just 26 percent of Guatemalan, Salvadoran, and Honduran asylum cases were granted in 2016, compared to the national asylum average of around 45 percent. Immigration judges were growing weary of gang-related persecution cases, because, as I once heard a judge say in court, "If I gave asylum to every person who came in claiming that they were afraid of the gangs, I'd be letting in all of Central America."

In other words, because gangs had become such a widespread and ever-present peril, the US immigration system no longer acknowledged gang persecution as an anomalous threat, but as a normative way of life in a land understood to be inherently violent. It was never acknowledged, however, that the US government itself played a foundational role in that violence. In 2009, for instance, the US Department of State—then led by Hillary Clinton—backed a coup to overthrow the democratically elected president of Honduras, Manuel Zelaya. His crime was daring to institute a series of progressive policies—including expanding the free public education system, increasing the national minimum wage by 60 percent, and guaranteeing free school meals for poor children—which enraged the Honduran elite and corporations operating in the country, who were worried that such reforms would cut into their profits. The coup was successful, right-wing politician Roberto Micheletti replaced Zelaya as president, and poverty in Honduras—which had continuously decreased under Zelaya's first term—rose again swiftly, as did the numbers of people fleeing the country. US courts were unwilling to grant Hondurans and other Central Americans asylum, because to do so would be obvious indictments of the failures of American foreign policy.

That left my organization with one other main legal option: SIJS, an abbreviation for special immigrant juvenile status, which was a visa exclusively for child migrants whose parents had abused, abandoned, or otherwise neglected them in their home countries. These visas were usually easier to win and faster than an asylum case, so determining if a child qualified for SIJS was generally the main focus of any intake I conducted. "Has one or both of your biological parents ever abandoned, abused, or neglected you?" I would ask the eleven-year-old in front of me, because that was how I was supposed to talk, at least at first. When they inevitably said they didn't understand the question, I would ask again more bluntly, "Did your mom ever hit you? Did your dad ever leave you?" Frequently, by the end of the interview, I had taken a child who'd spent little time ever thinking about his dad—or who maybe never even realized that his family had a "problem"—and revealed that his father had never actually loved him. Or that his mother was actually abusive. I did this week after week, wreaking havoc on scores of teary children, and many of them eventually received documents because of it.

An unspoken ranking system of trauma dominated the office, which was governed not by our own predilections, but by the US immigration courts' preformed prejudices against Central America. LGBTQ children were at the top, with bonus points awarded for how far down the acronym they identified, because it was understood that their asylum cases were the most straightforward of all. "The barbarians of Central America hate gay people" was a message that even conservative judges could get behind. Then came the SIJS kids, children who had been blatantly abandoned or abused by at least one of their parents, though both was ideal. "The barbarians of Central America are unfit to raise children," concluded the US courts. Finally there was the rare client with hard evidence of being targeted by government officials, such as a minor who had been raped by a police officer and carried the baby to term, and who even had a birth certificate with the man's name listed as the father—an actual case I had once, and which the courts could easily translate into "You see, these barbarians can't even govern their own countries." Then there was basically everyone else, the vast majority who were either poor, or abused by a relative, or threatened by the gangs. They usually had little proof of what happened and therefore didn't have much of a case.

My first intake was with a girl, eleven, who had fled El Salvador with her aunt after MS-13 started harassing her outside of school. The second and third were also girls, eight and sixteen, respectively, both of whom also stated that they were afraid of the gangs in El Salvador, though the sixteen-year-old said she'd never seen MS-13 in her neighborhood, as they were run by the rival gang Calle 18. None of these girls qualified for documents, because US immigration courts no longer recognized generalized gang persecution as worthy of asylum.

A short time after that, I interviewed another girl who said she'd started dating a boy in middle school, and by the time she was in high school he'd dropped out and was recruited into MS-13. If he didn't enlist, she said, they swore they would kill him, and then kill her, so he agreed. But soon after he joined, he started to change. He suddenly loved guns, which was confusing at first, and then one day he held a pistol against her temple. As a joke, he said. When they were having sex, he began to hit her. He didn't stop hitting her, or stop holding a gun to her head, so she left. She was sixteen. Her asylum claim was shaky at best, since she admitted that the boyfriend's behavior was more erratic and irrational than a series of overt, coordinated threats and that, despite it all, she still loved him.

Then there was the boy with long, dark hair that fell below his eyes, who told me that his father killed a man in front of him. He shot him in the head, the boy said in monotone, as he was sitting on the stoop. When I asked why, the boy said he didn't know, but that's when his mother—who had left for the US years ago to support the family—paid a man to bring him to DC. The coyote raped him, he said matter-of-factly, while they were somewhere in Mexico. Would that help his case? It would not help his case, but, fortunately for us, we could argue that the boy's father had "abused" him by forcing the child to watch an execution, and he received an SIJS visa.

One teenager was listed as "Female" on all the detention center files but was dressed in baggy men's clothing. A lot of kids came in wearing secondhand clothes, and so, not wanting to embarrass anyone, I continued the interview like normal. But after an hour I hadn't gotten anything substantial out of the kid, just a few grunts and sighs, a face quickly disappearing behind a hoodie, and finally I asked point blank if they really were a girl, or if they thought that, maybe, actually, they might sometimes feel like a boy. And then he told me, in an apologetic voice, his hoodie slipping down the back of his neck, that he didn't like being called a girl anymore, and could I please help him because his uncle, who he was staying with right now—who had driven him to this meeting, and who was waiting outside the office door at this very moment—had threatened to kick him out on the street if he didn't start wearing dresses again.

Despite the kid's obviously terrible home life, I couldn't help but feel a rush of elation—this was a slam dunk asylum case. That was the moment I realized that the intakes were having a paradoxical psychological effect on me. I began to hope that the most terrible things had happened to the children in my office. I was thrilled when they said that their parents had been murdered, or if they'd been repeatedly abused, or if they'd been stabbed while walking home from school. I obviously didn't wish such horrible things on them, but horrible things in the past meant the child could stay in the present. Normal and well-adjusted got deported. The right kind of traumatized got a green card.

I began to dread the intakes. The hundreds of small faces that passed in front of my desk, all of them in need of help, all of them a little scared and perhaps a little excited. Many of them had only been in air conditioning once or twice before they came to the US. They'd never stepped into a building that felt so fancy, or so intimidating, except for maybe when they went to immigration court and stood before the judge. Many lived in my neighborhood, or in adjacent neighborhoods, and I began to see them outside of work as well. I spotted a pair of twins—who had told me through tears that their uncle had molested them a few years previous—laughing and eating ice cream in Columbia Heights. I don't think they saw me. I ran into a boy whose father had been kidnapped and dismembered by MS-13 drinking a soda outside the 7-Eleven in Mount Pleasant. The father's murder actually made the news in El Salvador; the boy had carried the newspaper clippings across Mexico in his pocket as proof for his asylum case. Our eyes met and he looked away. Once, I had just picked up a pizza when I felt a tap on my shoulder, and behind me was the Honduran teenager I'd interviewed only a few days earlier, the one who'd told me that he'd dropped out of high school after someone stabbed his friend to death. He was smiling and wrapped me in a bear hug, which I wasn't expecting, and I almost dropped my pizza.

Every day I would go to work and another child would be waiting. Another child in their single new outfit and carefully combed hair. I'd lead them down the hallway to my office, close the door, and ask them to tell me about the most horrible things that had ever happened in their lives, things that they had never dared speak aloud before. Then I would weigh their words against the US legal system and decide their fate.

CHAPTER 22

SALMON AND ASPARAGUS AND BRIE

EVEN AS WE inched toward spring, Washington remained dull and frozen. Compared to the churning vivacity of Mexico City, the US capital felt like a little gray outpost at the end of the earth. Such an abrupt transition plunged me into an unshakeable and frenetic loneliness. It was like I was trapped in a giant pendulum, swinging back and forth. One moment I'd be dealing with a child under urgent threat of deportation, and the next Axel would text me a picture of himself with his arm thrown over the shoulder of a rifle-toting guerrilla, or email me a screenshot of another hack he was conducting for the Attorney. He was still hurtling through whatever Mexico threw his way, but back in DC, with the border between us, time had slowed to a standstill for me. All of our problems in Mexico had felt so palpable and immediate, as did their solutions. When I learned about the Southern Border Program, I marched against it on the Viacrucis. When Don Armando kidnapped Axel, I went to break him out. But DC had a way of professing to tackle all of the world's problems head on—from global poverty, to climate change, to mass migration—while actually holding them in perpetual abeyance. After work, I attempted to fill my empty life by attending talks about immigration in the city, hosted by various nonprofits or think tanks or universities. It seemed like the only thing this peripheral capital produced, besides bureaucracy, was slideshow presentations enumerating every apocalyptic disaster imaginable. As Donald Trump's campaign ramped up, everyone seemed to have a readymade solution to the supposed immigration crisis. And yet each presentation was more preposterous than the last. All that was needed, said a man in round spectacles, was an expansion of America's visa system, say by 10 to 20 percent. Another with white hair promoted extensive corporate tax breaks in Central America to invigorate the local economies. Someone with a PhD after her name insisted that the solution was for Washington to quash gang violence in Central America by funding an expansion of the region's military and police forces—which would be trained and equipped by defense contractors currently in Afghanistan and Iraq. There was never any mention of the Southern Border Program.

Then my own organization hosted a talk by a famous journalist who had recently published an article on Father Solalinde and how the good priest worked arduously to reduce abuses against migrants in both Hermanos en el Camino and Chahuites. Her speech was given at a wealthy synagogue. She spoke eloquently enough about the plight of migrants. She expounded upon their dangerous journeys through Mexico. She opined on the suffering of unaccompanied minors. Then she made an aside about the un-documented woman she'd previously employed as a maid. And she said that, just to be clear, she didn't support open borders or anything crazy like that. She believed in the rule of law, after all, and in bipartisan reform.

I looked around and waited for the punch line. Surely someone so knowledgeable about immigration wasn't suggesting biparti-sanship. Surely she knew that when George Bush created ICE af-ter 9/11, he was backed by patriotic bipartisan Democrats. Surely she understood that it was Barack Obama's bipartisanship that helped give birth to the Southern Border Program. But then she concluded her speech, and everyone clapped enthusiastically and lined up to take photos. I shuffled past the platters of hors d'oeu-vres, perfect little bites of salmon and asparagus and brie, and out onto the street. I tried to call Axel but he texted that he was busy doing something for the Attorney.

I sat on the curb and began to imagine the strangest things. I imagined the border patrol officer who had found Axel unconscious in the Texas desert. I envisioned his face. The lines that gathered along his forehead, his neatly trimmed mustache, the salt crystals from the dried sweat that collected along his eyelids in the heat of the day. I tried to conceive of an argument that might move him, of saying something profound and poignant enough to convince him to allow Axel to stay. Of anything at all that might change that man's mind and make him put down his gun. I couldn't think of a single sensible thing. Then I thought about stealing his gun and shooting him in the stomach instead. But that kind of violence was hard to picture, so I imagined leaning across the sturdy oak desk of a congressman, desperately making my case based on the economy or human rights, backed up by hard facts and figures, charts and statistics. But I kept getting distracted, checking my phone for a call from Axel that never came.

Later, I tried to recount the journalist's speech to a few acquaintances in a bar. Young professionals who worked in various nonprofits and governmental agencies in the capital. But I couldn't figure out how to portray the speaker correctly, or articulate my visceral reaction against her, and no one understood what the big deal was.

"Seems like a pretty level-headed talk to me," said one. "How else do you expect to convince conservatives to accept immigrants?"

"I don't know if it's about convincing," I said, trying to speak calmly. "I think it's really just about doing what needs to be done and not apologizing for it. I mean, am I the only one who feels like we're not really doing anything here? The world is on fire and we're up to our necks in policy proposals and paperwork. My whole job feels like nonsense."

There was an uneasy silence.

"Well, what do you suggest instead?" someone finally asked.

I surveyed the professionals in front of me. People who, like me, had yearned when they were younger to change and be changed by the world. But instead of going to Mexico, they had come to DC. And instead of being swept up in a migrant caravan, these young people were swept away by the endless tidal waves of governmental bureaucracy and law. They made and upheld that law in the name of the good. They were good people from good families who believed in good things and had never once felt the cloying desperation of illegality. The hardest people to reach are always those who genuinely believe that they are already leading moral lives.

And yet, Axel's existence was constantly up for negotiation with these good people. Every time I tried to explain why he meant so much to me, Americans never seemed to understand. Part of the problem was terminology. I had no word to describe Axel. "Friend" was too shallow. "Interlocutor" held an academic coldness that I detested. I was often tempted to call him my "brother," which is what Axel called me, but a white man calling a black man his brother, especially in his absence, only added an additional layer of discomfiture. The inevitable skepticism would begin: *Wait, you're not related to him? You only met him a year ago? Oh, are you two having sex or something?* Then I'd start to stutter and my face would burn. What I wanted to say was that being separated from Axel was like having a part of myself cleaved off. That I was experiencing his deportation in reverse, and that after I'd crossed back into the US his absence was like an open wound. This was the truth, but it sounded overdramatic.

What I realized in that moment was that everyone around me ultimately believed that this world was the best they could ever hope for, and all there was left to do was to make minor adjustments to it, to tweak and tinker with inevitable progress. But my allegiance lay elsewhere. In Mexico I glimpsed an entirely different world, one that cried out for something more, and between the world of DC and the one I witnessed with Axel yawned a titanic and fathomless gulf. In the end, however, I couldn't come up with anything sensible or practical to say, so we all went back to drinking our beers, and the conversation eventually turned to the incomprehensibility of the lame duck Trump campaign.

WHAT ME AND *the Attorney had done for Nestora kinda became a regular thing. The routine was always the same. Every couple a months the Attorney would text me that I had to drive her back down to Guerrero tomorrow, and when we arrived in Olinalá, I would wait outside the SUV while she went to her meetings. Eventually the Attorney would finish and then we would go buy groceries and pass them out to important community leaders, and the Attorney would take pictures with them to show her activist friends back in Mexico City. And then finally, only when all that was over, she'd tell me the instructions that Nestora's family had given her. Usually it was to deliver this thing or that thing to Nestora in prison—like a phone charger or some money to bribe the guards or something like that.*

But sometimes the CRAC-PC instructed her to help out other people too, like this dude named Gonzalo Molina. The Attorney said that he was another one of the leaders of CRAC-PC, just like Nestora, and he was also being held prisoner by the government. Except Gonzalo Molina wasn't in a normal prison. He was in a hospital, like a prison hospital, in Chilpancingo, the capital of Guerrero, cause he had something wrong with his health. Like his organs or something. I was never quite sure, to be honest, cause there was some rumors going around that he was faking it just so he didn't have to be in a normal prison cell, though I don't know if any of that shit's true or not. To be honest, he always looked pretty sick to me.

Anyways, the Attorney said that the hospital or prison or whatever it was, they wasn't letting him call his lawyers or families or nobody. And so she asked me if I could sneak him a phone, just like I did with Nestora. I said of course, baby girl, but I ain't sticking it in my butt this time. That was a one-time deal. And she could tell I was serious so she didn't push it. Fortunately, the security in Chilpancingo wasn't as strict as it was in Mexico City. They would just pat us down when we was at the entrance, so I told the Attorney to get me another watermelon, and I hid another StarTAC inside. It wasn't hard at all. And Gonzalo Molina, he was real grateful. He'd always ask me all these questions about myself. How I was doing, where I was from, did I have any family, things like that. He said my service proved I was a real guerrilla. Oh, and bro, did you know that in English guerrilla is pronounced like "gorilla"? How weird is that? Anyway, I thought you'd like it, since you never shut up about the tocayos thing. And in a way I guess they're both kinda similar. They both live in the mountains, far away from most people, and they're both in danger. Except one is in Africa and the other is in Guerrero.

And bro, Guerrero ain't no fucking joke. It's hard core. Like, there's a lotta poverty. People don't have hardly nothing. They live in tiny shacks with dirt floors and no indoor bathrooms. And the militias don't look nothing like any kinda actual military. It's mostly kids and grandpas running around with rifles. Their uniforms are just t-shirts. Life there certainly don't seem easy. But, at the same time, it's one of the only places I been in this whole country that I feel kinda accepted. Like when I'm down in Guerrero, there ain't nobody there who asks me where I'm from. Or, if they do ask, they're chill about it like Gonzalo Molina. They ain't asking me cause they're suspicious of my skin color or some shit, you know what I'm saying? Cause living in Mexico City, it's fucking hard. Everything is about skin color in this city. People see my skin, people hear my accent, and it's like they just immediately shut down. I'll walk into immigration to check on my visa application, or I'll try to open a bank account, and the people just tell me to get out before they even know what I'm there for. "Get out negrito, get out negrito." That's all anybody ever says to me. Even when I'm with the Attorney, people just assume that I'm her driver or her servant or her bitch before she even introduces me. And the thing that fucks me up the most is that they're right. I am her driver and her bitch. When I'm with her, I'm the fucking stereotype.

IN THE BASEMENT of my office building was a small, windowless gym that smelled of damp and disinfectant. Every day after work I trudged down the dimly lit stairwell, mostly because it was free and I had no money for a gym membership, but also because I was usually the only one there, and since leaving Mexico I enjoyed being alone. Just a year ago, I was on the Viacrucis eating only mangos and avocados, so skinny that I could run my fingers over the grooves of my rib cage. But after months of sitting at a desk, my body had changed. I would walk to the bathroom, pull up my shirt, and tug at the flesh of my stomach. It wasn't just about vanity, I muttered angrily to myself in the mirror. What if Axel had an emergency? What if he was trapped in a firefight in Guerrero and I had to go find him? I wouldn't be in good enough shape, I'd slow him down, maybe even be the reason he got caught. So I scrawled a workout plan on the back of a spare intake form, and every day after interviewing a child or writing up a report I'd descend into the gym.

The only other souls in the basement were the building's custodians, a quartet of women who arrived every evening at half past six. In the corner of the gym was a cramped walk-in closet that had been converted into a janitorial lounge, and the women had to walk across the gym's wall of mirrors, where I stood huffing and puffing, to deposit their purses and lunch boxes in the closet, chatting with each other about some family member, or how the ice on the sidewalks had inexplicably still not melted. At first, we only smiled at each other, them shyly, me apologetically for having invaded what was once their previously undisturbed refuge. I never spoke to them in Spanish, in part because I didn't want to talk, but also to give them a bit of privacy, or the illusion of it, so that they could chat freely without feeling that their space was even more encroached upon.

But after several months, I overheard one of the ladies—a sweet older woman, who wore a bow in her loose, gray hair—speaking from behind the cracked door of the lounge about her niece, who'd been detained crossing the border some months back. I gently tapped on the door and stuck my head inside. As luck would have it, I said, I worked for the organization upstairs, and if the woman passed along her niece's information, I might be able to help. The women looked confused, and at first I thought it was because they were surprised I spoke Spanish, but then one of them asked, very politely, exactly what organization I was talking about.

"The one upstairs," I said. "The one on the fourth floor that provides free attorneys to children in immigration proceedings." The one that they cleaned several nights a week.

They had no idea that's what we did.

I wrote down the niece's name, Rachel, and her phone number, and said that I would call tomorrow. The woman took my hand in both of hers and said that God would bless me. The next morning, I called the number and asked for Rachel, and the voice on the other end of the line said she was Rachel's mother. She'd been expecting my call, she said. Her sister had told her about me.

"Wonderful," I said. "If it's okay with you, I just need to start with some basic facts. Your daughter's full name, her age, when she entered the United States, those kinds of things."

Rachel's mother relayed the information back, reading everything off the immigration folder she was given when she picked her daughter up from the detention center.

"And how long ago was that?"

Forty-seven days ago.

"Have you enrolled her in school yet?"

Yes, of course.

"Where at?"

The mother told me.

"I'm sorry, could you repeat that? I haven't heard of that one."

Rachel's mother repeated the name again, slowly, and apologized if her pronunciation of the English name wasn't correct. I felt a sinking feeling in my chest. "I'm sorry, ma'am, I should have asked earlier, but what county do you live in?"

Loudoun, she said.

"Oh. Oh no, I'm so sorry, I didn't realize. Unfortunately, we can't serve people in Loudoun County. I would love to help, but it's just, it's that our federal grant stipulations are very strict, and we can only work with people in certain geozones specified in our funding. I'm really sorry. No, no, it's all my fault. I can send you a list of other organizations you can contact if you like. Okay. Have a good day, señora."

After I hung up, I sat in silence for a long time. I detested Don Armando for stringing migrants along with false promises of visas, but I found myself in a not-so-dissimilar position. Don Armando promised special access to immigration officials, we promised a specially trained attorney in court. Don Armando dragged migrants to fundraisers and forced them to sing his praises, we did the same in our promotional materials. The only difference was that Don Armando's operation existed in the gray areas of the law, and our nonprofit was supposedly the shining example of it.

After that, the cleaning women rarely made eye contact with me as they crossed the gym and entered the lounge, and I kept my head down too, silently lifting the dead weight in my hands over and over again, the border of Loudoun County between us.

CHAPTER 23

MIND BODY PROBLEMS

ONE OF THE first signs that I was starting to really lose it was when I couldn't bear to look at myself in the mirror anymore. Reflective surfaces are everywhere in DC—full-length mirrors in restaurant bathrooms, cheval glass in the entryways of apartments, the impeccably polished tinted windows of the city's squat and uninspired buildings. I would turn and see myself and instinctively grimace. Disgust would rise in my throat. I would raise my hand just to be sure that the jaundiced and miserable-looking thing in the reflection was me. I felt most wretched in the antiseptic tedium of my office, slouched over a desk, with my belt digging into the flesh of my stomach. Each day was an excruciating process of petrification. My weight began to swing, and the more it swung, the more aware I became of being trapped in my body. I wanted a different body. Or maybe what I really wanted was a different body for Axel. A body that had the power to move through the world without anyone hunting it down. I wanted his body to be able to do what mine could, to have the powers given to it at birth, like magic.

In my addled state, the only thing I could think to do was hit the gym harder. I was never fit enough, never ready enough. It was difficult to find the time and energy to stick to a strict workout routine, but this, I decided, was solely my fault. I simply needed to be more productive. I became gripped by the idea of efficiency.

I was agitated by idleness and wasted time. It was almost as if I believed that if I worked a little faster, and if I worked out a little harder, I could store that extra time and effort in my body, carry it across the border, and somehow share it with Axel. To say, "See, I've been saving up my life on the other side to give to you. I did not waste anything. I had no joy and partook in no pleasure so that we could do it together." I developed a method for putting my work clothes on with as few movements of my limbs as possible. In the shower, I noted how many times I lathered soap on my skin, and then tried to reduce the number. I counted exactly how many steps it took to walk from metro station entrance to my front door—fifty-one—and became enraged if an oblivious pedestrian cut in front of my path, forcing me to deviate into an inefficient pattern. I loathed my job and yet tried to work more quickly. There were so many clients, too many, a seemingly infinite stream of children in desperate need of help, and so I needed to be better, to do better, to work harder.

Because the other side of efficiency is austerity, I obsessed over money. Everything became about saving just a little bit more to send to Axel. Eating out was a sin, each cup of coffee a transgression. I demanded reimbursements for every shared beer or metro ride. Each cocktail I was socially obligated to shell out for, every grocery run I made, I insisted that Atlee pay me back to the cent. She did so quietly and with grace for months, and then told me she was worried, that she thought I was sick. I said she was overreacting. Eventually, she convinced me to take a break, and I conceded to visiting my dad for a long weekend in New Orleans on the condition that it remain a secret. I couldn't possibly explain such a luxury to Axel. I knew he'd never hold it against me—he'd probably even be happy for me in some respect—but he'd also ask me to take pictures for him, to show him things through the phone that he would never be able to see himself. I couldn't bear that.

On our last day in New Orleans, I was crossing the street when I heard someone call my name from the window of a passing car.

He said my name in Spanish, like "levee" or "levy," an echo from another world. I froze right there, in the middle of traffic, trying to squint through the tinted windshield. I didn't recognize the man until he pulled the rusty old Ford up onto the sidewalk and waved me over. James. A Honduran who'd lived in Hermanos en el Camino with his two sons while waiting on the results of their humanitarian visa applications. I had not seen him since the Viacrucis. He hopped out, clutching his head in disbelief, and began to recount everything in a rush, how he crossed the border with his two boys, how they were brave and didn't cry, how they drove through the night to New Orleans where his wife and eldest sons were waiting, and how his wife—his beautiful wife, he said, showing me pictures on his cell phone—was a bartender down-town, and that he found a steady job right away on a construction site. I was so dazed that all I could muster was, "That's wonderful, so wonderful" over and over again. James asked about my life and where I was living, what I was doing for work, and about—what was his name? Axel, that's right, Axel. Weren't you two friends? Had I heard anything from him?—and then I apologized and said that I had to go because I was about to miss my flight.

ONE MORNING THE *Attorney called me early as shit and said to get to her house immediately, cause the government was gonna release Nestora Salgado from prison. When I got to her house, I had never seen her so happy in my life.*

"We did it, Axelillo," she said. "After all this time, we finally did it."

But if I thought I was gonna get to celebrate with her, I was wrong. She said that Nestora's team was looking for something to make the photos of her release look badass. "We need a gun," she said, and handed me a giant stack of cash.

"Hells fucking nah," I said, cause I knew it was illegal for a guy like me to buy a gun in Mexico without a license. "I ain't bout to get my ass busted just so Nestora can look good for the cameras."

"You can keep the change," she said.

I dropped her off at the prison and headed straight for Tepito, where everybody knows you can go to buy a gun when you need one. And immediately all the hustlers there started showing me all these guns, just guns everywhere, and it got me freaked out, cause who knows how many of those things was used to kill someone in the past, right? So I said, "Nah man, these is gonna get me sent straight to jail. Tell me where I can get a BB gun that looks like the real deal."

And they sent me to this little place called El Conejo Salvaje or something like that. The Wild Rabbit in English. And sure enough they had this bad ass black air rifle on display, with a scope and everything. So I paid the owner in cash and rushed back to where Nestora was gonna give the speech, right? Her and her family was in this back room, strategizing on what she needed to say to the press. And then I busted in, sweating my balls off, waving around a big ass rifle, and for a second I thought all the guerrilla dudes was gonna cap my ass.

I had to shout, "Nah, man, nah, this ain't real. It's a gift for Nestora, for her photo opportunities."

And Nestora looked at me and I could tell for a second she was tryna figure out where she'd seen me before. "I'm the cell phone guy," I said.

"Oh my goodness," she said, and her cousin took the gun away. "You two are nuts."

When Nestora walked out to talk to the reporters, she was wearing the green shirt of the militia. Everybody cheered, and then her cousin handed her the rifle and she held it up over her head like she'd just won a battle. And the cameramen went crazy, snapping as many photos as they could. I didn't know it in that moment, but that would become a famous picture of Nestora. She became, like, an icon with that rifle. Pictures of her holding that gun up in victory would go all over the world.

Then she gave a speech. She said that the government was a buncha dumbass motherfuckers and that she was gonna keep fighting for as long as it took to end corruption. And then she said that she had some people she wanted to thank. The Attorney stood up straight, and started kinda rocking back and forth, and, like, even squeezing my arm in excitement and shit. Nestora said she wanted to thank her family, who was always there for her. And she wanted to thank her community, and all the people who had wished her good luck in prison. And then finally she said that she wanted to wish an extra big thank you to her legal team, cause they was the ones who never stopped fighting for a second for her, and that she coulda always counted on them. Different people was called and they came up and hugged her and sometimes they even said a few words for the cameras too. But the Attorney's name was never called. And then the whole thing was over, and Nestora walked right by us without even looking at the Attorney once.

Then we got back in the SUV and drove straight to Olinalá, where they was gonna throw a big homecoming celebration for Nestora. On the drive, I could tell that the Attorney was pissed, and I just kept looking at her, tryna think of something to say, but then she was like, "What the fuck are you looking at?" So I just stayed quiet.

When we got to Olinalá, Nestora started giving more speeches. And again she thanked this person, and then thanked that person, and it seemed like she'd thanked half the entire town before she stopped speaking. And once again she completely ignored the Attorney, even though it was obvious that she was standing right there in front of her. Then there was a humongous party, and everyone was crowding around Nestora, tryna talk to her, to laugh with her and drink with her, but it was like she had a sixth sense—every time the Attorney got near, Nestora would somehow float away, just disappear to another part of the party, or turn her back and block the Attorney out.

I'd never seen the Attorney so pissed. "That fucking bitch," she said after it was all over. "Two years of my life working for her and not even a thank you. Not even one measly thank you. That hija de puta. Who does she think she is, Axelillo? Who the fuck does she think she is?"

Over the next few days, the Attorney tried calling Nestora and her lawyers, but they never returned her calls. I guess Nestora was smart enough to know that getting involved with the Attorney was bad news. Of course, I ain't that lucky. After Nestora stopped talking to her, the Attorney went crazy. It was like everything she'd been forcing me to do all this time—all the hacking and cell phone smuggling and driving her ass to Guerrero and all that bullshit—it all went out the window. She didn't wanna talk about Nestora no more, she wanted to forget all about it. And having me around was just a reminder of how everything had gone wrong. Like it was somehow my fault. After that, she started to "forget" to pay the rent. She'd yell at me saying that I wasn't good for nothing, that I was lazy, that I needed to find a job. And then one day I got mad and yelled back how was I supposed to find a job when I was always working undercover for her ass. And by the way, she still hadn't gotten me a visa like she'd promised, so I couldn't even get a decent job if I wanted to. I'd risked everything for her and she still hadn't done shit for me.

And then she said, "Oh yeah? You're about to see what me not doing shit for you is really like, Axelillo."

And then she stopped returning my calls. Eventually, the witch land-lady kicked us outta the apartment. The teenagers all decided to bounce. Two of them went to go live with some girls they'd met in Mexico City. Another one said that he was gonna try to cross, and sure enough, a few weeks later that lucky motherfucker sent me photos from Phoenix. He had already found a job with a construction crew and everything. The last one had kinda gotten involved with some gangsters in Mexico City, and he said that they'd invited him to Sinaloa to do a job for them up there. The last thing I saw, he was posting pictures in a ski mask holding an automatic rifle or some shit in the back of a blacked-out car.

I asked Lalo what he was gonna do, and he said one of the girls he'd met in Chahuites had moved to Monterrey and that he was thinking maybe he was gonna go live with her. She worked as a bartender and had already convinced her boss to hire him as a waiter. "It's a real job," he said, "and we're even thinking about getting married, you know, so I can get my documents." He said all of it kinda looking down at the ground, right, like he didn't really wanna say it cause he knew it was gonna hurt my feelings.

"That's great, Lalo," I said, cause that's all you can say in that sit-uation. "Go on, kid. Go live your life. Go make something of yourself." I felt like crying, and I felt stupid for crying, cause Lalo was too young

to really be, like, a real friend of mine, but I still cared about him. We went to the bus station. He said he was gonna risk it tryna ride to Monterrey without getting caught by immigration, cause honestly what did he have to lose at this point. And I gave him a hug and wished him good luck and then he was gone. Long story short, he made it to Monterrey. And then I was all alone in Mexico City.

AFTER AXEL WAS kicked out of his apartment, he bounced between temporary shelters and park benches. I was furious with the Attorney and wanted Axel to cut off all contact with her, but now that Lalo had left, she was the only person besides me that he had. She answered his phone calls sporadically, just enough to keep him on the hook. I wanted to rush down to Mexico City to help, but my vacation time was paltry, and my pay was even worse. It was a more financially responsible decision, I concluded, to save the hundreds of dollars that my plane ticket and hotel room would have cost, and instead use that money to bribe a sleazy landlord in Iztapalapa—Mexico City's most dangerous borough but therefore one of its cheapest as well—to rent Axel a room. But even after finding a slightly more stable place to stay, living alone proved to be terrible for him. Axel would go days without ever leaving his bedroom, and began a habit of texting me lengthy, nearly indecipherable messages in the middle of the night. Messages about how lonely he was, about visions of his children's faces, and how the Attorney was angry with him. When we talked on the phone, his speech was erratic and nonlinear, like he'd forgotten how to conjure the words. I realized that, without any other Americans to talk to, Axel was starting to lose his grasp of the English language.

Meanwhile, spring turned to summer turned to fall, and Washington was fully swept up in the fever of the 2016 presidential election. Back at the office, speculation had it that our executive director was biding her time until Hillary won. She had supposedly been promised a position overseeing immigration in the new administration. The gossip wasn't surprising. The organization's promotional materials included endorsements from celebrities and tech conglomerates, and, like many large nonprofits in the DC area, we received over half our budget from federal grants, which allowed the government to outsource the immigrant question instead of address it. To keep those grants, our headquarters staff was chock full of middling DC patricians, the kind of hobnobbers who had lived in the capital for ages and attended enough of the right parties in the right neighborhoods to know which bureaucrat or lobbyist or socially minded corporate executive had money to burn on a good cause. Nearly all of them were middle-aged white women, and almost none of them spoke Spanish. Though, whenever prompted, they said with a smile that they were trying to learn. It was such a beautiful language.

"Oh," I said, stupidly taking the bait after one of the vice presidents remarked in the breakroom that she hoped to take a Spanish course the next time she was in the Yucatán. "Have you lived in Mexico before?"

"Lived?" she laughed. "Oh no, just vacationed. It's gorgeous there, but I just can't stand seeing that kind of poverty every day. It makes me so sad."

I thought about saying that, just because one chooses to look away from poverty doesn't mean that it simply disappears, but I stayed quiet. And it wasn't as if DC didn't have its own share of hardship. Just in my neighborhood alone, dozens of down-and-out Central American men would lounge outside the local grocery store, pressing themselves against the exterior walls to shelter from the chilly October winds that whipped down 14th Street. They mostly kept to themselves, so people mostly ignored them. But one day, I found one of the men writhing around on the sidewalk, clutching his stomach. He was wearing an old brown suit, with holes worn through the knees and elbows.

"Me estoy quemando," he screamed, tearing open his shirt and clawing at his skin. "I'm burning."

I called 9-1-1, but instead of an ambulance, two policemen showed up in a patrol car. The first officer was short and pudgy and dark skinned. Behind his reflective sunglasses, he looked exactly like the federal policemen who had laid siege to the Viacrucis. The second officer stayed in the car with the windows rolled down, watching us from a distance.

"What's going on here?" asked the first officer.

"Is an ambulance coming?" I asked. "We need an ambulance."

"It'll be here soon," he said, and then turned his attention to the man on the ground. "Sir, what is your name?" he enunciated from above.

The burning man arched his back and moaned.

"I don't think he speaks English," I said, and offered to translate.

The officer's eyebrows raised above his sunglasses. "You speak Spanish? Ask him where he's from."

"I'm not sure what that has to do with anything," I started to say. "He told me that his stomach hurts. That it feels like he's burning inside." But before all the words could leave my mouth, the second officer opened the door to the police car. He was tall and very pale. He put his hand on my chest and said that if I wasn't going to cooperate then I needed to stand back, that I was impeding their ability to do their jobs. Pedestrians rerouted their course to the other side of the street without so much as glancing our way. I looked around in desperation—whatever happened to this man, I knew it would be my fault—but fortunately the ambulance arrived. Men with white latex gloves rolled the burning man from the gutter onto a padded plastic gurney, then raised him up, and his body disappeared into the sterile cavity of the ambulance.

A few weeks later, as I was exiting the grocery store, I saw the man again. He was sitting on the ground with his back against the wall. He was unconscious, but so were many of the other men, and I didn't try to wake him. I just stood there for a while, staring. These were the men who were clever or lucky enough to have eluded Central America's various right-wing genocides and massacres in their youth. El Mozote, or Dos Erres, or Sumpul River, or all the others without names. Some even looked old enough to remember the CIA-backed coup of Árbenz in Guatemala, the first in a long line of right-wing military dictatorships that the agency orchestrated in Latin America. These were men who had crossed entire countries, who had left whole other lives and families behind, and then quietly slid into pools of their own vomit and excrement, politely tucking themselves away behind shopping carts and recycling bins so as not to disturb the shoppers. Simply making it to the US was never salvation, and finding Axel a coyote wasn't enough. We'd have to find him a life.

CHAPTER 24

MAGA

WHEN IT WAS clear that Trump had won, Atlee and I wandered out into the miserable night. No one else was outside. It seemed as if all the lights in all the windows had been switched off. At some point I realized our feet were taking us to the White House. A small crowd was already assembled, mostly young professionals who had come hours earlier to celebrate Hillary Clinton's victory. We wove our way slowly through the crowd, unsure where to place ourselves or focus our gaze, until we too stood dumb and slightly swaying, dispersed evenly from each other. The ground was slowly becoming littered with festive Hillary kitsch, hats and banners and kazoos. A young woman stumbled by in a t-shirt with Huma Abedin's face plastered onto Rosie the Riveter's body and was quietly repeating the word "no" over and over again. The White House, still illuminated in its constant shock of pure light, seemed too much to look at directly. I stared into the sky, muddied with chemicals and light pollution, and watched the commercial flights circle overhead, waiting to land at Reagan National. Off to the side, a local news crew was broadcasting live, but I couldn't hear what they were saying. Everything felt like the volume knob slowly turned down. Then the frat boys descended.

They arrived all at once, drawn to blood, a frenzy pouring out from the halls of Georgetown and George Washington and American University. For a moment we just stood there, unable to comprehend the yawps and howls. All of these boys in their MAGA hats, some of them as young as the teenagers I saw in my office, so close we could feel their wet breath on our faces. One boy snatched an American flag out of the hands of a teary-eyed woman and held it aloft, chanting, "This is mine, this is mine." And we understood that it was true. A pack of boys had surrounded an abject group clinging to a cloth banner covered in butterflies, which read "Migration is beautiful." The boys climbed into the trees and screamed, "Deportation is beautiful." Rage shot through me. The rage I had brought home from Mexico—all the silent fury that festered while I toiled away at my dead-end job choosing which children would be welcomed into the heart of American empire. Just for once, I wished that we really did have something to fear about immigrants, something that truly threatened our cloistered, pitiful lives. If only migrant caravans were actually filled with ruthless criminals, instead of the toughened but ultimately harmless souls doomed to decades of cooking and cleaning, to planting rose bushes on rolling lawns and changing diapers full of shit. If only they were coming to corrupt our children instead of serving them until they grew old enough to join fraternities and call for the death of immigrants. What I would have given for a caravan to actually invade then, to breach our borders en masse and overwhelm us. We who have done them so much wrong. But that would never happen. The Southern Border Program would make sure of it.

Axel 3:01 AM he won
Levi 3:03 AM im so sorry bro im so sorry
Axel 3:04 AM what are we gonna do?
Levi 3:04 AM whatever it takes i promise you that

The next morning, the doors to the attorneys' offices were closed, and the sounds of soft, muffled weeping slipped under the cracks and into the waiting room. A series of emergency meetings were called. Our executive director—who was most certainly not going to work in the White House now—somberly explained that our allegiance, no matter what, was with the children, and that this was just as true today as it was yesterday. This was a time to band together, to fight, to resist. But, of course, she said, now that the Republicans were going to be in power, the government grants that funded our work were in danger. In such uncertain times, the organization would have to insulate itself financially. This meant cutting back on certain expenditures, and headquarters was considering layoffs. Our health insurance would be restructured, and my premium was going up. Additionally, everyone's salaries would be frozen immediately. The paltry pay raise that I'd been promised in my contract—the one that I was counting on to pay for Axel's room now that the Attorney had cut him off—would be indefinitely postponed. Afterward I had to call Axel and tell him that I was too broke to pay his rent next month—"Don't worry about it bro," he'd said, "I'll call the Attorney and figure something out"—and when we hung up I was so distraught and ashamed that I threw up in the office bathroom.

We had entered what were supposedly the last precious moments of a Democratic presidency, and instead of any kind of actual resistance, instead of gritting its teeth and taking advantage of what invaluable time it still had left, the liberal guard of Washington was already handing over the keys. Not through force, not through coercion, but through barely veiled fear masquerading as fiscal responsibility, months before Trump ever took office. Meanwhile, the immigration courts hummed along unfazed, deporting more and more people every day, an impeccably rational machine, a judicious organ functioning perfectly.

AFTER THE ATTORNEY let me get kicked out onto the streets, our relationship didn't end, exactly. It just kinda became more complicated, you feel me? It became more based on, like, contracts. For instance,

I didn't have no contact with her for months—no calls, no texts, no nothing—and then one day out of the blue my phone rung. "Axelillo," she said. "Where have you been? What are you up to these days?" Like I'd just taken a vacation or some shit.

I said that I'd been keeping my nose clean and my hands dirty, just hustling life. Which was true, but I left out the part of always feeling alone and feeling like I was going crazy.

"Listen," she said. "I got a job for you."

She promised that if I helped her out, this time she woulda got me a visa for real, no bullshit. So I asked what she needed. And she said that she wanted me to hack Nestora. Since Nestora was outta prison, she musta switched phones and now the Attorney didn't have dirt on her no more. Can you believe that? Instead of helping Nestora, now we was supposed to hurt her. All cause she didn't wanna be the Attorney's friend. And I know it sounds stupid, like I'm just some gullible motherfucker, but I was desperate, man. I was out on the streets every day looking for food, and the Attorney knew it. Plus, I gotta be honest with you, it felt nice just to be with someone, even if I knew that she was taking advantage of me. At least I got the chance to look someone in the face and hear them say my name.

So I started hacking Nestora.

And again, this ain't the most sophisticated thing in the world. Nestora and the militia, they're rural people. They didn't know nothing about cybersecurity. I conducted most of my attacks through this platform called Maltego on Kali Linux, which basically identifies weaknesses in people's electronics and then helps you attack them over and over and over until you break through. And since the Attorney had all the contact information of everybody down in Olinalá, including Nestora herself, she also forced me to start phishing them. I'd send out emails from an account that looked like it was part of the CRAC-PC, and whoever clicked on the link would immediately hand over all their login info to me. Within days I had access to all their emails and group chats. I could sit there and watch them messaging each other in real time.

To be honest, nothing that they talked about seemed like that big a deal to me. But the Attorney had convinced herself that Nestora musta been doing some dirty shit, and that's why she didn't wanna work with her no more, and so the Attorney kept demanding for me to dig deeper, deeper, deeper. But all her messages was mostly just strategizing for how to get herself even more famous. She had political goals, that was kinda obvious, and she started to get involved in this new political party called MORENA. But politics takes time, and all the people she was talking to inside MORENA weren't part of the networks I had hacked. So the Attorney said I needed to hack them too, but I started to get real uncomfortable with the whole thing. It was clear that she was doing it just cause she was pissed at Nestora, and my visa still wasn't any closer to coming in, and with the money you was sending me now, Levi, I decided that I didn't always have to be her servant like I used to be. I knew that drove the Attorney crazy, cause she could never figure how I was earning enough money to keep myself, like, at least semi-independent from her. So when it came to MORENA, I was always just tryna stall as much as possible.

That's when things started to get really weird. The Attorney wasn't a trustful person at all, right? And one day, she came to me and said that she thought her husband was cheating on her, and she asked if I could look into him. I tried to act dignified and reassure her that I would do everything I could. But fuck that. I wasn't gonna get into none of that nutty business. And honestly, if I had to guess, I woulda bet that her husband probably was cheating on her, cause he's a super-rich guy who owns a big ass business and travels all the time. It's kinda obvious that those are the guys who usually cheat on their wives, especially in Mexico City. But I wasn't gonna get involved in it one way or another, cause I knew that when the Attorney got bad news she always took it out on the messenger, you feel me? So after a week I came back to her and said that I didn't find nothing that indicated her husband was cheating, which was technically true, cause I didn't try to find nothing at all. Well, that seemed to calm her down and she thanked me a whole bunch and invited me to dinner with her family. Then she'd stop responding to any *of my calls or texts for a few months, I'd be struggling to pay the rent, and then next thing you know she'd pop up again one day sniffling, talking bout how she still had suspicions, that she was sure her husband was cheating this time, and I'd have to pretend all over again that I was checking into it for her.*

But then things got even more ridiculous. One day she called me crying real hard, like sobbing all over the place. When I asked what was wrong, she put her husband on the phone. He sounded serious. He said that one of their teenage daughters had sent some naked pictures to someone. And even worser, he said, that person had shared them to the whole school, and next thing they knew the pictures was all over the internet. They was worried that it was gonna get around town that their little girl was experimenting with some freaky-deaky shit, and they couldn't let that happen, cause their reputations woulda been ruined. He said he was asking me man-to-man to wipe all the pictures of his little girl off the internet and preserve her honor. That's what he said, "preserve her honor." And then he said to please not be too horrified by what I saw, cause his daughter was trained as a gymnast and a dancer and the pictures was graphic and from multiple angles.

Honestly, my ass almost busted out laughing. Don't get it twisted, I felt terrible for the girl. What happened to her was a sucky situation, and on top of it she had to live in a messed-up family. But for the first time I felt like I kinda had some real power over the Attorney. What her and her husband was asking me to do was embarrassing to the max, and there wasn't nothing they could do about it. And you gotta understand, the Attorney's husband was this macho guy, and the thing macho guys hate most in the world is other men seeing their daughters naked, you feel me? And I loved to hear his macho ass pleading with me. So I just smiled into the phone and said that old Axel would see what he could do, but that this wasn't any simple task, and that I needed a decent laptop with some firepower to get the job done. He said anything, anything I needed was mine, just please hurry.

That same night the Attorney gave me a brand-new fancy ass laptop, and I got to work knocking off as many of her daughter's pictures

253

as I could. I did wanna protect that baby girl after all. Someone had done her wrong and betrayed her trust, and I wasn't cool with that, so I actually tried my hardest to scrub the internet of all her photos. I worked night and day to get everything taken down. After a week, it was almost impossible to find any pictures of her anymore. And, I'll be honest with you, I thought about saving the photos as like an insurance. As a way of protecting myself if the Attorney ever tried to fuck me over in the future. But I didn't. Honestly I didn't. I couldn't do that to that little girl. But I did keep the laptop. Hells yeah I did.

I DIDN'T HEAR from the Attorney for a freaking long time after that. When she did finally call, it was late at night. She sounded worried, so I asked what was wrong, and she said that she had a young man with her who was in trouble, and that he needed a place to hide. She said that she was gonna send him to live with me for a while, and that I should come meet him in the main square of Coyoacán. He'd be waiting next to the fountain of the two wolves. Then she hung up.

I didn't know what to do, so I walked upstairs and told my land-lord that I had a friend come into town unexpected, and that he was gonna crash with me for a little bit. He said that I'd have to pay some extra rent for having another person in the house. So I texted the At-torney, and she said the young guy would have the cash ready when we met up.

When I got to Coyoacán, the fountain was turned off for the night and he was sitting in between the two wolves in the darkness. He handed me the money from the Attorney without a sound. When we got back home, I took him up to my room and turned the light on, just so I get a good look at him. You could tell he was real poor like the people in Guerrero, which is saying something, cause by that time I was used to always being the brokest motherfucker in the room. It was hard to tell exactly how old he was, cause he was super-short, and that made me think he was young, like a kid, but at the same time there was something else that made him seem older. Like, by the way he looked at you, you could tell he had seen some real deal shit. Then he told me to *turn the light off, that someone mighta been able to watch us through the window if it was on.*

I was like, "Goddamn my dude, you more paranoid than me."

But he didn't laugh. Didn't even smile. So I turned off the light.

He basically didn't say nothing else for two days. He slept in my bed, ate my food, wore my clothes. And he was polite. He thanked me for all of it. But the way he said it, it was like a machine talking. Like he didn't actually care about none of that stuff, to be honest. Like if I wasn't giving him a bed and food and clothes, they never woulda even crossed his mind to begin with, right? Like it coulda rained right on top of his head and he woulda just stood in it without even flinching. Every night, we'd go to bed, and I could just feel him laying there, stiff as a board, staring straight up at the ceiling. And then as soon as I started to drift off, I could feel him get up all quiet and walk over to the window and stare out onto the street again. And every time a car drove by or a person walked down the road he just frozed up and watched them until they disappeared.

And so eventually I just said it. "Look, baby boy, I ain't tryna be rude or nothing, cause you seem like a decent kid, but you freak me the fuck out. I'm risking my neck for you. And my landlord's starting to think I'm some kinda pervert for keeping a boy as young as you in my bedroom. So please, I'm begging you, tell me what's going on. What's on the other side of that window you're so worried about?"

And the boy turned and looked at me and said that he'd killed somebody. Three people, actually. He said it like it wasn't nothing. Not like he was proud or ashamed or nothing. Then he turned back to the window. The next night he told me that he was seventeen and from Guerrero, like I'd guessed. That he was part of a militia, like I'd also guessed. And that he was already married and had kids, which I definitely had not guessed. The night after that, he said the men he'd killed were part of a cartel. The cartel had kidnapped a family who owned a farm in his village. They wanted to use the land to grow poppies. After several days, they let the family go instead of killing them. Who knows why, he said. But when the family was released, they went straight to the militia and

255

said that the cartel had tortured them and stole their land. And the boy and the rest of the men loaded up a buncha trucks with machine guns and drove to the farm. There was a shootout. Six cartel members died, he said, and he'd killed three of them himself.

I asked him what it felt like to kill somebody. I knew I shouldn't have, but I couldn't help it.

And he said that it didn't feel like nothing at all.

The next night he said that he needed to stay in Mexico City until things in Guerrero cooled down. That word had been spread out that he had committed murder, and that both the cartel and the government was searching for him now. That's why he was always looking outta the window. And every single night he kept watch, staring at the street, which was fine with me, cause he was worser when he was asleep. I swear to god sometimes I thought he was on drugs. He'd go to sleep and start screaming and crying and rolling around, and then he'd jump up and run to the window, still yelling like a demon bout how they was watching us, how they was climbing inside. His eyes was wide open, but he wasn't awake, and I'd have to shake him until he calmed down.

He lived in my bedroom for four months. Then one day he said that his wife had called and told him that it was safe to go back to the village again, that there wasn't nobody there looking for him anymore, and he left, just like that.

ONE NIGHT, WE threw a party in our basement apartment, and a man I didn't know appeared in our windowless living room. He was wearing a particularly ugly tie that drooped past his belt. He said his name was Adam and that he was the deputy director of communications for the Trump administration. I had no idea who had invited him. Adam got drunk and claimed that Trump didn't actually hate immigrants at all, that it was just a calculated gimmick to whip up his base. Adam's wife got drunk and said that she was a Democrat and didn't share her husband's political views. I got drunk and considered punching Adam in the face. But I didn't. I was afraid he'd press charges. The next morning,

I was furious with myself. If I ever saw the sniveling rat again, I vowed, I'd deck him on sight. Then, by chance, I did see Adam at another party. And again I did nothing.

I was ashamed. I was ashamed of what I was doing, and I was ashamed of what I was not doing. I was a coward in a city full of cowards. After work I would roam the streets, hoping to find some glimmer of tangible outrage, but the boulevards remained tranquil and well swept. The few marches organized in protest of Trump were pitifully placid affairs that made the Viacrucis look like an invading army. There was no turmoil or struggle here. It was like I'd wandered into a little provincial capital filled with little provincial people. Well-informed voters jogged through well-policed neighborhoods and dined in well-reviewed cafes. It seemed that nothing could halt the clockwork manufacture of immaculately poached eggs and watered-down mimosas steadily ticking out onto brunch tabletops. If there was ever an occasional shout from a far-off place, it was quickly drowned out by the sound of tinkling glass and measured conversation.

I WAS EXERCISING in the basement gym when Iván Hernández called. He asked if I'd spoken with Ever recently. I said no.

"He's missing," said Iván. "We had a fight a couple weeks ago and he left for the border. Nobody's heard from him since."

I searched for Ever's name in ICE's Online Detainee Locator System, but I couldn't find him. I imagined him wandering through an arid desert, his clothing covered in dust. I imagined him collapsed, face down in the cracking earth. I imagined a black committee of vultures perched atop his small, white skeleton. For two agonizing weeks, I held my breath and prayed. Then I got a call from Farmville Detention Center. It was Ever. There was no time for sentimentalities, he said, because he was only permitted two minutes on the phone. He asked if I could find an attorney to help him file for asylum, and if I might be able to visit him in the detention center. I was the only person he knew in the US.

By chance, Farmville was only four hours from DC. I rented a car and drove into the Virginia countryside. The town was mostly a collection of dilapidated brick buildings baking in the southern heat. If the detention center were included in the town census, the detainees would have comprised a quarter of the total population. But it wasn't, so they didn't. I parked in the visitor section in front of a van that had a "Farmville Dancer" sticker in the back window. Nearby was a gleaming white BMW with a vanity plate that read "GODABLE." In the air-conditioned lobby there was a metal detector and a guard who patted me down. Fox News played in the background. When they finally let me in, Ever was sitting in the far corner of the visitation room. He was wearing a yellow prison uniform that engulfed his feeble frame. We talked for an hour. About his trip through the desert, during which he hid in a bush for an entire night while a helicopter circled overhead. About how he wasn't actually caught crossing the border—they nabbed him several days later after he hopped on a northbound bus outside of McAllen. About how the nonprofit I'd put him in touch with might take his case. Then a guard came and told me to leave.

Three months later, Ever was released on bail, which was paid for by an acquaintance of a family friend who'd agreed to lend him the money with interest. She lived in the Midwest and was willing to rent Ever a spare bedroom while he fought for asylum. He stayed for one night on a blow-up mattress in my living room. By the time he arrived it was very late, and he looked exhausted. Our conversation was brief.

"I'm nervous," he said wearily.

"About your asylum case?"

"About living in the snow."

He asked if it snowed in DC, and I said yes, it could get very cold compared to Honduras or Georgia, which was one of the many reasons I was hoping to leave. In fact, I'd just applied to grad school.

"Anthropology?" he asked.

"Anthropology," I confirmed. But it seemed utterly ridiculous to talk about something like grad school at that moment, so I said, "Axel sends his best. He actually tried to trace your phone when you went missing. He mapped your route all the way up to the border, but then your signal disappeared."

"Oh, is he in DC now too?" asked Ever hopefully.

"No," I said. "No, he's not."

In the morning, I bought Ever a train ticket and gave him all the spare cash in my sock drawer. A year later, he was granted asylum and moved into an apartment with his new American boyfriend. He was the only person from the entire Viacrucis, as far as I know, who won his immigration case in the US.

CHAPTER 25

ISABELA

THE CASE THAT forced me to finally quit was Isabela's. I conducted her intake, which didn't seem particularly abnormal at the time. Isabela was seventeen, from Honduras, and had fled with her infant child, Miguel, after Miguel's father, Adrián, was murdered by a local gang. She had a decent shot at winning asylum, but her case had quickly become a problem not for any particular legal reason but because she was shy. Too shy. Even when I asked for her full name, Isabela had fumbled the words, accidentally switching her two middle names. Shy clients were always a problem. Asylum interviews could be arduous affairs, in which applicants were asked a litany of questions about the most traumatic experiences of their lives. To prove that she deserved to remain in the US, Isabela didn't just have to regurgitate the minutia of her case accurately—which was hard enough for anyone to do on the fly, but especially for her because she hadn't attended school since the age of thirteen. She also had to provide a narrative about her trauma that was interesting and held the officer's attention. That was the thing about the asylum system, I'd come to realize. You had to take a constellation of seemingly random events that couldn't possibly be explained adequately—how could you ever really articulate the terror and confusion of your partner being murdered on a gang member's whim?—and convert it into a good story, one that was chronological, with dates and a perfectly logical series of events.

It didn't matter if you were an adult or a child, a PhD student or a dropout, you had to provide a narrative about yourself that kept the pace and held the asylum officer's attention, a story that included those aspects of your life that you hoped would seem both entertaining and entirely tragic. The key was to provide details that moved the officer, that made them want to cry, even if they weren't allowed to cry. And at that moment, the very instant they felt their eyes going red and welling up with tears, you should cry instead. This was the game. To tell a good story, and to tell it so well that you became it.

Helping a child tell a story like that required extensive prep time, evenings upon evenings of extra work. All unpaid, of course. Unfortunately, Isabela simply wasn't getting it. Try as she might, she couldn't understand which bits of information about herself, or about Adrián's murder, would likely be deemed crucial or interesting by the US immigration system. She'd veer off on a tangent or jump back and forth between events seemingly at random. Fortunately, however, we'd landed a top-notch attorney to assist us with Isabela's case pro bono. He was a corporate lawyer at one of DC's top firms, who, after Trump took office, began dedicating his free time to representing unaccompanied minors. He had won every asylum case he'd taken, and his schedule had cleared just enough to represent Isabela as well.

For Isabela's preparation, we convened in the penthouse board room of the attorney's office building, which had a sweeping view of the city. Isabela reached out and lightly touched the twenty-foot-long glass conference table as if it might disappear at any moment. She'd never been in such a lavish space in her life. As we strategized, the attorney asked my boss if she knew who the asylum officer presiding over the case would be.

"No," my boss said, but hopefully it would be someone we'd worked with before. An officer who was familiar with our organization and respected our professionalism. "I actually went to law school with someone who works there now," my boss said.

The attorney grimaced. "Someone shelled out two hundred grand for law school and then became an asylum officer?"

"It happens more than you'd think," said my boss. "You don't make the grades and then none of the DC firms will hire you."

It was a well-known fact in immigration circles that a not insignificant share of asylum officers were law school washouts who couldn't cut it in the private sector. The government, by contrast, was eager to hire anyone with a law degree, no matter their grades, in an attempt to lend a sense of legitimacy to the whole process. It was essentially the white-collar equivalent of what happened with the border patrol. Border patrol agents were wannabe soldiers. Asylum officers were wannabe lawyers.

My boss explained to Isabela that I would translate her interview, and that she anticipated it would go fairly quickly—hopefully no more than an hour and a half.

"Sound good?" she asked after I translated everything. Isabela nodded and looked out the window as the corporate attorney patted her hand reassuringly and followed her gaze across the rooftops of DC, the national monuments and government agencies, the luxury hotels and public museums, extending as far as the eye could see.

THE DAY OF her interview, Isabela, the attorney, and I spent hours in the Arlington Asylum Office waiting room before someone opened a door and called her name. I wasn't looking forward to the process. I had translated several other interviews previously, which were all somber and woebegone affairs, full of desperate melancholy. We walked through a maze of hallways leading to various offices, all completely stark, and then another door was opened and we were ushered into a small room, just large enough for a desk and four chairs. A man in a blue suit entered and said that he would be the asylum officer. His accent was posh and from sub-Saharan Africa. I guessed Nigeria. His tie was silk. Behind the officer's desk were two large filing cabinets stuffed with packets and briefs. Other than that, there were no decorations. The cabinets were gray, the walls were white, the desk was black.

The officer explained the basics of the meeting to us in English and that he was going to patch through the government-appointed virtual interpreter, who was listening on the other end of the line to ensure I was translating accurately. He would not speak unless I mistranslated something, or if I needed help translating a word I did not know. "You see?" said the asylum officer. "He's here to make sure you don't fool me."

I didn't know if the officer was joking, so I smiled nervously. "I won't," I said, but the officer held a finger to his lips.

"From now on," he whispered dramatically, "you no longer have permission to speak, except when translating."

We set about verifying Isabela's basic information.

"What is your name?" asked the officer in English.

"What is your name?" I repeated in Spanish.

Isabela said her name.

"No, louder, I cannot hear you," said the officer.

"No, louder, I cannot hear you," I said.

Isabela said her name louder.

"Louder."

"Louder."

Isabela said her name a third time, and I repeated it a third time.

"And your date of birth?"

"And your date of birth?"

From the corner of my eye, I could see the attorney check his watch. Basic information checks were just a way to get the interview going. They usually only lasted a few minutes, but almost twenty had already passed. "Sir," said the attorney, attempting to speed up the process, "we have already submitted a copy of my client's birth certificate, which clearly has her name, and well as many other documents that verify her identity."

"You don't dictate the questions," snapped the officer, and made Isabela repeat her current address three times. I wondered what it would be like to have access to the addresses of all the immigration judges and asylum officers, the way that they had the addresses of our clients. After nearly an hour, Miguel squirmed out of Isabela's lap and tugged at his diaper. The room started to stink.

"Sir," interrupted the attorney again, "if I may, I understand that it's standard practice, after verifying a small child's basic information, to allow them to leave the room. So we might avoid any unnecessary disruptions."

"You find this process unnecessary?"

"No sir, of course not."

"Of course not. I want little Miguel to stay. I'm sure he'll be a very good boy," he said. Then, as if making sure Miguel understood him, he asked, "Won't you, Miguel?"

I paused, unsure if I was supposed to translate the question.

"Interpreter," barked the officer.

Isabela looked at me, confused. "Levi, is he speaking to me?" she asked.

"Levi, is he speaking to me?" I said in English.

"The interviewee will only address the interviewer," the asylum officer said, and I parroted his words.

"No, Levi, I don't understand. Am I the interviewee? Are you the interviewer, or him?"

"No, Levi, I don't understand. Am I the interviewee? Are you the interviewer, or him?"

"I am the interviewer," snarled the asylum officer. "And you will not directly address the translator again, do I make myself clear?"

"May I remind you, sir," cut in the attorney, blessedly deadpan, "that Miguel does not speak English or Spanish, as he is a baby."

After nearly three hours, we finally arrived at Adrián's murder, and I had no idea how I was supposed to interpret Isabela's crying. If she said something through tears, I wondered, should I try to imitate the sorrow in her voice, the cadence of her sobs? Should I also stare at the ceiling and catch my breath, just like she did? I became nervous and began to stutter. I was so focused on translating everything literally, precisely, word-for-word, that my English became disjointed, then unraveled entirely. I started missing the overall meaning of certain phrases. I translated "bélico" literally to "warlike" without thinking and had to backtrack when I remembered that in Honduras it also meant "cool." And then I stupidly did the same thing a few minutes later, translating "caballo" as "horse."

"The guys who killed Adrián were horses," I said. "No, sorry, interpreter's correction. The guys who killed Adrián were oblivious, idiots, like men who do things without thinking about their consequences."

I was sweating profusely in my blazer, the only blazer I owned, and I had an impulse to dive over the table, tackle the officer out of his chair, and slam his head into the ground. I imagined making him feel as desperate as Isabela felt, as caged and suffocated as all the other people he had trapped in the very seats we were sitting in now. But I didn't. Instead, I dutifully listened to every question the officer asked, processed it, and repeated it again to Isabela in her own tongue.

Then Isabela said a word I didn't recognize. I asked the officer for permission to clarify, but I still didn't understand. The attorney shifted in his seat. Isabela wiped a tissue across her nose. My shirt was soaked through with sweat. Then the virtual interpreter chimed in that he believed the word was Honduran slang for a getaway vehicle. "She said that she believes Adrián's murderers drove off in a getaway vehicle as she fled the scene."

"Slang?" said the officer. "Like gang slang?"

The virtual interpreter said he did not know if it was gang slang, and then the asylum officer said that the interview was over.

"That concludes the interview," I repeated in Spanish. "You are free to leave."

We exited the perfectly air-conditioned building without a word and walked into the sunshine, all of us knowing we had lost, the attorney already vowing to appeal the decision—"How could he speak like that to a little girl, Levi, Jesus Christ, what is this goddamned world coming to?"—and me feeling like somewhere inside a devil had taken hold, as if it had spoken through my own mouth.

I DON'T KNOW what happened with Isabela's asylum case because a couple months later I quit. Asylum applications frequently take years, and the appeals process years more. The official complaint against the asylum officer was that he had put Isabela through a highly unprofessional and unusual interview process. Isabela's interview was undoubtedly unprofessional, but its outcome was in no way unusual. Asylum denials had been steadily rising across the country since Obama's second term, and they continued under Trump. In 2016, for instance—the last fiscal year of Obama's presidency—US immigration courts denied over 70 percent of all the men, women, and children who looked an asylum officer in the eyes and said that they would be killed if they were deported to the Northern Triangle. And in my home state of Georgia, from 2013 to 2018, Atlanta's two immigration offices rejected close to 95 percent of all asylum cases. Unlike Isabela, most asylum seekers are courteously offered water and listened to attentively. They are called ma'am and sir. Their cases are weighed with the utmost dignity. And then they are still deported. Deported politely. Deported with propriety. After interpreting Isabela's asylum interview, I could no longer deny that I too, regardless of my intentions, had played a role in that silent slaughter. I brought children like her to court. I put them in front of a judge. And if they didn't win their case, I had essentially helped deport them. That was really what my job was about. To help the state keep tabs on migrants. To keep them churning in the machine.

I didn't say any of this to my boss when I told her I was leaving. I wasn't blaming or implicating her. She and all the other attorneys at my organization were working around the clock to fight deportations, even though they could have walked across the street to a corporate firm and landed a job that paid four times as much. My boss had even offered to take a look at Axel's immigration file. But after scanning his record, she shook her head in dismay. His chances, as she saw them then, were nil. We were caught up in a losing game, a rigged game, and I was done playing.

"I've been accepted into a PhD program in California," I said when I handed in my letter of resignation. "I start in the fall."

"What will you do until then?" she asked.

"Well, as you know," I said, "I've got a friend in Mexico. I think I'll crash with him for a while."

PART IV
THE ANTHROPOLOGIST

CHAPTER 26

TOCAYOS

WHEN I LANDED in Mexico City, Axel wasn't waiting in the airport like we'd planned. After calling him for almost two hours with no response, I hailed a cab and rode alone to the room I'd rented in a boarding house. It was late in the evening when Axel finally called back, apologizing profusely and saying that he'd gotten the time wrong and overslept.

"Overslept?" I said. "Axel it's almost nine at night. My plane landed at two." But I shrugged it off. I only had enough money to rent the room for a week, and I wanted to take advantage of our time together, not bicker. When Axel finally showed up, it was nearly ten, and he was dragging a suitcase full of clothes behind him. He tossed the suitcase onto one of the twin beds and we embraced. He smelled like he hadn't bathed in forever. To my surprise, he said that he'd been evicted again and was now sleeping in a tent in the middle of the city.

"What?" I said. "You told me not to worry. You said that you'd worked something out with the Attorney."

"Yeah, bro, we did. That was what we worked out."

Through her Guerrero connections, the Attorney had heard about a group of protestors squatting in a local park. They were Teachers—just like the ones who'd fought the police on behalf of Father Solalinde and the Viacrucis—and had come from southern states like Guerrero and Oaxaca to strike for better wages.

The Attorney asked if they would allow Axel stay with them in the park where they were squatting. It was like a tent city, said Axel, and he managed to make a little money repairing the Teachers' phones and laptops, which inevitably broke because of exposure to the damp and generally rough living conditions. When Axel finally gave the Attorney some incriminating evidence on Nestora, she said, they would talk about moving him back into an apartment again.

"Of course now I ain't got no internet signal in a freaking tent," he spat while collapsing onto the bed. "So I don't know how she thinks I'm gonna be able to hack for her."

I felt terrible. I'd been so wrapped up in my work in DC that I hadn't thought to ask Axel where the Attorney had put him. The next morning, I got up quietly so as not to disturb his sleep. It was the first time he'd lain on a mattress in months. I took a shower and ate a bowl of cereal in the communal kitchen, but Axel still hadn't woken up, so I took a walk around the neighborhood. When I returned Axel was still asleep, so I read Roberto Arlt's *The Seven Madmen* in the kitchen for a couple of hours. Then I went into the bedroom and shook him awake.

"Dude, it's noon," I said. "Go take a shower and then we'll go grab your stuff."

"My bad bro. I don't need to shower."

"You sure you don't want to change your clothes or brush your teeth? I brought you some extra toothpaste."

"Nah buddy I'm good, let's bounce." So we bounced.

When we got to the park—which was sandwiched between the Biblioteca de México and the Ciudadela, a famous souvenir market—the tent city was mostly empty. "Everyone must be out on a protest," said Axel. He led me to his "room," which was constructed with tarps tied around nearby trees.

"Dude, I didn't know things had gotten this bad. Why didn't you tell me the Attorney was forcing you to live like this?"

"Guess I didn't want to bother you with some more bullshit."

"No man, this is not okay. We've got to find you a different place to live."

I considered calling the Attorney and yelling at her, but what was the point? Better, I thought, to simply make a clean break. I'd figure out some way to get Axel into stable housing and pay for it myself, and we'd never have to speak to her again. Over dinner that evening, a friend of a friend recommended a hotel in the city center that had somehow managed to remain reasonably affordable. When we asked the proprietor if Axel could rent long term, the man said that was fine, so long as Axel took a room on the top floor, which was otherwise empty on account of its faulty plumbing and the fact that the maids thought it was haunted. The nicer rooms on the first and second floors, which had reliable toilets and fewer ghosts, were for short-term guests only. We agreed, and to make small talk as the landlord readied the contract, I asked about the carved stone inscription down the street that commemorated where Moctezuma first met Hernán Cortés. The proprietor thought for a moment and said that, yes, they supposedly met somewhere near where the hotel stood today. Then he paused for a moment longer and asked if we knew the real reason that Tenochtitlán fell.

No, we said.

It wasn't because the Spanish had horses or armor or gunpowder, he claimed. It was because, as the conquistadors began to pillage everything in sight on their march to Tenochtitlán, the thousands of people burned out of their homes fled to the Aztec capital. Welcoming all those refugees quickly depleted the city's resources and, in such miserable and cramped quarters, sickness and hunger spread. Then he said, almost absentmindedly, as he pointed on the contract to where Axel and I needed to sign, that if the Aztecs had turned all of those people away, Tenochtitlán might still be here today. We nodded solemnly, with our mouths shut, and laid down enough bills across the counter to pay the first and last month's rent, plus a deposit. Axel would move in at the end of the week, after I headed back to the US.

In the meantime, we passed the days strolling around Mexico City. Axel especially loved the National Museum of Anthropology, which housed the world's largest collection of Aztec artifacts.

"Bro, the things these people made was so magnificent," he said, excitedly surveying the Tōnalpōhualli. "Hernán Cortés was such a bitch."

We ate meals that Axel couldn't usually afford. Actually, they were meals that I couldn't usually afford either, or meals that I would have felt too guilty to eat without him. So we ate them together. But the fancy restaurants didn't always have the desired effect. Once, at a swanky Italian joint, Axel went quiet and didn't touch his pizza. When I came back from a trip to the bathroom, his chair was empty. I found him in the kitchen, pestering our waiter about how much he earned and if the restaurant had any openings. The waiter, who was tall and light skinned—all the waiters in the fancy restaurants seemed tall and light skinned—shook his head no, bemused.

After dinner, as we were walking back home, I asked Axel if everything was alright.

"Waddya mean, bro? Axel's just chilling. Everything good with you?"

I hesitated. "I don't know, man, it just feels like things are a little off."

"Yeah, Levi. Maybe things are a little off."

I only realized after the fact that the restaurant had been a shock for Axel. Rather than being a treat or celebration, as I had stupidly intended, our meal was a reminder of just how far he'd fallen. "I used to save up and take Monica on dates to places like that in New York," he said later. "I didn't even know they existed in Mexico City. I've only seen the bad places."

That night, after we went to bed, Axel shook me awake. "You were screaming," he said. Later in the night, I woke up again. This time, it was because Axel was the one moaning in his sleep. I had a sudden sensation that something or someone was hiding in the room with us, something concealing itself, but when I flipped on the lights there was nothing there.

My last day in the city, Axel slept in again. When I woke him, he asked whether it was finally June.

"No, dude," I said, confused. "It's September."

"Oh," he said, pulling the sheets back over his head. "I thought it was June."

I hailed a cab and loaded Axel's luggage into the trunk. Then we drove to the hotel and dropped him off. I said that I would come back as soon as I could. On the way to the airport, the peculiar feeling I had continued to grow and grow until it felt like it was filling the whole taxi and I had to roll down the window for some air. I wasn't sure if Axel was on drugs or just starting to go crazy, but something had changed.

After a month in the hotel, Axel called to say that he heard sounds outside his room, pacing and scratching and whispering in the hallway, but when he opened the door there was no one there. Then the knocking began, quietly at first, and then a little louder and more insistent. And again he would open his door and no one would be there. He said that he wasn't sure what was worse, the knocking or the fact that opening a door to an empty hallway was a reminder that he was all alone.

"I'm a ghost," Axel would text me. "Ghost ghost ghost."

Then one day the ghost of his daughter walked through the door of his hotel room. That's how he explained it to me over the phone—"the ghost of my daughter, bro, even though I know she ain't dead." The ghost of his daughter walked through the door, stood in front of his bed, and told him to kill himself. She said that he wasn't her father anymore, that he wasn't a father at all, and all that there was left to do was man up and pull the trigger. Axel saw her four times in seven months, and then the hotel proprietor said he was raising the rent, which we couldn't afford to pay, so Axel moved across the city to Iztapalapa, and fortunately the ghost of his daughter didn't follow him there.

YEARS WOULD PASS.

ATLEE AND I found a studio apartment in Oakland, and I began grad school. From our window, when the red sunset cut through the fog of the San Francisco Bay, you could just make out Alcatraz, a lonely prison in dark waters. I started to read. I picked Roberto Bolaño's *Savage Detectives* back up—the book I'd tried to decipher over and over again in Mexico, the book that had always confused and confounded me—and I finally understood. Then I devoured everything else by Bolaño. I developed a game. Whenever possible, I paired anthropologists with one of their tocayos. I read Roberto Bolaño with Robert Redfield. I read E. E. Evans-Pritchard alongside e. e. cummings, Eric Wolf with Thomas Wolfe, Franz Boas with Frantz Fanon. And, of course, I read Claude Lévi-Strauss with Primo Levi and Larry Levis. Tocayos who were not quite tocayos. Tocayos whose names never fully matched.

With the stipend I earned as a PhD student, I figured out a way to cover Axel's rent without having to rely on the Attorney's intermittent charity, and he was finally able to cut her out for good. His hacks were over. I don't know how much money I sent Axel in total. Easily enough for the down payment on a nice house in my hometown. Or another metric: enough money that I could have paid off my sister Ani's medical bills when she was diagnosed with cancer out of the blue. That's the thing about deportations—they make you choose. Which family member deserves the money more, as well as who merits your attention, your time, and your energy. I was the oldest of my parents' four children, and the only one to have graduated from college. I'd made it out of Georgia and seen some of the world. I was supposed to help support the family. Instead, the money went to Axel. I didn't tell him about Ani's health for a long time. I guess it was like my version of sleeping in a tent city. Not that it was equivalent—I just didn't want to bother him with things that were beyond his control. But after the insurance company declined to cover her medical bills, we held a fundraiser, and Axel saw a picture of Ani's shaved head online. He immediately refused to withdraw the last wire transfer I'd sent him.

"Nah bro, give the money to her," he said. "She needs it more than me right now."

During her chemotherapy, Axel would message Ani occasionally, just to wish her well, and even after she recovered, they kept in touch. They shared something, I think, that even Axel and I didn't. I'd brushed against death while in Mexico, but Axel and Ani had both, in their own ways, been forced to stare it in the face.

But, of course, Axel was really facing something that none of us could comprehend. Alone in his room, Axel would go feral, not bathe or shave for weeks at a time, and have visions. Whispers, shadows, things he'd never seen until he'd been deported. And then I would eventually return and slowly resocialize him. Through caring for Axel, I was able to let go of at least some of the pain and anguish I had been lost in since DC. He became the embodiment of what I felt I could do at the time. I could not fix the US immigration system or destroy the Southern Border Program, but when I was in Mexico City, I could buy Axel his groceries and cook him his meals. I'd give him money for new clothes and shoes. I'd purchase toothbrushes and toothpaste, floss and mouthwash, deodorant and lotion. I'd bring fresh towels and soap and shaving cream and razor blades. Axel would use the toiletries for a day or two and then forget all about them, and I'd have to drag him out of his room every night and force him to brush his teeth. He had a habit of dowsing his feet, which blistered and cracked in the arid Mexico City climate, in baby powder. At his lowest, Axel would disappear into his room for days at a time, and I'd only know that he'd finally left—to go to the bathroom, or to buy cigarettes—because in the morning there would be delicate powdery footprints trailing across the floor. The footprints of a ghost.

"My feets never healed from the Viacrucis," he explained once.

I peeled off my socks and showed him my own feet, which were red and flaky. "Ever since the Viacrucis, I've had terrible eczema. It won't go away."

From then on, we couldn't help but notice that we had strangely parallel ailments. Once, when I was in the US and Axel was in Mexico, my lower back began to ache. Then Axel called to say that he thought there was something wrong with his kidneys. He hadn't been able to leave his bed in days. Finally, a doctor at UNAM's School of Medicine took pity on him and ran several diagnostic tests for free. But Axel never returned for the results.

"You have to go back," I pleaded. "There could be something seriously wrong with you."

"I ain't got the money to pay for whatever the fuck's wrong with me, bro, so it's just better not to know."

Axel developed a small phobia about drinking water. For a while, he refused to consume any liquid except Coke, which rotted his teeth. Then one day a tooth came loose and fell out of his head. The weirdest thing, he said, was that it didn't even hurt. By coincidence, I had a dental check-up around the same time.

"You've been grinding your teeth to nubs," said the dentist. "You must be stressed. And—what on earth? Half your molar is missing."

"Huh?" I grunted, with his hand still digging around in my mouth.

"Half of your back molar is snapped clean off. Why didn't you come in sooner?"

I had no idea that it had happened. There were other strange parallels: aches in our left knees, twitching in our right eyes, and night terrors—sometimes even what seemed to be the same dream, in which we were being hunted by unknown assassins in a pitch-black mansion.

"We're falling apart," I said.

YEARS WOULD PASS.

WITHOUT HAVING TO hack for the Attorney all day, Axel set out to find other work. But it was a fleeting and confounding thing. Over half of the Mexican economy is informal, meaning that the jobs are unregulated and untaxed, and, at the time, Mexico had the second-lowest minimum wage in the Americas, behind only Haiti. The glut of cheap citizen labor meant that bosses never needed to hire immigrants of any kind, let alone ones who were undocumented. Axel was turned away from sleek call centers and humble cantinas alike, with many bosses unapologetically stating that they'd never hire Central Americans because they were un-trustworthy, especially black ones like him. Instead, Axel's best chance at finding work was if somebody missed their shift. At night he'd circle the nearby restaurants, stopping at each to ask if they were short staffed. Sometimes he'd get lucky and pick up a few hours washing dishes in the back. Usually his payment was whatever leftovers he could eat off customers' plates before they were plopped in soapy water. There were other odd jobs: waiting tables, installing internet in a new office building, mopping the guts and blood from butchers' stalls, mending busted television satellites, and scrubbing neighborhood fountains. The compensation was scattershot. Mostly food, but occasionally pesos, as well as things he could haggle for—a blanket during the winter, a jacket, shoes, several broken smartphones, an old computer, and once, a bottle of Cuban rum, aged seven years.

Eventually, I landed Axel a part-time gig with my friend Mike, who had started a company that hunted an invasive fish species in the Mexican state of Tabasco. The company processed the fish and turned it into jerky. Axel was supposed to handle the in-country logistics: shipping the frozen fillets from Tabasco to Mexico City, storing them in various industrial freezers, and all the payments in between. But after a few months, money started disappearing. We never exactly figured out where it all went—if Axel was just losing his mind, or if he was skimming something off the top, or if it was a bit of both—but eventually Mike had to let him go.

There were other strange occurrences. Bizarre sagas about mysterious men following him. Or that the narco evading a nation-wide manhunt just so happened to be hiding out in the apartment across the hall. Before Axel cut off all contact with the Attorney, she once informed him that Beto Donis, Father Solalinde's right-hand man, was dead. He died in a car crash, the details of which were suspicious, at least according to her. There was a rumor going around that Solalinde had quietly fired Beto months earlier from the shelter, presumably because his transgressions had grown too conspicuous for the priest to ignore any longer. But Beto's departure had been so swept under the rug that most people still didn't know that he'd ever left the shelter in the first place. Father Solalinde held a memorial service for him at Hermanos, as if he hadn't been fired. Later, Axel said that he'd heard Beto's car was seen flying down the road, like he was running from someone, and when first responders arrived at the scene, they found the sides of the vehicle riddled with bullet holes. But Solalinde didn't want something as scandalous as Beto's cartel assassination to get out, Axel said, so he covered it up and strong-armed the media into reporting the accident as a one-man car crash.

Afterward, I reached out to some journalist contacts, who all confirmed that there were no bullet holes in Beto's car. One had seen the crash with his own eyes. It was just an accident, he insisted, that was all. Again, it was hard to know if Axel made up the fantastical details himself, or if he was repeating a rumor the Attorney told him, or if he was simply confused. That was the thing. I could never quite tell where I stood in relation to him anymore, or where he stood in relation to the rest of the world. I felt like I was losing him.

Things came to a head when, while I was visiting, Axel suddenly disappeared. All I got was a text message that said he was sorry, but he'd just been offered a construction job in the state of Guanajuato, and he had to leave immediately. A week later, after I was already back in the US, Axel sent another text saying that he'd been duped. The job offer was a trap. The "boss" drove Axel to a remote warehouse in the middle of the Guanajuatan desert, and then, with no other witnesses or transportation around, claimed that the original job had "fallen through." Fortunately, however, he had another opportunity. He pulled out a bag of cocaine and instructed Axel to sell it in the nearby city of Celaya. Axel said that he had to escape on foot, leaving behind his backpack, which was packed with the clothes I'd just bought him, a tablet I'd given him weeks earlier as a gift, a laptop, and the 5,000 pesos I'd left for next month's rent. I also had to pay for an Uber worth an entire month's wages in Mexico—immigration almost never hassled the rideshare companies, loath as the government was to anger its new tech colonizers—to sneak Axel back into Mexico City in the dead of night. But then Axel claimed that he couldn't return to his current apartment, because the boss knew where he lived, and he'd need to move somewhere else. So we lost the deposit and the rest of that month's rent, plus the fridge and cooktop I'd bought him. All in all, the losses added up to at least 60,000 pesos.

I was near my breaking point.

"What the fuck is going on with you?" I seethed over the phone. "In case you forgot, I'm a student. You can't just blow money like this."

"Well excuse me," he retorted, "for tryna support myself and then almost getting kidnapped."

"This isn't easy for me either, you know. I'm still skipping meals to send you money, and then this is what you go and do with it? I need you to be smarter than that."

"I truly do apologize that you had to go hungry, my brother. That must be difficult for you."

YEARS WOULD PASS.

IT WASN'T ALL bad. There were times when Axel's eyes gleamed with the sharp brilliance that I'd first seen on the Viacrucis. One night, in a fit of spontaneity, we decided to sneak into a new boutique hotel, because we'd heard that they had a jacuzzi on the rooftop. But after we slipped past the staff and tiptoed up the stairs, my hopes were dashed. The hot tub was there, but it was filled with a foot of brown leaves and sludge.

"Don't worry bro," said Axel, rolling up his sleeves. "You just relax on the patio and I'll work my magic."

I don't know how he did it, but somehow Axel eventually got the jets humming again, good as new. For a brief moment, soaking in the jacuzzi, it was almost like things were back to normal.

Just weeks later, after I'd already returned to the US, there was a massive earthquake. Axel's room shook until it nearly split in half, but he was unhurt. When the ground settled again, he ran to the city center, where whole buildings had collapsed, and frantically helped dig through the rubble. Axel would turn over slabs of concrete and find dried pools of blood. He and a stranger uncovered what they determined to be a body of a woman, because of what was left of her dress and shoulder-length hair. No one knew that the dark-skinned civilian risking his life in the heaps of debris was an undocumented migrant. After two days of nonstop excavation, Axel returned home. His landlord never fixed the crack that ran the entire length of his room, and he lived there for nine more months.

Sometimes misfortune worked in our favor. Once, as I was scrambling to figure out how I was going to pay both my rent and Axel's for the month, his landlord's toddler climbed onto a stovetop, slipped, and somehow fell feet-first into a pot of boiling water.

The family couldn't afford the hospital bill, and so they cut Axel a deal: if he forked over next month's rent within twenty-four hours, they'd only charge him half the normal amount. For three months afterward, the girl's feet needed to be washed and bandaged daily, but the family couldn't bear to do it themselves. So they proposed the same deal—half the rent if Axel cared for the girl. Every day, Axel held the soft flesh of the toddler's feet in his hands. He cleaned it and kissed it when she cried. Her skin eventually healed, she learned to walk, and then the family raised the rent and Axel was out on the street again.

At his next apartment, the landlord agreed to rent to Axel on the condition that he provide proof that he was in the country legally. We decided that the best thing to do was to photoshop my passport and give the landlord a scanned black-and-white "copy." I was able to paste Axel's headshot over my own with relative ease, but I wasn't skilled enough to convincingly change the name. I couldn't find the right font, and even when I used an approximation, the new typeface warped the passport's watermark. Anyone who inspected the scan would immediately realize something was up. So I just left the name: Levi David Vonk. Axel memorized my date of birth and passport number, in case the landlord quizzed him, and came up with some story about how Axel was just a family nickname. His landlord bought it. How stupid, I thought, that this was all it took. One small lie—just a single photocopied sheet of paper that cost nothing to print— meant everything.

"Does this make me your tocayo?" I asked.

"That don't even make sense, Levi. Tocayos are people with the same name."

"But we do have the same name now," I said. "On paper at least."

"Yeah, but not in real life."

"Okay, but hear me out, what if we were tocayos with different names? Everyone's always confusing us anyway. Remember how people on the Viacrucis would call you Levi by mistake, and me Axel? And then the Shrew did the same thing. And the Attorney too. It's like we're a paradox, right? Tocayos with different names."

"Whatever you say, bro, but honestly you're overthinking it. To me we're just brothers."

"Brothers," I repeated. "Impossible brothers."

YEARS WOULD PASS.

CHAPTER 27

LÓPEZ OBRADOR

IN THE SUMMER of 2018, Mexico elected a new president, Andrés Manuel López Obrador. I was with Axel at the time, and we gazed in awe as the streets of Mexico City filled with celebratory crowds. There were streamers and banners and fireworks. I'd never seen Mexico this hopeful before. During his campaign, López Obrador promised to fight the hallmark corruption of the country's long-ruling conservative party, the PRI, the same party that struck a deal with Obama to enact the Southern Border Program. His incoming administration had even vowed to create an easier path to legalization for Central Americans and to "respect, in unrestricted terms, migrants' human rights." I desperately wanted to believe him, so I believed him.

"Come on bro," I said to Axel the night of the election. "Let's celebrate. This could be the end of the Southern Border Program. You might finally get documents."

"I'll believe it when I got the papers in hand, my brother. Until then my black ass is staying locked up inside this apartment."

Shortly before López Obrador took office, another migrant caravan entered Mexico. It had been organized in Honduras and was led entirely by migrants and activists. It was also massive, evolving into a kind of super-caravan, with estimates of over ten thousand Central Americans traveling in waves across Mexico from October 2018 to February 2019. US reports characterized the caravan as if it was entirely alien, a lumpen horde hell bent on swarming the country. And though López Obrador initially offered to aid the migrants—even granting them the opportunity to apply for humanitarian visas—he quickly stationed soldiers in northern Mexico to stop them from entering the US. It was possibly in an attempt to appease Donald Trump, who was threatening to end trade agreements with Mexico if the caravan wasn't halted immediately. Things were quickly becoming tense with the new president.

I decided that I had to meet the caravan when it arrived in Tijuana. One of their base camps was at Enclave Caracol, a community center in the middle of downtown. When I arrived, a group of journalists was crowded around one of the entrances, where a man with dark, hooded eyes was giving a speech in front of the cameras.

> **Levi 2:21 PM** dude you'll never believe this
> **Levi 2:21 PM** irineo is here
> **Levi 2:21 PM** i just got to TJ and he's like the first person i see
> **Axel 2:44 PM** omg that mofo keeps poppin up everywhere
> **Axel 2:44 PM** Be careful bro

Irineo's status as a migrant activist had grown significantly since the last time I'd seen him. In fact, it seemed that the more Trump raged about the invaders threatening to flood our borders, the more Irineo's face appeared in US media coverage. Throughout 2018, he was quoted in the *New York Times*, the *Los Angeles Times*, the *Guardian*, the *Washington Post*, *Time* magazine, and even *Teen Vogue*. Later that evening, I was walking up the stairs of Enclave Caracol when I almost ran straight into him.

"Irineo," I said, extending my hand. He grabbed it absentmindedly and then went back to typing on his phone. "Irineo," I said again, "do you remember me?"

He gave a grunt, which sounded like neither a yes nor a no. I stood there on the bottom step, gazing up at him, unsure of what to do. He never once looked at me. Then I turned around and left. Over the next few days, I watched Irineo give more speeches and interviews to journalists. He announced that he and several other migrants were conducting a hunger strike near the San Ysidro port of entry until the US government allowed everyone to apply for asylum. He clearly positioned himself as an authority figure within the caravan and held great sway over some of its members, which worried me. I decided that I had to tell someone what I knew about him. But how to explain something so complicated? I ended up confiding in a friend, Carlos, another anthropologist working in Tijuana, and he put me in touch with a woman who said that she worked for the American side of Pueblo Sin Fronteras. When she called me on the phone, I was wary of speaking with her, but I didn't know where else to turn.

She asked exactly what my accusations against Irineo were, and I first tried to explain his overall demeanor during the Viacrucis, especially what I believed to be his recklessness and general disregard for others' safety. Then I told her about the boy I'd seen sitting on his lap, who seemed to be no more than twelve years old, and how the boy had approached me afterward, how it sounded like someone was forcing him to talk to me. Finally, I recounted the other rumors I'd heard about the shelter in Chahuites, and the fact that it had even been shut down recently and Father Solalinde's name quietly removed from the walls. The woman listened wordlessly, and when I was done, she asked if I had any proof for my accusations. I said that I could only tell her what I'd seen and what dozens of other migrants had told me over the years. Then she said that, though the claims concerned her, Irineo was currently facing many lies because of his activism. She needed hard evidence and wanted to speak directly to some of the people he'd allegedly abused.

I tried to stay measured. "I get that you want evidence," I said, "but that's just not how these things work."

"Do you think," she asked, and I could sense antagonism in her voice now, "that these accusations might exist because Irineo is gay? And that people tend to be, you know, homophobic in Mexico?"

"Homophobic? Who's homophobic? Me? The migrants?" The insinuation upset me, but I was much more incensed that Irineo's destiny lay in the hands of Americans. I didn't know a single person in Mexico who respected Irineo at all. But north of the border, he could hold fundraisers and press conferences, and no one asked questions. "Listen," I said, "have you ever actually lived in Mexico before? Or traveled with migrants?"

The woman replied defensively that she'd visited Tijuana a couple times.

I tried to explain that I couldn't just get in touch with the people who'd made accusations against Irineo, because they'd disappeared. Migrants migrate. They leave. Even if I could track some of them down, I said, I didn't think that they'd trust some random person in the US with their story. We were at an impasse. There was nothing else to say, so we hung up.

IN MAY 2019, López Obrador announced the launch of the National Guard of Mexico. It was a new military force that in theory existed to handle all matters of national security but in practice quickly became Mexico's primary means of combating migrant caravans. In early 2020, another caravan crossed into Mexico and was brutally beaten by the National Guard at the border. Watching coverage of the bloody clashes from the US, it was astounding just how much better funded and trained Mexico's anti-immigrant forces had become since 2015. Essentially, the Southern Border Program had taken what was once a ragtag band of immigration agents and replaced them when necessary with a ruthlessly organized army.

But Father Solalinde—who was rumored to have recently been long-listed for the Nobel Peace Prize—publicly defended López Obrador. During the president's campaign, Solalinde was one of his highest-profile endorsers. To reward the priest for his loyalty, López Obrador proposed that he head the National Human Rights Commission, the same institution where the Viacrucis filed their official complaint against the immigration and federal police forces. But Solalinde eventually declined the appointment. The Catholic Church was reticent to relinquish its clergy to the state, and, from a secular perspective, the constitutionality of a priest heading a government institution was legally ambiguous at best. But from then on, it was an open secret that the priest was a close, if technically unofficial, advisor to Mexico's president. As López Obrador's open suppression of caravans continued, Father Solalinde was asked by Salvadoran journalist Carlos Martínez about his position on the violence.

Migrants were very important, said the priest, "but Mexico must come first."

The statement sent shockwaves across Mexico's high-profile human rights community. Activists like Don Armando and the Attorney had spent years competing to become Solalinde's right hand, but it turned out that the priest had been jockeying for position in a much bigger game. And now that migrants didn't matter politically to Solalinde in the same way anymore, both Don Armando and the Attorney were left out in the cold.

Someone who the election served very well, however, was Nestora Salgado. López Obrador's party MORENA nominated her to be a senator for the state of Guerrero. She officially became one of the most powerful people in the entire country. Countless news stories were run about Nestora's heroic arc from state prisoner to guerrilla senator, enumerating her various court cases and legal battles. But none of them mentioned the nameless migrant who had ensured—at the very moment the state was denying Nestora her right to counsel—that she remained in touch with her legal team. Without Axel, Nestora's case would have likely dragged on much longer than it did, and she might not have even been released from prison until years later. Similarly, if Axel hadn't hacked the police jammer during the Viacrucis, things might have gone very differently for Father Solalinde. If not for Axel, the police could have invaded the shelter and detained everyone, and what was one of Solalinde's greatest triumphs would have been his most public failure. Two of Mexico's brightest political stars—two people who now held the destiny of Mexico in their hands—owed their fortunes to an anonymous migrant in Iztapalapa who couldn't even afford to feed himself.

One month after the creation of the National Guard, in June 2019, Irineo was arrested by the Mexican government and charged with human trafficking. Six migrants were apparently cooperating with the prosecution, some of whom claimed that they paid Irineo to smuggle them through Mexico. I was conflicted. On the one hand, there was no doubt in my mind that Irineo was an egotistical creep who had no political vision beyond his next television interview or quick buck. Everywhere he went, he left a trail of chaos and slime. On the other hand, it seemed fairly obvious that the López Obrador administration was not punishing Irineo for his past transgressions so much as attempting to ruin his life and shut him up for good. If López Obrador got his way, Irineo's conviction would set a precedent that allowed the government to arrest anyone who aided migrant caravans in the future, Axel and me included.

"Do you think Solalinde had something to do with this?" I asked Axel.

"Abso-fucking-lutely," he said.

It was certainly clear that the priest thought Irineo was guilty. In his interview with Carlos Martínez, Solalinde bizarrely insisted that he'd seen a video in which Irineo or other Pueblo Sin Fronteras members were bribing Hondurans with US dollars to join the caravan. It was all an elaborate scheme, he asserted, to discredit the López Obrador administration. I scoured the internet for the video, but it simply didn't exist.

"That's low," I said to Axel. "Solalinde knows good and well that even if Irineo was helping organize the caravan, he certainly wasn't paying them to travel. He's never spent a buck on someone else in his life. It's all just a blatant lie."

"He's doing it to make people forget," said Axel.

"Forget what?"

"That he was the one who made Irineo in the first place. He was the one who helped him build the shelter in Chahuites. He created that fucking monster. But don't none of the news channels ever mention that."

After living in Mexico, I was baffled as to why Solalinde received near-universal adoration, especially in the English-speaking press. Eventually, I thought, someone must realize that something was amiss and begin asking the real questions. But then again, I remembered how I felt when I first arrived in Mexico, so full of shock and despair at the violence I witnessed, and so filled with hope when I heard about the priest. But it wasn't Solalinde who had changed me after all. It was marching on the Viacrucis Migrante, even in spite of it being led by someone like Irineo. That was worth defending. But Solalinde, who had made his name by standing up to the government on behalf of migrants, was now calling for the criminalization of others who did the same. In the span of four years, the priest went from being one of the most prominent voices against the Program to its implicit proponent. What I'd come to understand was that Solalinde was idealized not for what he really was or what he really did but for what he allowed us not to do. If the priest was a hero, if he was a lion-hearted soldier peacefully fighting the good fight, it meant that we were not obligated to enter the trenches ourselves. No need to look too closely or to dive in too deeply. Solalinde had it covered, so we didn't have to care.

A week after he was arrested, Irineo was released from jail. Government prosecution dropped their charges due to insufficient evidence. None of the original six migrant witnesses had shown up to court. They'd disappeared, like migrants do.

ONE EVENING, AXEL and I visited the house of some friends, Frank and Jovi, who were throwing a small dinner party. The guests were mostly journalists, and so the conversation inevitably turned to the new presidential administration, and to Father Solalinde, and what the right combination of hope and pragmatic skepticism was for the country. Axel—who until that point had surveyed the dinner with the differential reticence of an anthropologist in the midst of some unintelligible tribe—chimed in that he didn't have very much hope for Solalinde at all, actually. He proceeded to divulge some of his experiences with the priest on the Viacrucis, experiences that now seemed utterly and unbelievably bombastic when ripped from the unseen margins of southern Mexico and dropped without warning into our smartly decorated dining room. The journalists listened with expressions that seemed halfway between bafflement and fascination. Then someone asked Axel a question, then another, and another. At the end of the night, one of the journalists took our hands and said that she and many others had heard whispers about Solalinde for years, and that even if what Axel had just told them was only half or a quarter of the truth, it had the potential to be a monumental story in Mexico. But journalists here, she said, would never be able to break a story about someone as powerful as Solalinde themselves. The priest was too well connected, and the media was largely under the control of whichever presidential administration was in power.

"But maybe," she said, "if you two were able to get Axel's story out in the US first, the cracks would begin to appear here as well. Have you ever thought about writing a book?"

ONE DAY, AXEL and I were eating lunch at a café when I noticed a message from an account I didn't recognize. The woman said that she was Monica, Axel's ex-wife. She was trying to find Axel and asked if I knew where he was. I was wary. Disclosing Axel's whereabouts to a random account could still be dangerous. I wouldn't have put it past Don Armando or the Attorney to try to trick me with a fake account. But I also didn't want to ignore her, so my answer was cagey. I said that I wasn't sure if I knew much about Axel or not. I asked if he'd told her where he was planning on going before he left.

To the US, she said, where he used to live.

Didn't she used to live there as well? I asked. Didn't she have a visa to travel back and forth?

No, she said. She never had a visa. She'd only ever lived with Axel in Guatemala. But he had a problem with his DPI, and so he couldn't get steady work there either, and that's why he left for the US again.

After lunch, Axel and I had a massive fight in the apartment.

"Look at these messages," I fumed. "She says she was never in the US at all. That your kids weren't born there. That everything you ever told me was a lie."

"Bro, you gotta believe me. She's the one lying to you. So it looks like I abandoned her. She's just tryna make you feel sorry, like, pretending to be the poor Guatemalan woman so you give her more info on me."

"Come on, man, you can't expect me to believe that."

"I don't know what else I gotta say to convince you. I'm telling you that she was in the US. I'm telling you that my kids was born there. I wish I could prove it to you, bro, I really do. But look around. Look at where you are, look at who I've become now. I'm a nobody in the middle of the nowhere. What proof do I have?"

"I don't think I do believe you."

Axel punched the couch. "You seriously think I'd lie to you for years like this?"

"Look," I said, "if you didn't tell me the truth before, it sucks, but just tell me now. Please. I'm here to listen."

"You know what, bro? Fuck you and fuck your Mr. Listening Anthropologist bullshit. Always tryna fact-check me, always second guessing the shit I tell you. I would never abandon my babies. Never. You think this is easy for me? You think it's fun for me to tell you about the most horrible, embarrassing, messed up shit in my life? You think I like that?"

"No," I stuttered. "Of course not."

"You're the one who's always being a nosy bitch all the time. You ever think that sometimes I don't tell you things cause I don't wanna talk about them? That it might be fucking hard for me to relive some of that shit? So if you don't like the answers, fuck you, bro. I don't need this. I never laid down any guidelines before, I never told you nothing was off limits. But I'm telling you now: If you talk to Monica, that's it. I'm done with this. You won't need to come back down here no more."

Then he walked into his room and slammed the door.

We didn't speak to each other for days. I wasn't sure what to do. I wanted to trust Axel, but I also didn't want to dismiss this woman or her children. The old fears crept in again. What if Axel really had abandoned them? What if I was now complicit in that abandonment? Axel had a hard life, and Monica had a hard life. There was no doubt that if I talked to her, I would receive a very different picture of Axel, a darker one. Maybe that version would be true, or maybe it would be exaggerated, or maybe, as Axel insisted, it would be mostly lies. But whatever he had done in the past, Axel was in front of me now. It wasn't even about forgiveness. It was prior to forgiveness. Without me, there was a good chance Axel would end up homeless or dead. Not because I was some hero or savior, but because I had money. I didn't earn that money because I was good or honest or pure. I earned it because

I was a US citizen. I had done bad things in my life, I had hurt and betrayed others, and yet I was still allowed to live, and to live unquestioned. I wondered if Axel was still hacking me, if he had access to all my emails and bank statements. I wondered if he had seen all the times I hadn't told him quite the whole truth about myself, all the times I said I didn't have any extra cash when maybe I could have spared just a bit more. If he had, he never said anything or held it over my head. He never questioned our discussions or checked with Atlee to confirm that I was telling the truth.

After several days, Axel emerged from his room. I looked at him and suddenly felt as if I was gazing upon myself. Or at some distant, inconceivable version of myself, like I was adrift on a boat swept far out to sea, and I could just spot Axel's body, which was also my body, peering out from the dark shoreline. I realized that I was never going to fully apprehend what had brought us together in the first place. The more I tried to decipher it all, the more it eluded me. Every time I dug deeper, every time I grasped at some kind of essence or innermost kernel, it all melted into air.

"I'm never going to ever really understand you, am I?" I asked.

"I could say the same about you," he said.

"You remember the day we met? What made you talk to me? Why did you choose me?"

"Why did you answer?"

"I don't know," I said. "Sometimes I feel like I don't know you at all."

"You know me," he said. "At least, you know enough."

"I'm okay with that," I said.

SO HERE'S WHAT really happened. Or at least my version of what really happened. Me and Monica would fight, right? And I ain't talking just a little disagreement, like "You make me feel sad" or "You never take me out to the movies" or whatever. I'm talking bout the kinda fights that feel like the whole world is collapsing all around you. Cause I loved her. No matter what you think about me after I tell you this story, or even if you believe it at all, Levi, believe me when I say that I loved her from the bottom of my heart, and my kids too, and love makes you truly insane. It ain't an excuse, it's just a fact.

Anyway, I met Monica outside the mall one night. I was walking in, and she just happened to be walking out with this girl I knew. And Monica was looking fine as hell, right, and I had just got paid from washing some yachts, so I stopped to say hello and respectfully ask what the girls was up to on this Friday night. They said not much. And so I said why didn't they go shopping with me inside the mall, I'd buy them something nice. Well one thing led to another, and after the mall we went to the club, and then after the club I took Monica home. I could hardly believe it, cause I'm just an ugly old bald guy and she was freaking beautiful, so far outta my league. Well it turns out, we didn't use protection, and I got her pregnant that first night. Very first night. Just old Axel's luck. But I wasn't even tripping over it. I never really had a dad, and I wasn't bout to let that happen to any baby of my own. In fact, I was kinda excited, if I'm being real with you. I thought I'd hit the jackpot, and I told Monica that. Life had been such a hustle up until that point, and I hadn't been with many other girls since Jen. I mean, a little thing here and there, but girls in the States could always, I dunno, sense that there was something wrong with me, like that I didn't belong, and they'd never stick around. But when I told Monica that I was originally from Guatemala, she was chill about it, since she was from Guatemala too. And I thought, my god, I've found this gorgeous shorty who don't even care that I'm illegal? I'm in heaven.

But when Monica found out she was pregnant, she asked what was the process to get married, cause she had a visa to be in the States, but not forever, and now she wanted to make our relationship legit and become a citizen. And that's when I realized that when I told her I was originally from Guatemala, she musta thought that I was like a dual citizen or something. I don't know why she thought that. I guess she just assumed cause I had lived in New York for so long. So then I had to tell her that I didn't have documents, and that we couldn't get married in the US cause I didn't exist, right, and the whole fucking mood shifted on *the spot. I wasn't ever tryna hide it from her, I swear. We barely even knew each other. But she felt like she had got tricked. She said it straight to my face: "Of all the ugly motherfuckers in New York, how'd I end up with the one who was also illegal?"*

And things was bad from then on out. I said that since she was pregnant, she should move in with me, and that I'd figure out a way to get a bigger place for the baby and pay rent and everything. But every time she came to stay, we'd have a fight. She'd say the apartment was trash, and then I'd try to find more work to afford a nicer place, and then she'd say that if I was gonna be gone working all the time she might as well get with someone else. Then she'd move out to live with her relatives in Jersey, and I'd be stuck all alone in an expensive ass empty house I couldn't afford.

When my baby boy was born, I remember I was tiling a swimming pool for some rich guy in order to hustle up extra bucks. Monica wouldn't tell me what hospital she was at for three whole days, can you believe that? But eventually her family said they couldn't commit to supporting her and a new baby, so they kicked her out and she was back on my doorstep. And that's how it was. When she was in the house, I was so happy, even if she wasn't, cause I got to play with my son. I'd take him to the pool or play soccer and just be part of his life. I'd hold his little feets and feel like I had meaning in this world. And I loved Monica too, I really did. But I'd eventually do something that woulda pissed her off again, and she'd take my baby boy and leave. Or she'd kick me out the house and I'd go sleep on one of the yachts I was cleaning, and hope the owner wasn't gonna show up. Things only kept getting worser, and I started to suspect that she was seeing somebody else behind my back. Then one day she told me that she was done with me for good, and that she was gonna go back to Guatemala. And next thing I knew, she hopped on a plane with my baby boy and bounced.

Well, I fucking lost my mind. I couldn't just let that shit happen. So I went back too. I guess I ain't proud of it. I know it makes me look crazy. That's why I don't tell nobody. But I did it. I followed them to Guatemala. And I found Monica. She was living with some of her family down there, and when I knocked on their door Monica was shook. She couldn't believe that I had left the US. I said it was cause I loved her, and I convinced her to come back. It was easy for her and my son to return—she had the visa and he had his passport. I had to get a coyote. But back then, it wasn't like what it is today, the US border wasn't nearly as scary and there wasn't any bitch ass Southern Border Program in Mexico, and so I made it back in.

But soon enough I caught her texting another dude on her phone and we had a big fight and she went back to Guatemala again. And I went after her again. I don't know how many times this happened, like three or four. And then somewhere in there, my baby girl was born. So when you saw pictures of my kids on my account, Levi, that's what it was from. From Monica running away and me tryna get them back. It was the most embarrassing thing in the world, chasing them around like that. Monica's family hated me for following her, and my mom hated Monica for running away. My mom was always tryna get me to leave her, but I kept telling her I couldn't just give up my babies like that.

Not long after my little girl was born, I started to suspect that Monica was seeing this one dude whenever I was out at work. So one night I came back early and sure enough there was this strange car parked out front. So I snuck around the side of the house and started looking in all the windows. And there they were, right there in our bedroom, butt ass naked together. And I don't know why I did it, but instead of busting in there and beating the shit outta this dude, I just stood there and watched. Like a pervert or some shit. I just couldn't stop watching. And I even took out my phone and started recording. Cause I knew that when I stood up to Monica later, she was gonna deny everything on the spot. But also, I just needed to record it. For me. So that later, when I wanted it not to be true and started tryna convince myself to stay, I coulda watched it and felt that pain again. It sounds disgusting or crazy or some shit but that's what I did. I waited until after the dude left, and then I walked in the house and said I knew what she'd been doing. Monica denied it, so I showed her the video, and then she freaked the fuck out like I'd never seen before, calling me every name she could think of, saying that I was sick, that I was a fucking nasty freak bitch who shouldn't never be around children.

Then the car accident happened, and I got deported. Perfect timing. When I finally got the money and the balls to call Monica and tell her what had happened, you know what she said? She said to just keep my ass in Guatemala, cause she already had a man who was supporting them better than I ever could. And I asked her if it was the man I had seen in the house and she said yes. And then she went for the kill shot. She said that he was the real father of my little girl, not me. That's why my son looked like me but my daughter didn't. Cause biologically she wasn't mine at all.

And that's when I really lost it, bro. For a month I tried to stay strong and hustle up some money. Washing cars, selling fish, whatever I could find. But after I got a gun pulled on me by MS-13, I didn't wanna keep living no more. So I went to the market and bought these little gray tablets. Farmers use them to kill insects eating their crops. I swallowed half a packet on the spot and waited to die. For some reason, and don't ask me why, I wandered over to this office where I knew one of Monica's cousins worked, and that's where I passed out, in the grass in front of the building. I woulda died, but he happened to be coming back from lunch and found me and called an ambulance and they pumped my stomach and I lived. I spent weeks recovering in a bed somewhere in the city. My mom sent some money and paid for it. But after that, she said me tryna kill myself was the most selfish thing in the world.

"Don't never expect nothing from me ever again," she told me.

That's why she don't send me money here in Mexico, or try to help me out with a coyote or nothing. She says that I ain't really her son no more. That she's done with me. And that's why I don't never wanna talk about this shit with you, Levi. Cause when things get real bad, I start thinking bout it too much. I start thinking that maybe I should just do it again. After I got scammed the last time out in Guanajuato and they stole my tablet and computer and everything else from me, I was kinda certain I was gonna do it. I was gonna kill myself for real this time. When I got back home, it was so dark. I only had one lightbulb for the whole place, and I was just sitting there on the floor underneath it, tryna figure out how I was gonna kill myself with no money. I was too broke to even afford suicide, can you believe that? And then I saw someone step outta the shadows. I looked up, and I was standing in front of myself. But it was a different Axel. It was like an Axel who was well dressed, you feel me? He had on some tailored khaki pants and a collared shirt. He was clean and tall and, no lie, he had a full head of hair. Like thick, black, curly hair that was washed and combed and taken care of. It was like the version of Axel if Axel had stayed in the States and became successful. Like he hadn't never been deported cause he had documents all along. And I looked up at him and said, "I think I'm gonna kill myself."

"No you're not Axel. You don't die tonight." And then he started speaking all the things I couldn't say, things to counteract all the sadness bursting out from my chest. Things I can't even repeat back now, cause they wasn't even words exactly. They was like words that was inside and outside of my body at the same time. We talked for hours, under that one little light bulb, me sitting on the floor and him standing up above me. And for some reason we started talking bout my childhood and the first time I did cocaine. I had to tell him the whole story cause he said he didn't know it.

I was twelve and had got kicked out the house for one of the first times, and I was looking for a place to sleep, right? It was summer, and so I wasn't too worried—I wasn't gonna freeze to death or nothing— and I was just wandering around tryna find something to do. And I passed these dudes chilling on their front stoop, right? They was always there, always drinking. Typical broke ass neighborhood dudes. And they saw me, and they was like, "Yo little man. Come hang with us." And they asked if I was thirsty and I said yeah, so they gave me a beer. And then they got real excited saying they was gonna take me out with them, to do something I ain't never done before. They asked if I'd ever seen the

Twin Towers up close, and I said no, cause to be honest I wasn't even exactly sure what the Twin Towers was anyway. I was just a kid, right? And they said, "Not for long, little dude" and we hopped on the train direct to Manhattan. And on the train they was drinking, partying, acting out, and then one guy pulled out a little bag and sniffed this powder from it. I asked what was it, and he said I should give it a try, and so I snorted it like he showed me. And honestly, it made me feel freaking awful in the beginning, but at some point it turned into a miracle drug, cause I thought there was no way I was gonna go to sleep that night, which is what I was most concerned about. But then quickly the miracle feeling was over and I was thirsty as shit. Somebody gave me a beer and I chugged it and asked for another one. I didn't know what I was doing no more.

By the time we got to the Twin Towers I was, like, legit hammered, and the neighborhood dudes had to hold me up, with my arms around their waists. And I stood there just staring up at the towers, so humongous and quiet with the city lights reflecting off them. It was one thing to see them from a distance, and another to see them up close and touch them, you feel me? And I felt like I coulda just stood there forever, watching the lights slide across the glass, but then as I was looking up I started feeling super dizzy, and the lights started spinning, like the world was turning upside down, and I asked why these towers in specific was important, like what did they do—cause they ain't exactly pretty or interesting in a normal sense, you feel me, they're just so freaking huge that you couldn't never get a complete look at them, especially when you was drunk like me. And then the guys laughed and said I was just a kid talking nonsense, but to be honest I could kinda tell that they didn't really know what the towers was for either, and then I started to feel real sick and someone scooped me into his arms and carried me back to the train super gentle.

And for some reason I can't explain, I told that whole story to the other Axel, the American Axel, standing right there in front of me. But he didn't say nothing, he didn't even react, just kept staring at me with his big, white eyes—eyes that wasn't yellow and red like mine—so I just kept talking late, late into the night. And at some point I fell asleep. I had no dreams and when I woke up the light was on, the American Axel was gone, and I was still alive.

SOME NIGHTS AXEL and I would take long walks and play a game we nicknamed "Spot the Migrant." We'd look for nondescript figures around Mexico City—standing on street corners or reclining on park benches—people who blended into the background, but who, upon a second glance, seemed to be trying a little too hard to do so.

"That dude is definitely a migrant," said Axel, pointing to a guy underneath a jacaranda tree wearing baggy jean shorts. "Only Hondurans wear clothes like that. Oye catracho," he called out, and sure enough, the man responded and asked if we had a cigarette.

Near the Alameda, Axel pointed to another completely ordinary person and said, "Guatemalan. Just got in a few days ago."

"How can you tell?" I asked.

"Cause the dude's shoes. His clothes is new, like he just bought them, but his shoes is still busted as fuck from walking."

Back in 2015, it was much easier to spot migrants in the city. It wasn't uncommon to see groups of them talking excitedly in front of the Palacio de Bellas Artes, or taking photos to send to their families next to the Torre Latinoamericana. But the slow and steady march of the Southern Border Program forced them underground, even in the liberal capital.

"I still see migrants everywhere though," said Axel. "There's more here than ever. We just gotta shut the fuck up and blend in now."

Without meaning to, we ended up at the Zócalo. To the side of the cathedral, next to the open excavations of destroyed Aztec pyramids, were a group of shirtless men. They had broad leather belts and bright sashes around their waists, which they used to hit a dark rubber ball across a line drawn between them. The game was called ulama, a Mesoamerican sport that had been outlawed after Tenochtitlán was conquered. We stopped to watch them play.

"You know, the thing I still can't really wrap my mind around," I said, "was that the Aztecs weren't an ancient society. They'd only been around a couple hundred years when Cortés showed up. Tenochtitlán was younger then than the US is today. And then it was all destroyed."

"Like if aliens came down and blasted everybody," said Axel.

"Exactly. Like all of Manhattan was just leveled to the ground. The skyscrapers, the cathedrals, Central Park, all of it torn down and the rubble of the city used to make something completely foreign."

"Where'd everyone go?" asked Axel.

I pointed to the men playing the ball game. "They didn't go anywhere. We just don't see them as Aztecs anymore."

WHILE VISITING AXEL, I'd occasionally trek to a migrant shelter and talk with people who said they were headed north and planned to ask for asylum. When they learned I was from the US, they would say without fail that they had faith in the judges and policemen and border patrol there. They believed that deep down they were good people, and they knew that if they just told the truth, they would be listened to fairly.

"That's where you're wrong," I'd say. "We are not good people, and you cannot tell the truth. You need to lie."

So we'd sit for hours and discuss what happened to them—the poverty, the gang violence, the inescapable evils that the US court system found to be banal. And I would insist that this was simply not enough to win asylum anymore. So we came up with other stories, embellished stories, stories that were built on truths, or half truths, or truths of truths, but stories that would give them an actual chance of convincing an immigration judge to let them stay. To let them live. And when the migrants began to shift uncomfortably, when they insisted that they couldn't possibly lie like this, that it was against God, and I would grab them by the shoulders and say that they were right, that it was all horrible lies. But it might also keep them alive, and keep their children and parents and siblings alive as well, and I didn't believe something like that was against God at all. Then it would grow dark and someone would shout that dinner was served, and I would brush the dust off my pants and shake their hands goodbye. I don't know how many of them ended up standing before a judge, or what kinds of stories they told, or if any of them worked. I just wished them luck and walked back home to Axel.

ONE THING I never fully understood was why Guatemala refused to recognize Axel as a citizen. Axel swore that he went to the embassy several times to plead his case, but they always turned him away. After witnessing him unable to leave bed for days, however, I wasn't sure if I completely believed that he'd tried as hard as he insisted. Or maybe, I thought, the bureaucratic mumbo-jumbo had just confused him. It was against international law, after all, for embassies to simply turn away their own citizens. So I offered to accompany Axel one time. After commuting for an hour and a half—the Guatemalan embassy was located in one of the fanciest neighborhoods in Mexico City, far removed from any kind of public transportation, which I suspected was intentional—we were immediately denied entry.

"Excuse me," I waved to the guard, as he tried to slide the little reception window closed again. "I'm an anthropologist from the US following this man's story. Why exactly are you turning him away?"

"What's an anthropologist?" said the guard.

"It's someone who keeps coming back to ask more questions," I said.

We were let inside. The guard apologized. To me. I wondered how many Guatemalan migrants who didn't have white people following them around were denied. Probably dozens every day, thousands upon thousands of people over the course of a year. A man in a suit appeared. He introduced himself as Secretario Walter Arturo Estrada and asked how he could help us. I said that Axel had been trying for years to obtain his birth certificate through the embassy, but each time he was told they were unable to help him. I said I didn't understand how this could be possible, since Guatemala was legally obligated to issue him a birth certificate upon request. Secretario Estrada listened with an attentive expression of concern. He asked Axel for his details, shook our hands, and promised that he'd do everything in his power to resolve the issue right away.

We submitted all the documents required and heard nothing for several weeks. Then Axel received an email from the embassy stating that there was simply nothing they could do.

"You see?" said Axel, entirely unsurprised. "Kinda makes you wanna go crazy, huh?"

Axel petitioned the Guatemalan embassy for his birth certificate and passport for more than five years. They never helped him.

ONE EVENING, AS Axel was walking home from a shift he'd managed to land at a taco stand, a motorcycle hit him at full speed. He was thrown into the air, and the driver accelerated and disappeared down a rainy street. Axel managed to stumble home before vomiting blood all over the apartment building's single shared cabinet de toilette. The landlady summoned a taxi and sent him straight to the hospital, but in the chaos, Axel left the door to his room unlocked. When he returned a few days later—heavily bruised but fortunately with no detectable internal bleeding—the landlady stated unapologetically that she'd found a folder in his room containing denied immigration documents. When he'd applied to be a tenant, Axel had used the photocopy of my doctored passport and said that he was American.

The landlady waved a form from the Guatemalan embassy in Axel's face and said that she couldn't have a liar living in her building, least of all a "fucking migrant."

"Bro, I can't do this anymore," Axel sobbed over the phone. "If I stay in this city a second longer, I'm gonna die."

I sent him enough money to get to the border. It was risky, but there was no other option. In the four years that Axel lived in Mexico City, as the tourists poured in and the metropolis's bourgeois center was luxuriously remodeled, he was evicted five times. He was robbed on six occasions, twice at gunpoint. He worked seventeen odd jobs in nine different neighborhoods, not including his side hustles of hacking and fixing electronics. He visited the offices of fourteen various agencies, both governmental and nonprofit, which professed to serve migrants, but none of them helped him in the end. He slept on the street more times than either of us could count. And now, with only a garbage bag of clothes to his name, and just months until his five-year ban from the US would expire, he was back on the migrant trail.

He made it to the border.

CHAPTER 28

ACROSS

AXEL'S FIRST STOP was Tijuana. It was by no means salvation but, compared to Mexico City, it was something of a temporary relief. Axel was now a stranger in a city teeming with strangers. In 2018, the Trump administration announced Remain in Mexico, which was an expansion of an Obama-era policy that illegally limited the number of people permitted to enter US ports of entry. As tens of thousands of asylum seekers were forced to wait in Mexico indefinitely, migrant encampments sprang up throughout Tijuana, tent cities with no plumbing or electricity. The majority of them were Central Americans, but the new anti-asylum policy stranded people fleeing from all over the world—Haiti, Russia, Ethiopia, Cameroon, Ghana, Peru, and more.

The most insidious aspect of Remain in Mexico, however, was not that it was simply illegal under international refugee law—which requires that anyone be allowed to cross into any country at any time to ask for asylum—but that it was mostly a ruse. All of the migrants "stuck" in Tijuana could have picked up and crossed the border elsewhere, even just a few miles east, and if they were detained, they could request asylum right then and there, rather than waiting months and months while living on the street. It was basically just bureaucratic smoke and mirrors deployed to confuse people into delaying crossing the border. Immigration had convinced everyone that they were engaging in some kind of legitimate process, but there was none. It was all made up.

The one upside was that, in this new melancholy melting pot, Axel didn't stand out nearly as much as he did in the rest of Mexico. He found a room in a nondescript apartment, and, this time, the landlord didn't ask for any documents—he was used to renting to migrants. When I visited, we would stroll along the beach until the border stopped us. Axel's health had visibly improved, and I credited it in part to living near the ocean again. He occasionally braved a dip in the icy Pacific waters, diving deep beneath the roiling waves that washed over him and broke across the metal wall that extended into the sea. Happiness was elusive, but I hadn't seen him this sharp in years. We would sit in the sand and stare at the border for hours. There was no chance of getting over it in Tijuana. It was too militarized there. We'd have to find another way.

In theory, acquiring a coyote in Tijuana was easy enough, but finding one we could actually trust felt impossible. The price of smugglers continued to skyrocket under the Southern Border Program, and, in such a bullish market, new traffickers appeared in the city every day, each swearing that they were the best in the business. But whenever Axel inquired about a fee, he received quotes as high as $10,000, with no guarantee that he would make it across safely. During his time in Tijuana, Axel met five people who eventually hired smugglers. Two were detained in California. The other three he never heard from again.

For years, all I'd dreamed of was helping Axel return to the US. But now it seemed that none of our plotting or scheming had brought us any closer to getting him across. Things just kept changing too quickly on the border, even as they simultaneously seemed frozen in time, and there were several false starts. We'd nearly finalized a plan when the pandemic hit. Some of the first places in the US to be ravaged by COVID-19 were immigration detention centers, where border guards were intentionally denying immigrants adequate medical care. So we postponed. Then Biden was elected president. He'd hinted at some kind of immigration overhaul, and so we again delayed, but, as the months dragged on, he did nothing.

While planning the crossing, our conversations would inevitably return to our three failed presidents. Barack Obama was like Father Solalinde, we agreed. The high priest of the liberal order. He talked about peace when it was politically advantageous, and then went quiet when it wasn't. Trump was like Don Armando, obviously. He was loud and dirty and genuinely deluded, but his cartoonishly evil deeds were also wholly dependent on the elegant foundations laid by his predecessor. Biden was like the Attorney. He moved in the right circles and promised the world, but he was also aloof and held those promises in perpetual postponement, which in practice allowed his administration to continue all of Trump's most insidious immigration policies with just a fraction of the criticism. In the end, his administration offered nothing that would actually help someone like Axel. When it came to immigration, Obama and Trump and Biden weren't all that different. When it came to immigration, they were like brothers.

ONE OF THE strangest things about the US-Mexico border wall is that much of it is not built on the border proper. If it were, then migrants could sit atop the wall, straddling it, and immigration agents theoretically couldn't touch them, since they'd technically be in some in-between space, partly subject to the laws of the US and partly escaping into the sovereign territory of Mexico. To avoid this ambiguity, portions of the wall are built several feet into the interior of the United States, which ensures that agents can wrench migrants down without any qualms or legal repercussions. What this means, however, is that a sliver of the US is left on the other side, a tiny forfeited fragment, a nowhere.

Whenever I visited, Axel and I made a pilgrimage to the middle of this nowhere. There was nothing to indicate where the true dividing line was. We walked toward the wall together, and at some point we crossed the border, but we never knew where exactly, or when.

"I don't got nobody waiting for me up there no more," said Axel. "No wife, no kids, no nothing."

"I'll be waiting for you," I said, trying to cheer him up. "Hey, I might as well be the love of your life, you know." I meant it as a joke, but the words came out differently than I'd expected. Sadder, maybe.

"I guess so," he sighed.

"I'm sorry," I said.

"Me too," he said.

We stayed until the sun set and the wall glowed in the eerie yellow haze of the border's spotlights. From behind the iron bars, we watched immigration patrols stalk the terrain. It used to be that enemies of the state were lined up against a wall and shot. Now the firing squads waited on the other side. I turned and followed the line of the wall up and over the hills to the east. I saw it all in a flash. I saw the border stretch itself violently across the entire continent, and then slither into the Gulf of Mexico. I saw it span the Atlantic, snake through the Strait of Gibraltar, and cut the Mediterranean in half. I saw it surge into Turkey and then become confused and turn over on itself, writhing into a giant knot in the Middle East, like a thousand or a million nooses intent on hanging anything that crossed its path.

But then I saw it differently. The border was not an entity unto itself. It was something that was made. I saw all of the caravans and the centuries of struggle that proceeded them. I saw the creation of the border wall to keep them out, and the hands that built it. The hands of people, real people, who mapped the topography and leveled the terrain and erected a wall where one didn't used to exist. I thought about what dismantling something as violent as this border would require. I thought about what peace meant, the peace preached by so many activists and advocates, from Father Solalinde to the humanitarian organizations of Washington, DC. That kind of peace was never going to end something as horrific as what was in front of us.

"What do you want to do?" asked Axel.

"I don't want to pretend anymore," I said. "I want to tear down this wall. I want to take it apart piece by piece."

"I meant for dinner," he said.

"Let's go get some steaks," I said.

That night, neither of us could sleep. We stayed up and gazed out at the twinkling sprawl of Tijuana, a ramshackle and disquieted mass abutting a great darkness in the distance, the black abyss that marked the beginning of the taboo land awaiting us. I couldn't conceive of what it meant to desire a country. It made no sense. It was madness. A country is nothing. You can't touch it or hold it. A country melts away at the idea of itself. And yet Axel still desired it. And I still desired him to find it. Did I suddenly trust him? Did I believe that finally he was now telling me the truth about himself, the real truth, the thing that he'd so desperately kept hidden all along? No, I don't think I did. But that didn't matter anymore. Because when confronted with a border like the one that loomed before us, I knew I had glimpsed something of a truth there with him. A deeper truth, a truth that comes only in the unexpected encounter with the brute violence of this world, the violence I had been trained not to see since birth, to avoid and dismiss without question. It was a violence foundational to all countries, which preordained that someone like Axel should be made to bear great suffering, and that, if he wanted to escape it, he had to articulate the truth of his agony perfectly, to demean himself before those who did not suffer, to confess and apologize for all his sins, as if somehow I held the power of absolution. I did not, and I would not.

The truth was also that I loved him. It was a tumultuous and occasionally blinding love, as all true love is, a love that comes only in moments of quiet desperation, when one feels utterly and hopelessly alone. But we were not alone. We were together.

"Bro, are you sure you want to do this?" I asked, because I was scared. "Maybe you don't have to go back. You could stay here. We could find you a nice place by the beach. You could swim every day. Maybe we could bribe an official to forge you Mexican documents."

"Levi," he said quietly, "I have to go back."

I wasn't listening. "Every time I think we've found an answer, there's always just another problem waiting at the other end. Even if we do somehow manage to get you into the US, then what? You'll be undocumented for the rest of your life. You'll have no healthcare and no real job. You'll live in constant fear of being deported again. That's not a solution, that's not solving the problem."

"Bro, you know what we have to do."

"It's not going to be what you remember. You're not going back home. It's all different. Everything is changed in ways you can't imagine. You're not the same person, and it's not the same country."

"No, it ain't, Levi. But I still gotta cross. I gotta try."

I looked at him as if I was looking at myself. His trembling hands looked like my hands. His face looked impossibly like my face. Even as it didn't. Even as it couldn't.

"Do you really mean that?" I asked. And then, because I already I knew the answer, I said, "I'll always be here for you."

"I do," he said. "Do you?"

"I do," I said.

Eventually, Axel left Tijuana for good, and we moved to another town along the border to scout for a better place to cross. We waited as long as we could, which wasn't much, and prepared as best we could, which was even less, and then one day it was time.

312

IMAGINE THIS: MAYBE I did get a coyote. Maybe it cost me $3,000. Maybe it cost me $10,000. It's the basic kinda migrant story, right? I go alone, or I'm with a buncha other people who's broke as fuck and scared as fuck and who don't talk to each other, which is basically the same thing as being alone. We cross in the middle of the nighttime. We swim through the river, we get wet, and we run for a while. Maybe in the deserts of Texas, or maybe across the mountains in Arizona. And we get lucky, cause border patrol ain't out that night, and we make it through. And then Levi's waiting for me on the other side. In reality he'd probably have to be waiting in a busted up old van, so that we coulda blended in. But since we're imagining it, shit, it's a badass cherry red Camaro. Nah, even better, it's a freaking Ducati motorcycle, and we fly down the road.

Okay, now you gotta imagine the sad shit too, cause that's more realistic. Maybe I don't try to cross. Maybe in the end I just can't risk it. The border wins. Or I do cross, but immigration shows up and I have to run back to Mexico and wait for another day. Or maybe I cross and get to where Levi's supposed to pick me up, but he's not there. He chickens out like a little bitch boy academic and stays home. He ain't what I thought he was, and I'm all alone again. Or maybe Levi waits all night, but I'm the one who never shows up. I get caught and that's it. Boom. Done. The dream is over. I get deported to Guatemala again, and I stay there and try to hustle up a life, or I cross back into Mexico, or I just kill myself to get outta all this bullshit. And when you think of me, you have to think of the dead body.

Now don't think about that no more. Instead imagine that I don't cross alone cause Levi comes with me. Maybe we both make it, and then we drive to Los Angeles or Atlanta or wherever. As long as it's a place to make a clean start, it's good with me. But then Levi says goodbye, cause he's got responsibilities and a job and all that back where he is. And so he leaves. And he still calls and we see each other a little bit, right, but it ain't exactly the same as it was before. Maybe I figure out how to get my GED or some shit after all this time. Maybe I start hacking again cause it's the only way I can hustle up some money. Maybe Axel even finally finds a nice little lady for himself and settles down and she eventually gets him documents. Hey, anything's possible, even for old Axel.

Or maybe we try to cross and get murdered by the cartels. It happens to migrants all the time. It coulda happened to us too, or at least to me. They coulda killed us and left our bodies for the vultures, or they coulda buried us in the desert, or maybe they coulda tried to kill us but we faked dead the whole time, and then when they leave we get up and keep running.

Now imagine that, actually, border patrol shows up before the cartels can find us and busts the whole shit wide open. Levi runs one way, I run another, and that's it. I get caught and never see Levi again. Or maybe we don't split up and we run together and then some pasty-faced fucker yells, "Freeze," and we drop to the ground and he handcuffs us. I get arrested and Levi gets arrested. I get deported and Levi gets let go. Or maybe not. Maybe Levi goes crazy, cause the way he's been talking these days, I think he's kinda starting to go cuckoo, you know what I'm saying? And he doesn't freeze and instead he just loses his goddamn mind and beats the shit outta the immigration dude. And he just keeps hitting him and hitting him over and over. And then we drag his body into the bushes so the drones don't see nothing and we get the fuck outta there real quick. And cause of what Levi did we get away, we don't get caught, and we don't never tell nobody bout what happened.

Shit, I can make the scenario even crazier. Maybe imagine that we steal a truck from the Mexican federal police and drive into the US spraying bullets. Imagine we bring a big ass can of gasoline and burn down the entire freaking border wall. We dump a buncha oil into the Rio Grande until it's black and then we light it on fire. Oh, you can imagine a ton of migrants dead in the desert but you can't imagine that? It's just thoughts, baby, they ain't gonna hurt you.

Now imagine we ride off into the sunset together, the most beautiful sunset you coulda ever dreamed of, and for a moment the world is quiet and calm and peaceful. Imagine that eventually we pull up to a diner and walk into the air conditioning and order some nice juicy steaks.

Maybe that's what really happened. Maybe it ain't. Maybe I made it all up. What? You thought you was gonna get to know how it all ends? You thought I was just gonna tell you straight up?

You wanna know the truth?

Fuck you.

ACKNOWLEDGMENTS

AXEL AND I could never possibly hope to thank everyone who helped with this book. We list only a few names here. Thank you to all the marchers of the 2015 Viacrucis Migrante, especially the migrants and activists who did not appear in this book because of space limitations, including Julio Campos, the Mendoza family, Ximena Natera, and los patinetos.

Thank you also to Francisco Goldman and Jovi Montes for your love and support for both of us. Jon Lee Anderson, DW Gibson, Adam Hochschild, and Tim MacGabhann for your wisdom and encouragement at the start of this project. Ted Rosengarten, my "literary father," for teaching me how to write, and Dale Rosengarten, for your steadfast encouragement and kindness. Professor Lisa Samuel for always being there. Seth Holmes, Stefania Pandolfo, and Ian Whitmarsh for your intellectual guidance and for supporting such a nontraditional academic project. Gustavo Capela, Raphael Frankfurter, and Jaleel Plummer for your anthropological solidarity, as well as Summer Brenner, Diego Castro Oliva, John Flanagan, Stephanie Friede, Joe Friedman, Mara Kardas-Nelson, Mike Mitchell, Martha Pskowski, and Francisco Trejo Morales. Mesa Refuge for granting me a retreat space at the early stages of this project. Amelia Atlas, my agent, for fighting for this story when so many others didn't believe. Katy O'Donnell for taking a chance on it. Lisa Kaufman, my steadfast and incisive editor, to whom this book owes so much, as well as the rest of the Bold Type team.

And to Atlee. For everything, and everything else.

NOTES

I have provided a selection of endnotes below that document, contextualize, or otherwise help explain various statements in the book, as there was simply not enough room to include everything. These endnotes are meant only to provide additional detail and grounds for further discussion and do not have the same function as academic citations.

CHAPTER 1

As far as I have been able to tell, there is no recorded history documenting when exactly Viacrucis Migrante pilgrimages started. My best guess is that they began sometime in the mid-2000s in southern Mexico, because when I began asking about them in 2015, many people told me that they believed they'd been happening "for about a decade."

In addition, many of the details surrounding the Southern Border Program remain a mystery today. However, for more literature on the Program, please see my previously published pieces:

"Mexico Isn't Helping Refugees: It's Depriving Them of Their Rights," *Foreign Policy*, February 2019.

"Long Walk to Deportation," *Foreign Policy*, January 2016.

The Washington Office on Latin America (WOLA) has also been covering developments regarding the Southern Border Program since 2015. Their reports and essays on the Program can be found at wola.org.

CHAPTER 2

In this chapter, I claim that the Southern Border Program was established with "no clearly defined policy, law, or centralized supervision." To clarify, the Program was originally overseen by the Coordinación para la Atención Integral de la Migración en la Frontera Sur (CAIMFS) and headed by former Mexican senator Humberto Mayans. After a year, however—and after failing to heed repeated calls for transparency from the media—Mayans announced that he would be stepping down from CAIMFS and suggested that the agency would be disbanded and integrated into other preexisting governmental organizations. The office never published any detailed plans about, or findings on, how to carry out the Program, and Mayans returned to his old Senate seat. What CAIMFS was actually doing (if anything at all)—and what was within its legal purview—was always contested and unclear.

At the time of publication, Irineo Mujica is one of the leaders of the organization Pueblo Sin Fronteras, a binational nonprofit that raises money in both the United States and Mexico. When I first met Irineo, he was a relatively unknown activist, and not much information about him or Pueblo Sin Fronteras was readily available. But over time, he has cultivated a growing presence in the media. On July 9, 2019, Hannah Critchfield published an interview with Irineo for the *Phoenix New Times* about the basic facts of his life and activism, entitled, "Interview: Phoenix Migrant Activist Irineo Mujica on U.S. and Mexico Crackdowns."

In this chapter I also briefly mention my anthropological goals. To clarify for the few anthropologists who might read this book: I do not claim that *Border Hacker* is an overt work of anthropology. It is not, even as it also depends upon an intensive ethnographic approach. Rather, this book is in the service of anthropology. It works to justify, encourage, and validate anthropological methodology in the hopes of reinvigorating and relegitimizing the discipline after decades of systemic marginalization, a marginalization that—let's face it—most anthropologists, brilliant as they are, have been terrible at fighting against. My overtly anthropological research on migrant caravans will hopefully be published in the next several years, after the completion of my doctoral dissertation.

CHAPTER 3

After I witnessed the boy sitting in his underwear on Irineo's lap and then had a brief conversation with him the next day, I never saw him again. While I was back in Chahuites living with Axel (see Chapter 11), I actually did briefly search for the boy at Irineo's shelter when I heard that Irineo was not in. After strolling through the shelter and asking about the boy's whereabouts, I was unable to find him, and no one there seemed to have seen him, as the migrants there had arrived only up to three days prior.

It has been widely reported that the shelter Irineo Mujica ran in Chahuites was started by Father Alejandro Solalinde and affiliated with the Hermanos en el Camino network throughout its run. In 2017, Chahuites mayor Leobardo Ramos Lázaro ordered the shelter to be shut down so as to "stop bothering the neighbors," despite Father Solalinde's public reproach of the decision. (See: Gisela Ramírez, "Alcalde en Oaxaca ordena cerrar albergue de migrantes para 'no molestar a vecinos,'" *Conexión Migrante*, May 12, 2017, https://conexionmigrante.com/2017-/05-/12/alcalde-en-oaxaca-ordena-cerrar-albergue-de-migrantes-molestar-a-vecinos/.)

After the shelter in Chahuites was shut down, Irineo has been affiliated with at least two other migrant shelters in the northern Mexican state of Sonora, and they are not affiliated with the Hermanos en el Camino network.

CHAPTER 4

The transwoman I describe as "Shakira" in this chapter and others really did go by that name, at least to us on the Viacrucis. She told me that she had lived in Miami for four years before being deported at the beginning of 2015 and that she had a boyfriend there, who she hoped to return to. I was never able to confirm that her murder (discussed in Chapter 6) really was at the hands of the police, or even if she was killed at all. Shakira, if you're reading this, Axel and I still think of you.

CHAPTER 5

Alberto "Beto" Donis's life has been well covered in both the Mexican and US media. He was frequently in contact with organizations like Amnesty International, which often wrote stories about Beto's time in Hermanos en el Camino that labeled him a "human rights defender," as well as "Urgent Action" statements when the organization deemed that his life might be in danger.

CHAPTER 6

In this chapter, Irineo Mujica refers to a certain law in the Mexican constitution that supposedly either protects pilgrims traveling in Mexico or bans government officials from setting foot in "humanitarian zones" such as migrant shelters. After carefully reviewing the Mexican constitution and discussing the matter with a Mexican attorney, I have not been able to find any such law. It was a claim that I often heard repeated in Mexico, however—even once by a police officer—and one of the goals of my doctoral dissertation is to trace exactly how such a fiction came to hold real power in Mexico. If anyone has any ideas on the subject, please reach out.

I wish I could thank the pharmacist who saved my life by name, but alas I never learned it. Soon after he gave me the medicine that stopped my anaphylactic shock, he shuttered his business abruptly and left. For anyone who believes that they might be able to identify him, the pharmacy was located on the bottom floor of Carlos B. Zetina 80, Colonia Escandón, Mexico City. I would love to thank him in person one day.

CHAPTER 7

The people described as "the Teachers" (los Maestros) by Axel in this chapter are a well-known group of activists in Oaxaca and the rest of southern Mexico. They have engaged in a long struggle with local and federal officials alike over, among other things, indigenous autonomy and taxation. This struggle reached a boiling point during the 2006 Oaxaca protests, during which the police opened fire on a nonviolent protest led by a teachers' trade union. Since then, many more Teachers have been killed and incarcerated by the state.

CHAPTER 8

After the Viacrucis arrived in Mexico City, we concluded the march by worshipping at the Basilica of Our Lady Guadalupe, one of the largest pilgrimage sites in the world. It is said that in 1531, near where the Basilica is today, the Virgin Mary appeared to Juan Diego Cuauhtlatoatzin in a series of apparitions that would later come to be characterized as the great unifying symbol of Mexico. One could interpret Father Solalinde concluding the Viacrucis at the Basilica of Guadalupe as a symbolic act that cemented its status as a pilgrimage, as well as a statement that every Viacrucis could potentially be united with the Mexican project under the image of the Virgin of Guadalupe.

Since the National Human Rights Commission's granting of amparos to the 2015 Viacrucis Migrante, I have tried to verify whether other migrants refer to amparos by the nickname that we did—"la visa véte." As you might imagine, tracking down other migrants who have received a twenty-day visa has been incredibly difficult, and so I have not been able to verify it one way or the other.

CHAPTER 9

In my research for this book, I submitted a request for Axel's complete immigration file under the Freedom of Information Act (with his consent, of course) and had it reviewed by several immigration attorneys. The basic outline of his claims—that he was first "deported" through Voluntary Departure and only received his first official deportation when he crossed back into the US after marching on the Viacrucis—are substantiated by his immigration file.

The text messages I send Axel in this chapter are based on the real texts that he actually asked me to send him the night of the Fight of the Century. Unfortunately, the record of those original text messages was lost. But the ones in the book are roughly composed from what I can remember writing at the time.

Axel's assertion that he was attacked by narcotraffickers, though lacking in hard evidence, is corroborated by many other migrant accounts of traveling through the US-Mexico borderland. The bodies of Central American migrants frequently turn up in mass graves just south of the US border, and Los Zetas cartel is often assumed to be responsible. (One such incident has come to be known as the 2010 San Fernando massacre, in which the bodies of seventy-two migrants were found in a mass grave.) The fact that Axel was hit with some kind of bat or other blunt instrument—rather than immediately shot on sight—might have to do with the fact that he was within US territory and possibly still within earshot of US immigration officials.

CHAPTER 13

In 2021, Mayor Leobardo Ramos Lázaro—who Axel alleges asked him to hack his political opponents—was shot to death by unknown assassins while driving his truck in Chahuites. No suspects have been identified as of the time of publication of this book, but the assassination is thought to have been politically motivated. (See: Elías Camhaji, "Asesinado en Oaxaca el alcalde Leobardo Ramos Lázaro," El País, February 4, 2021, https://elpais.com/mexico/2021-02-04/asesinado-en-oaxaca-el-alcalde-leobardo-ramos-lazaro.html.)

CHAPTER 14

As this book goes to press, Armando "Don Armando" Vilchis Vargas is still operating a "shelter" out of his auto shop in Metepec, a suburb of Toluca, and it is still affiliated with the Hermanos en el Camino network. His son, Armando "Armando Jr." Vilchis Moreno, continues to be somewhat involved with the "shelter" as well, judging from social media posts.

CHAPTER 15

Nobody Beats the Wiz was a chain of electronics stores in the Northeast of the United States, founded in 1977. The stores filed for bankruptcy in 1998 and closed permanently in 2003, which fits within Axel's general timeline.

CHAPTER 17

Axel's chosen pen name for this book—"Kirschner"—is my paternal grandmother's maiden name. She was also an immigrant to the US, which is one of the reasons we thought that she would make a good tocaya.

When Axel mentions Meme's boast of killing Miss Honduras, he is referencing a real crime. In November 2014, Maria Jose Alvarado, the current Miss Honduras, was murdered. In 2017, her sister's boyfriend Plutarco Antonio Ruiz admitted to the murder and was convicted. It is unknown whether Meme had anything to do with her killing or disposal of her body, but Ruiz never implicated him.

CHAPTER 18

Day of the Dead began picking up steam as a Mexico City–wide holiday after a James Bond film shot a chase scene there in 2015, in which Bond must avoid would-be assassins by weaving through a Day of the Dead parade. The Mexico City tourism board liked the idea so much that it threw its first official Day of the Dead parade in 2016.

CHAPTER 20

Nestora Salgado's story has been widely covered in both the US and Mexican media since Salgado also holds US citizenship. For more information on Nestora Salgado's life and militancy, see Alexis Okeowo's 2017 piece in the *New Yorker* entitled, "A Mexican Town Wages Its Own War on Drugs," as well as David Agren's 2016 piece in the *Guardian* entitled, "Nestora Salgado, Community Leader Battling Cartels, Freed from Jail."

CHAPTER 21

I have not included in this book any identifying information about the immigration nonprofit that I used to work for in Washington, DC. I did this because I do not believe that they deserve any special attention or unique criticism. The issue is systemic, and immigration attorneys, in my experience, are in an impossible bind. I do wonder, however, if all of the hours and resources currently spent on engaging with dishonest government bureaucracy might somehow be put to better use. What would be possible if we fought the government outside the normal channels of the law?

Special immigrant juvenile status, or SIJS, was created in 1990. As asylum has become an increasingly impossible option for many immigrant children, the use of SIJS has surged in recent years, especially after the 2014 border crisis. (See: Alexandra Starr, "With Asylum Out of Reach, Some Minors Seek Out Special Visas," NPR, November 22, 2015, www.npr.org/2015/11/22/456669013 /with-asylum-out-of-reach-some-minors-seek-out-special-visas.)

CHAPTER 22

Gonzalo Molina González's imprisonment, like Nestora Salgado's, was also covered widely in the press, though almost exclusively in Mexico. He was freed after being held in prison for five years for "suspected terrorism." (See: Zacarías Cervantes, "Gonzalo Molina, preso hace 5 años por supuesto terrorismo, queda libre en Guerrero," *SinEmbargo MX*, March 1, 2019, www.sinembargo.mx /28-02-2019/3543909.)

CHAPTER 23

Nestora Salgado's release from prison was covered internationally, and the picture of her at her press conference, holding what appears to be a black rifle above her head, was published around the world and turned Nestora into something of an icon in Mexico. From the photos of the event, it appears that what she might be holding is a version of the FX T12 Synthetic airgun, which would substantiate Axel's claim.

CHAPTER 24

Yes, the Adam I reference is that Adam, the one who you can easily find by searching for him on the internet. Let's not talk about him too much, or I'll start saying things that will worry my publisher.

Instead, let's talk about Ever. When I visited him in the Farmville Detention Center, I was accompanied by my friend and fellow writer DW Gibson, who, because of space limitations, was not included in my account of the visit. At the time, DW was beginning a project that eventually became his book *14 Miles*. Though Ever's story was ultimately not covered in *14 Miles*, some of their conversations did help spur DW's work forward.

Ever and I still speak from time to time, and he is doing well. He still loves Rihanna.

CHAPTER 25

In this chapter, I make several claims about shrinking rates of asylum approval across the US, and for Central American migrants in particular. It has only become worse since my time working in DC. For instance, during the 2021 fiscal year, the Arlington Asylum Office, just a few miles from Joe Biden's White House, denied approximately 75 percent of asylum seekers. All data for these statistics was retrieved from TRAC Immigration, an invaluable project conducted out of Syracuse University.

It is not uncommon for immigration attorneys to appeal the decisions made by asylum officers. However, I wish to stress that the interview I translated for Isabela was roundly denounced by all the immigration attorneys involved as one of the most unprofessional interviews they had ever been a part of. The interview was irregular in almost every way—from its incredibly lengthy duration, to the overt antagonism of the asylum officer and his general distrust of my interpretations. That being said, I translated for several of our clients during their asylum interviews, and each was a generally tense and unpleasant affair.

I still do not know what happened to Isabela's asylum appeal. I will never know, as I am no longer privy to her case information. I wish her all the best.

CHAPTER 26

The claim of the proprietor of the hotel where Axel stayed for a time—that Tenochtitlán would have survived if it had turned away the refugees fleeing Cortés's slaughter—is a story I have heard from time to time in Mexico, mostly by people who identify as right-wing. I am shocked to find that similar claims are now being made on some English-language "history" channels on YouTube as well. I believe the claim is fantastically and stupidly false.

My depiction of Axel's generally erratic behavior in this chapter may cause some to ask if Axel was secretly using drugs. I myself had suspicions at first, and—though I would not necessarily have blamed him if he was using—at one point, I even began dropping by unannounced at his apartment to see if I might be able to catch him in the act. Or, when he was staying with me, I would knock on his door at odd hours, just to see what kind of state he was in. Though Axel showed clear signs of anxiety, paranoia, and occasional delusions, he never once exhibited any obvious signs of inebriation. Axel insists that he has never used any substances harder than nicotine in Mexico, and in all the years we've worked together, I have never once found any evidence that would indicate otherwise.

CHAPTER 27

The full translated interview of Father Solalinde accusing Irineo Mujica or other Pueblo Sin Fronteras members of bribing migrants to join caravans was published by *El Faro* on January 29, 2020. It was entitled, "Migrants Are Very Important, but Mexico Comes First." The interview was originally conducted by Carlos Martínez and translated by Max Granger. In the article, Solalinde also alleges that Irineo's organization Pueblo Sin Fronteras participated in human and drug trafficking in the past.

In 2019, Irineo—as well as Cristóbal Sánchez Sánchez, another 2015 Viacrucis Migrante activist who was not included in this book because of space limitations—was arrested in Mexico after the López Obrador's foreign minister arrived to conduct negotiations in Washington, DC. Many believe that the arrest of Mujica and Sanchez was, at least in part, a bit of theatrics to "prove" to the Trump administration that Mexico took the threat of migrant caravans seriously.

As already clearly stated in this chapter, one of the reasons Axel had such a hard time resettling in Mexico was because he was continuously denied a legal birth certificate from Guatemala. Despite a push from the López Obrador administration to provide more migrants with temporary legal documents like humanitarian visas and work permits, Axel did not qualify for these programs because the Mexican government required that migrants present a valid birth certificate. For instance, after the Lopéz Obrador administration announced that migrants would be able to open bank accounts, I once followed Axel to fifty-seven various bank branches in Mexico City, all of which turned him away under the auspices of having the wrong documentation, which in turn led Axel to lose job opportunities.

CHAPTER 28

What to say about this chapter, the conclusion of the book? Obviously, we have tried to obscure the details of Axel's potential crossing as much as possible to protect him legally, as well as to protect him from anyone who might wish him harm after this book is published. All I am able to say is this: Axel and I have prepared for many years for his crossing back into the US. We have tried to plan that crossing as carefully as possible, despite the great risks associated with the act. Understand that regardless of the outcome, Axel is still in an impossible situation. He is either undocumented in the US, without recourse to all the things that might help make a comfortable life—a living wage, healthcare, social security, free education, and the like—or he is in Guatemala or Mexico. And our book already covers that agony. You do not need me to describe it again.

Levi Vonk is an anthropologist, writer, and doctoral candidate. He lives between the US and Mexico.